Art and Imagination

Other works by Roger Scruton from St. Augustine's Press

An Intelligence Person's Guide to Modern Culture
Philosopher of Dover Beach: Essays
The Meaning of Conservatism
The Aesthetic Understanding
Xanthippic Dialogues
Perictione in Colophon
On Hunting

Art and Imagination

A STUDY OF THE PHILOSOPHY OF MIND

Roger Scruton

ST. AUGUSTINE'S PRESS

South Bend, Indiana

Manufactured in the United States of America

2 3 4 5   23 24 25 26

Cataloging in Publicaiton Data
Roger Scruton
Art and imagination: a study in the philosophy of mind /
Roger Scruton
p. cm.
Originally published: London: Methuan, 1974
Includes bibliographical references and index.
ISBN 978-1-890318-00-0 (cloth: alk. paper)
ISBN 978-1-58731-032-4 (paper: alk. paper)
1. Judgment (Aesthetics). 2. Philosophy of mind.
3. Empiricism. I. Title.
BH301.J8S37 1997
111'.85–dc21   97-37824

ST. AUGUSTINE'S PRESS
www.staugustine.net

Contents

Preface

My intention in this work is to show that it is possible to give a systematic account of aesthetic experience in terms of an empiricist philosophy of mind. I have derived great benefit from several authors, in particular from Wittgenstein, whose influence is everywhere apparent, and from Kant, whose views have inspired the theory defended in Chapter Ten. While I have attempted to avoid unnecessary jargon, the approach to aesthetics that is presented here is frequently technical. I only hope that this will not deter the reader unfamiliar with the more specialized areas of modern philosophy. The problems that I deal with, while often phrased for clarity's sake in the language of philosophical logic, are the perennial problems of aesthetics, the problems of the nature and value of art. In order to make the reader's task less difficult I have tried, so far as possible, to make the three parts of this work independent of one another. Those interested in the philosophy of mind may, therefore, prefer to begin at Part II, while those interested in the philosophy of art may prefer to approach the whole book in reverse.

A version of this work was presented as a doctoral dissertation to the University of Cambridge in October 1972. I wish to thank the Master and Fellows of Peterhouse for the award of a Research Fellowship, and hence for the leisure to work on the dissertation. I also wish to thank my supervisors, Dr M. K. Tanner and Professor G. E. M. Anscombe, for guidance and suggestions; my examiners, Professor Stuart Hampshire, and Professor B. A. O. Williams, for painstaking and helpful criticism; Dr J. E. J. Altham and Miss Hidé Ishiguro for stimulating discussions;

Dr Hans Kamp, Mr Mark Platts, and Professor David Hamlyn for comments, and especially Dr M. J. Budd, who patiently criticized an earlier draft, suggesting many improvements. My greatest debt is to Dr John Casey, who has read and criticized this work at every stage, making substantial suggestions and guiding my thought in so many ways that I am indebted to him on almost every page.

London, (July 1974)   Roger Scruton

CHAPTER ONE
Introduction

The purpose of the present work is to sketch a theory of aesthetic judgement and appreciation in terms of an empiricist philosophy of mind. For philosophers of an idealist cast aesthetics has never detached itself from the philosophy of mind: such philosophers have produced theories of thought, feeling and imagination that give a central and intelligible place to the activities of aesthetic judgement and appreciation. Empiricists, on the other hand, have found it difficult to account for these activities except by reducing their importance in a way that few will find acceptable. Aesthetics becomes, for such philosophers as Hutcheson and Hume, a matter of 'sentiment': of liking this thing rather than that. Taste is an isolated and inexplicable segment of human psychology, and it is simply a curious but philosophically uninteresting fact, that human beings enjoy some things (such as tragedies, strawberries and fine weather) and recoil from others. 'Beauty,' wrote Hume, 'is such an order and construction of parts, as either by the *primary constitution* of our nature, by *custom*, or by *caprice*, is fitted to give a pleasure and satisfaction to the soul.'[1] Having no philosophy of thought and feeling that could make our experience of art intelligible, it seemed natural to such philosophers that aesthetic appreciation should find no place in the intellectual part of human mentality. Thus Hutcheson was happy to say that 'the origin of our perceptions of beauty and harmony is justly called a "sense" because it involves no intellectual element, no reflection on principles and causes.'[2]

[1] *Treatise*, II, 1, viii.
[2] *An Inquiry into the Original of our Ideas of Beauty and Virtue*, section 1, para. 13.

Modern analytical philosophy has inherited the weaknesses of its empiricist origins. There have been few works of philosophical aesthetics in this century that cast any light on the topic, and many of those that do (Croce's *Aesthetic*, for example, and Collingwood's *Philosophy of Art*) borrow the intellectual framework of idealism. It is clear that, for all its rejection of the sceptical and Cartesian presuppositions of traditional empiricism, analytical philosophy has more in common with the thought of Locke, Hume, Berkeley and Thomas Reid than it has with that of Hegel, Fichte or Croce. It is no longer possible to accept the philosophy of mind that made Croce's account of aesthetic judgement plausible: and yet the rival account of human mental processes that derives from Ryle and Wittgenstein gives no clear picture of the place which aesthetics can occupy. In the following chapters I wish to suggest how this lacuna might be filled.

Philosophical aesthetics seems to divide into two parts: firstly, there is the study of aesthetic appreciation, the aesthetic attitude, taste, the aesthetic emotions, and so on. In other words there is the philosophical analysis of an area of human experience, the area involved in our responses to the objects of aesthetic interest. It is a philosophical question how far it is possible to give a description of these attitudes and preferences that is not trivial, and how far it is possible to set them apart as an autonomous segment of mental activity. Secondly, philosophers attempt to analyse our judgements about the *objects* of aesthetic feeling and appreciation. We make value judgements about these objects, and we describe them in various ways which seem to have a peculiar relation to their aesthetic significance. We must discover what these descriptions and evaluations mean, and how they might be supported if they can be supported at all.

Immediately we seem to have made a large assumption. Is it really so obvious that we can describe aesthetic judgement and aesthetic appreciation independently? It will be one of my contentions that we cannot. Certainly it would be a rash philosopher who claimed that ethics divides in a similar way – into the study of moral attitudes and feelings on the one hand, and the study of moral judgements on the other. For there are strong arguments for saying that we cannot understand moral judgements except in the context of certain attitudes and feelings, and that we cannot understand these attitudes and feelings until we have a firm grasp of their expression in moral judgements. To understand the one is to understand the other.

But to establish the precise connections between judgement and appreciation in aesthetics is difficult – more difficult even than it is in ethics. One source of difficulty is the obscurity of such heavily theoretical notions as 'aesthetic appreciation' and 'aesthetic experience'; yet it is on an analysis of these notions that an empiricist aesthetic must be founded. Moreover, certain far-reaching assumptions have to be made about the concept of meaning if aesthetic judgement is to be explained at all. That there is *some* connection between the meaning of our utterances and our mental states is undeniable; but in the case of aesthetic experience the connection proves hard to describe. The first part of these investigations will, therefore, be concerned largely with questions in the theory of meaning, while the second part will be given over to the philosophy of mind. Only by these roundabout means can an empiricist theory of mind be brought into relation with the problems of aesthetics.

It will be asked 'What place has art in such an investigation? Where does the concept of art fit in with those of aesthetic experience and aesthetic judgement?' Certainly it would be foolish to treat aesthetics in such a way that it becomes an irrelevant fact that the principal objects of aesthetic judgement and appreciation are works of art. It is precisely this that has made empiricist aesthetics unacceptable. No reader of Hegel can fail to admire the brilliance and sureness with which he argued for the central place of art in human experience, and with which he derived from purely philosophical premises a theory of the nature and limits of the various art-forms. Nevertheless, it is not certain that the empiricist assumption that art and the appreciation of art can be independently described has really been refuted. If Kant is important in the history of aesthetics it is partly because he was the first philosopher to attempt to give a systematic account of aesthetic appreciation, without describing its material object, and without lapsing into 'Sentimentalism'. It will become clear that a great amount hangs on the question whether Kant's enterprise can be carried through. It is characteristic of empiricism to regard mental processes as intrinsically divisible into separate categories – the cognitive, the conative and the affective, for example. For idealism these are at most only mutually dependent aspects of a single process, and the empiricist's assimilation of the 'aesthetic' to the 'affective' is simply a refusal to acknowledge that all mental activity is equally cognitive. Aesthetic experience is a form of knowledge, and is to be defined in terms of its object. The experience and its objects are so intimately connected, the idealist will say, as to cohere completely, forming an autonomous sphere of mental activity. Thus Croce (and following him Collingwood) argued that the connection between art and aesthetic appreciation is logically necessary: the object of appreciation is 'expression', and expression is the prerogative of art. In what follows I wish to show that the Kantian approach to aesthetics not only can be resuscitated, but also can be given a firm analytical basis.

Before beginning I shall describe certain philosophical pre-suppositions of the arguments in later chapters, and indicate briefly why these presuppositions are near to the tenets of empiricism. Any serious philosophy of mind must enable us to answer questions of the form, 'What is thought?', 'What is belief?', 'What is sensation?', 'What are the moral emotions?', 'What is aesthetic experience?', and so on. I shall assume that answers to questions such as these involve analysis of the meaning of 'thought', 'belief', 'sensation' and similar terms. That is, I assume one of the principal doctrines of analytical philosophy. However, not all explanations of the meaning of 'thought', 'belief' and 'sensation' are philosophically adequate; we do not wish to know just *any* facts about the usage of these terms. I shall assume that, apart from certain very important exceptions, which I shall discuss in Chapter Five, the interesting features of the meaning of a term, those features that a philosopher is concerned to discover, are the features which govern the truth and falsehood of sentences where the term occurs. We are interested in the meaning of terms only because we are interested in the truth of sentences. Only if we know the conditions under which it is true to say of someone that he is thinking (for example) do we know what is important about the meaning of 'thought'. If we know these conditions then we are in a position to say *why* we have a term with this meaning: we have learned something about the *concept* of thought. We can point to relations and coherences among the truth conditions that make the concept of thought intelligible. It is partly because philosophical arguments are about truth conditions that they are not just verbal quibbles.

Now an important tenet of the kind of analytical empiricism that I shall assume is this: we suppose that there is a central category of sentences, including many present tense singular declarative sentences, that are essentially tied to truth conditions, in that no account can be given of the meaning of one of these sentences, or of what it is to understand one of these sentences, that does not refer to the conditions for its truth. There are, perhaps, other sentences the meaning of which does not have to be explained in this way, but it is essential to our language, and indeed to any language in which information is to be transmitted, that there should exist this central category of declarative sentences, the meaning of which derives from the conditions for their truth. And giving sense to sentences of this class is a condition of giving sense to any sentence whatsoever.

It is for this reason that a philosophical inquiry into the meaning of terms will tend to concentrate on their use in present tense declarative sentences – we wish to know when it is true to say of someone that he is now thinking, in pain, afraid, and so on. The hope is that an understanding of certain general features of the language – rules governing the introduction of tenses, connectives, moods and so on – will enable us to derive the meaning of the sentences that remain. The empiricist will argue that this privileged class of sentences has the important place that it has because these sentences are intimately connected with the foundations of our knowledge. It is with these sentences that the idea of a truth condition is given epistemological content.

But here we must distinguish two notions of a truth condition, the first epistemological, the second merely formal. Empiricism involves an attempt to explain our understanding of language. But we must be careful not to confuse it with the more formal approach to the concept of meaning that makes no reference to understanding. From the point of view of formal semantics there is a sense in which almost any system of signs can be assigned a truth condition for each of its sentences, whether or not such a system could be used or understood as a language by intelligent beings. It is sufficient that for each sentence '*s*' another sentence '*s*'' should be found, such that '*s*' is true if and only if *s*'. We could think of '*s*' and '*s*'' as sentences in two isomorphic but uninterpreted languages. Or we could think of '*s*'' as some arbitrary sentence introduced into the language for precisely this purpose (a sentence that has no sense apart from the sense given to it by its equivalence to '*s*'). In the limiting case '*s*' and '*s*'' might even be taken as identical. Thus, provided it makes sense to *say* '*s* is true', then the sentence '*s*' has, in this purely formal sense, a truth condition, namely the circumstance that *s*. But philosophers who argue whether the sentence '*a* is good' has genuine truth conditions do not mean to deny that '*a* is good' is true if and only if *a* is good, nor do they mean to deny that '*a* is good' is true if and only if *p*, where '*p*' stands for some other sentence – such as '*a* is desirable', '*a* is a fit object of preference', and so on – which presents the same epistemological difficulties.

Furthermore, this 'formal' notion of a truth condition can be strengthened without yielding any substantial conclusions. For a language can be collated with a semantic theory, so that every sentence in the language is assigned a truth condition in the theory. If we can construct a semantic interpretation for some language or system of signs, then this enables us to assign truth conditions recursively to the sentences of the language, in a way that is no longer trivial. But this assignment of truth conditions will give us the means of understanding the original language only if we first understand the semantic theory with which it is collated. And to understand the theory will equally involve the ability to assign truth conditions, in some stronger, less formal sense, to its sentences.

The empiricist argues that we can understand a language only if at least some of its sentences are given truth conditions in a stronger sense: conditions which show how a sentence should be verified. We must ascribe meaning to certain sentences directly, without the mediation of others that 'give their truth conditions' in a purely formal manner. We must explain the referential and descriptive function of sentences in terms of observable features of our world. It is not the fact that '*s*' is true if and only if *s* which enables us to understand the sentence '*s*'. It is rather the fact that there is some state of affairs which guarantees the truth of '*s*', and which can be identified not just by the use of equivalent sentences but also directly, as it were, by observation. In other words the idea of a truth condition is filled out, or given content, in terms of the observable states of affairs that make sentences true. It is an essential tenet of empiricism that the formal notion of a truth condition can only be filled out in this way, by referring to states of affairs that could be located by observation.

Throughout the following chapters I shall lean heavily on the distinction that is here emphasized, between the formal theory of semantics and that part of the theory of meaning which belongs more properly to the philosophy of mind: the theory of understanding. The first contains, I suggest, no presuppositions of an epistemological kind, whereas the second requires an account of human knowledge. If we consider empiricism as a theory of understanding, then we can see why it is that a central class of sentences – present tense singular declaratives – has such importance for a philosophical inquiry of the kind we shall be engaged in. For these sentences can be given ostensive explanations: their truth conditions can be identified ostensively, by pointing to observable features of the world. It is by reference to these observable states of affairs that the meaning of elementary sentences is taught, and without this relation to an observable situation the meaning of those predicates and referring expressions that are essential for the understanding of a language could never be learned. It follows that the meaning of these primitive sentences must be given in terms of the observable states of affairs that make them true – these states of affairs are essentially involved in the teaching and learning of the sentences in question. There is, therefore, a sense of 'truth condition' in which a truth condition of '*s*' is connected to the established use of '*s*', and hence to the meaning of '*s*'; it can, therefore, be distinguished from mere evidence for the truth of '*s*'. Of course, a truth condition of '*s*' will also refer to a state of affairs that is evidence for the truth of '*s*'; but it is evidence that is connected with '*s*' in a particular way, such that were it to cease to be evidence we should be forced to conclude that the meaning of '*s*' had changed. In the epistemological sense of 'truth condition', then, we can see why it is that the meaning of a declarative sentence is (in at least these central cases) given by the conditions for its truth.

Now language learning is dependent on a certain natural understanding of the situations with which sentences are correlated: there is no *a priori* determination of what may be taken for granted. The child's future practice is the criterion of what he has understood, but at no point is practice logically determined by what has gone before. It would seem to follow that we cannot derive from the merely ostensive connection of a sentence with truth conditions a description of conditions that are both necessary and sufficient for its truth. The necessary conditions will subsist as a vaguely understood and unarticulated background to the teaching situation, while sufficient conditions could only be stated if we had some means of describing what it is about the situation that we have located by ostension. And that is to suppose an understanding of other sentences presenting precisely the problems of those we are trying to explain. However, the impossibility of *stating* necessary and sufficient conditions does not imply that such conditions do not exist: on the contrary, the argument seems to suggest that they do exist, and that they are what determine the sentence's meaning.

The connection of present tense declarative sentences with truth conditions, in the epistemological sense, perhaps accounts for the significance of Wittgenstein's notion of a 'criterion'. I take it that a criterion of intelligence, say, is a feature of a man which necessarily gives a reason for describing him as intelligent: this is part of what we mean by intelligence so that, were this fact or feature to cease to give a reason for the judgement, the concept of intelligence would thereby have changed. This definition is, as it stands, not very satisfactory, for the notion of a reason is contextual – what is a reason in one context may not be a reason in another. For example, it could be that having horns is a criterion for something's being a cow: but in other circumstances it might be part of the reason for saying of something that it is a goat and hence not a cow. We must explain, therefore, how a criterion is conceptually connected with a certain judgement. We might say that it is a conceptual truth that, in the absence of any reason to the contrary, the presence of a criterion gives a reason for the truth of the corresponding judgement. In calling this a conceptual truth I mean to point to the fact that it is through grasping the relations between a term and its criteria that a man is said to understand the term. A conceptual truth is a direct consequence of the way in which we fix the meaning of a term.

Now it follows from this that a criterion for the application of the predicate F is *also* a condition governing the truth of the sentence $F(a)$. The criteria which define the meaning of the terms employed in present tense declarative sentences also give the conditions under which those sentences are true. (These criteria are generally neither necessary nor sufficient conditions, though both necessary and sufficient conditions are related to them asymptotically.) Wittgenstein thought that the presence of criteria in anything must be detectable: they serve, therefore, to close the gap between epistemology and logic. Hence to discover the criteria for the application of a predicate is to discover what is philosophically interesting about it.

The problems of aesthetics will be answered in a way satisfactory to empiricism if the notions that trouble us – such as 'aesthetic experience', and 'the aesthetic attitude' – are elucidated in terms of their criteria, the observable states of affairs that warrant their application. But this brings us to a final assumption that may seem to make the empiricist programme impossible to carry through. This is the assumption that criteria must be publicly observable facts or features: aesthetic experience, and the aesthetic attitude must, therefore, be elucidated primarily in terms of their expression. It might be objected that we cannot possibly prove anything by approaching the subject in such a roundabout way. Surely, it will be argued, the important point is the experience or attitude itself, and this is something independent of its expression, an inner process discoverable by introspection alone. If we wish to know the essential nature of aesthetic experience, it will be said, we should embark on a phenomenological investigation, discovering what the experience is in itself, its 'noematic structure' as this is revealed to phenomenological study.[3] The plausibility of such a view is reflected in the fact that the most influential and ambitious works on aesthetics outside the idealist tradition have been works of phenomenology, such as Sartre's two treatises on imagination, Mikel Dufrenne's *Phénoménologie de L'expérience Esthétique*, and Roman Ingarden's *Das Literarische Kunstwerk*.

Phenomenology attempts to clarify the notion of aesthetic

[3] Cf., for example, the method adumbrated in E. Husserl's *Ideas*.

experience by means of a 'phenomenological reduction' of the experience itself. The experience is subjected to an 'epoché' or 'bracketing', which is to say that all reference to outer objects is excluded from its description, in which terms must occur with their ordinary reference suspended. Whether or not we espouse extensionality as a necessary condition of analysis – as modern empiricists, such as Carnap, have usually done – it is nonetheless clear that the systematic search for truth conditions in other than a formal sense will be undermined by the existence of intensional contexts for which we possess no rule of replacement. Hence phenomenological reduction, which must inevitably produce such contexts, will be avoided in this work. Moreover, there are independent arguments that support a purely extensional approach. For although an experience is supposed to be 'reduced' by phenomenological examination and hence separated both from its material object and from its outward expression, there can be no coherent description of what it is reduced *to*. The phenomenological 'descriptions' of experience, when they are not simply disguised references to public expression, are elaborate metaphors that tell us nothing definite about the experiences to which they refer. Indeed, if we assume the truth of Wittgenstein's famous argument against the possibility of reference to 'private objects' (objects statements about which are only contingently connected with statements about what is publicly observable), then this is exactly what we must expect. The 'noematic' structure of experience is no more than a metaphorical translation of the fact that experience is essentially constituted by outward circumstances.

Certainly aesthetic experience has 'intentionality', and involves a particular mode of apprehension of its object. But there is no reason why this feature should not be explained in terms of criteria that are applicable equally to the first-person and the third-person case. Indeed, I hope to make various suggestions which will show how these criteria could be produced. I shall assume that no meaning can be attached to a term of a public language – such as 'experience' – except by referring to publicly observable criteria for its application.[4] Since it is impossible to refer to 'private objects', it follows that the truth conditions of

4 See L. Wittgenstein, *Philosophical Investigations*, No. 293.

sentences about experiences and other mental states must be given in terms of publicly observable states of affairs. To put this point another way: there are no facts about mental states which are not facts that I can know and observe in another as well as in myself. Phenomenology in the tradition of Husserl attempts a study in depth of the first-person case, independently of the criteria that must be invoked in giving the meaning of any psychological term. But as Wittgenstein's discussion makes clear, we must not attempt to answer such questions as 'What is the aesthetic experience?' by looking inwards. Our knowledge of our own experiences is immediate, based on nothing. It, therefore, rests on no *features* of experiences whereby we recognize them for what they are. The noematic observation of experience can tell us nothing about it. The only facts about experience are facts about the experience of others. If we attempt to describe aesthetic experiences in our own case alone, if we attempt to discover features of our experiences that are not publicly observable, and yet on the basis of which we are supposed to classify them into kinds, then we simply characterize our experiences by means of elaborate metaphors, or through the intermediary of some special technical language (such as that invented by Husserl) whose field of reference can never be defined.

In the following inquiry, therefore, I shall refer to phenomenology only where it provides a convenient method of summarizing facts that might equally be stated in terms of what is publicly observable. I shall borrow from phenomenology the term 'aesthetic object', but I shall use it only in a material sense, to refer to the item (whether work of art or not) that is the material object of aesthetic interest. However, this does not mean that I shall be disagreeing with those phenomenologists (such as Ingarden and Dufrenne) who have argued that the work of art and the 'aesthetic object' are distinct. In the sense in which they intended this assertion it is entirely true. The phenomenologist's distinction will correspond at least in part to a distinction I shall make between the work of art and its aesthetic character.

This brings us to the end of the unargued assumptions that will dictate the method of ensuing chapters. It may be that these assumptions are not as obvious to some as they are to the author; and it may be that they express only part of the truth. However, this should not deter the reader, since questionable assumptions must be made in every treatise on aesthetics, which is only a branch of philosophy and not philosophy itself. Furthermore, it will not be without interest, even to a philosopher who imagines that all experience is in part at least irremediably 'private', to see how far the public and observable aspect of aesthetic experience can be described.

PART I
Aesthetic Judgement

CHAPTER TWO

The Individuality of the Aesthetic Object

There is a tradition in aesthetic philosophy, which perhaps derives from Kant's *Critique of Judgement*, that seeks to define the concepts of aesthetic judgement and appreciation in terms of the 'uniqueness' of the aesthetic object. In viewing something aesthetically, it is said, I am viewing it as it is in itself, divorced from any practical interest, and from all comparison with other things. I see the object as an isolated, unique occurrence, and to the extent that I appreciate it aesthetically I neither bring it under concepts nor relate it to any practical end. Associated with this view is a theory of the aesthetic attitude that has dominated aesthetics until the present day. This is the theory which seeks to define the aesthetic attitude by contrasting it with scientific (cognitive) attitudes on the one hand, and with moral (practical) attitudes on the other. I shall begin by discussing this theory, for it will show us where the main problems of the subject lie.

Clearly the theory involves two separate views. First there is a contrast between aesthetic and scientific (or cognitive) activity. When I appreciate an aesthetic object, it is said, I am not interested in comparing it with objects of a similar kind: I have no concern to derive universal laws. Kant went further, insisting that in aesthetic judgement the object is not brought under concepts at all. Hence the faculty of appreciation is quite distinct from that of the pure understanding, and involves a sort of mental leap in which the individuality of an object is seized and made present to thought. This part of the theory survives in an altered form in much recent philosophy, in particular, in the expressionism of Croce and Collingwood, with its celebrated contrast between intuition and conception. Of course, for the expressionist the object of appreciation is not the individuality of the work of art so much as the individuality of what is expressed by it, but since neither Croce nor Collingwood give a criterion whereby expression and content may be distinguished, their theory amounts to no more than a resuscitation of the Kantian standpoint. In fact, it is no exaggeration to say that all the dogmas of aesthetic philosophy in the romantic tradition are presaged in Kant's great work.

The second part of the theory is the postulation of a contrast between aesthetic and practical attitudes. Kant said that I approach the aesthetic object with my interests in abeyance. I do not judge it as something which will serve as a means to some end that is external to it, nor do I treat it as a stimulus to emotion. My attitude is one of disinterested contemplation, whose main ingredient is pleasure.[1] This aspect of the theory has received perhaps even more support than the other. Schopenhauer, for example, thought that a man could regard anything aesthetically, so long as he regarded it in independence of his will – that is, irrespective of any use to which he might put it. Regarding it thus a man could come to see the 'Idea' which the object expressed; and in this knowledge, Schopenhauer thought, aesthetic appreciation consists.[2] Of a piece with such a view is the popular theory of art as a kind of 'play' activity, where creation and appreciation are divorced from the normal urgencies of practical and moral life. 'With the agreeable, the good, the perfect,' said Schiller, 'man is merely in earnest, but with beauty he plays.'[3]

Associated with the distinction between aesthetic and practical attitudes is a more specific distinction, between what is aesthetic and what is moral. In fact, philosophers in the Kantian tradition have tended to concentrate on this distinction, partly, I think, because it is supposed that aesthetic and moral attitudes are so close that if a distinction can be made between them the task of defining the aesthetic attitude is near fulfilment.

Before discussing this approach there is a point of method that

[1] I. Kant, *Critique of Judgement*, bk. I.
[2] A. Schopenhauer, *The World as Will and Representation*, bk. III, sections 34–48.
[3] F. C. S. Schiller, *Letters on Aesthetic Education*, p. 107

arises whenever we theorize about aesthetic judgement or appreciation. It will be said that any philosophical theory of the nature of the aesthetic must inevitably have a remote and abstract quality since the notion it claims to discuss is absent from our common thought. There is no ordinary concept of the aesthetic. We do not, in common thought and speech, divide human mental life into those areas in which aesthetic appreciation plays a part and those in which it does not. Terms like 'aesthetic' and 'appreciation' are technical terms, which are perhaps given sense within the context of a philosophical theory, but which can be employed outside such a theory only in an arbitrary way, to denote activities and attitudes that may well have little in common. Why must we assume that our attitudes and feelings towards music are in any way comparable to our attitudes and feelings when reading a poem, or standing before a landscape? It seems that, before the investigation has really begun, we have already classed together, by a philosopher's sleight of hand, a bewildering multitude of mental items, as though ultimately they must exhibit a common structure. But why must they? What is there to explain that demands a unitary account of all these feelings and activities?

One suggestion is that, unless we can give a unitary account, we will be unable to explain why we describe and evaluate so many different things (pieces of music, poems, pictures, landscapes, people) in such similar ways. There is a language of appraisal in common to all the philosopher's examples of 'aesthetic appreciation', and perhaps this entitles us to assume that a particular kind of preference is evinced in each of them. We speak of works of art as 'beautiful' or 'fine'; we refer to a man's taste in paintings, music, landscapes and interior decoration; we criticize the execution of pieces of music, of paintings, of poems and so on in the same language, by referring to what it is right or not right to do, to what goes, or fits, and so on. This roughly uniform activity of aesthetic appraisal might seem to suggest an underlying attitude in common to its instances.

This view must surely have been taken for granted by Kant, who laid as great an emphasis on the concept of the beautiful as he did, in another context, on such concepts as law, freedom, good, out of which he supposed the notion of morality to be constructed.

It has been the habit among philosophers to follow Kant in this, and this has led to a great many attempts to delimit what is aesthetic in terms of an analysis of the concept of aesthetic appraisal, since this is where ordinary language seems to give most grounds for the supposition that aesthetics is indeed a unity. We might compare the attempt in recent philosophy to describe the moral area of human experience in terms of a peculiar kind of evaluation which is supposed to be characteristic of it, an enterprise which has several times been called in doubt, but which continues to attract a great deal of philosophical thought.

The emphasis on evaluation gains support from the fact that, difficult as it is to find agreed criteria of relevance governing our interest in art, it is at least accepted that art has some kind of autonomy, which is to say that we appreciate art not as a means to some end, but as an end in itself. Even if there are examples of works of art – buildings, martial music and jars – that have characteristic functions, in treating them as works of art we do not judge them simply as means to the fulfilment of these functions. If this intuition is widespread, then perhaps the basis of the aesthetic can be explored by uniting it with the view that there is some one unitary activity of aesthetic appraisal. Of course, we are still some way from showing that aesthetic appreciation and judgement involve the attribution of a uniqueness (in all the various senses derived from Kant) to their object, and that it is this, above all, that distinguishes aesthetic from moral and scientific attitudes. But we will have shown, at least, that there is a notion of aesthetic appreciation that can be derived from ordinary ways of thought and which, nonetheless, shows some similarity to the philosopher's construction.

Confirmation of this second intuition – that the aesthetic object is not treated as a means, that a proper appreciation of art (for example) must grant it a measure of autonomy – can be found among the commonplaces of modern critical thought. Someone who reads Homer merely in order to learn the elements of Greek theology, and who thereby treats Homer's works as a means for conveying information, is said to be uninterested in the poetry as poetry. In other words, he does not appreciate it as it is made to be appreciated: he may be blind to its nature as an aesthetic object. Again, it is customary to argue that pornography cannot, except exceptionally, be art, since the aims of pornography and the aims of art are incompatible. Pornography is essentially a means to the stimulation of sexual feeling, whereas art is the means to the stimulation of nothing at all. The arguments for aesthetic autonomy can be carried further. It is said, for example, that the Italian peasant who adorns a statue of the Virgin cannot, to the extent that he treats the statue as an object of religious veneration, appreciate it from an aesthetic point of view. For to the extent that his interest is religious he must treat its immediate object as a surrogate for something else. He sees through the statue to what it represents and is interested in it only in so far as it evokes a true conception of the Virgin. The statue serves the peasant as a means for the transmission of a religious thought: it can have value as such a means to the extent that it succeeds in inspiring the thought, whether or not it also has value as a work of art. It follows that the question of good or bad taste need not arise, and the presence of an adored St Dominic in plastic beside an overlooked Virgin by Sansovino is not in itself a sign of the corruption of aesthetic judgement. This way of thinking – which opens the way to the expressionist view that representation is in itself alien to the aims of art – is again one of the mainstays of romanticism.

This argument for autonomy may be taken so far as to begin to sound absurd. Thus it might be argued with Kant,[4] and with many modern philosophers, that aesthetic interest cannot be interest in an object as a means to the evocation of emotion, and hence that to treat a play, for example, as though it were a vehicle for arousing pity and terror is to fall into the error of the heteronomy of aesthetic judgement. The play is not a means for arousing dramatic emotions, and hence to the extent that one's enjoyment of a play consists in the experience of these emotions it is not aesthetic – for the play might equally have been replaced by some other object of similar feelings. Thus the defence of autonomy can lead to a blanket condemnation of emotion in art. In fact, it can lead to a theory that aesthetic appreciation is nothing more nor less than totally disinterested contemplation, about which nothing more can be said than that its object has certain formal properties. Alternatively, if it is still admitted that

[4] Op. cit., bk. I, section 13.

there is something that might justifiably be called the 'experience' of art, this experience is itself made autonomous, impossible to assimilate to any of the normal categories of emotion or thought, having nothing in common with anything that might be felt in another situation.[5] So that, if art *is*, in some minimal sense, a means for the arousal of aesthetic experience, it is still a means that cannot be replaced by any other. Hence an interest in art is no less an interest in art for its own sake. The work of art is still not considered as a means to the production of anything that is identifiable apart from it. This, in brief, is the Crocean version of autonomy, which carries with it a masterly condemnation of the popular prejudice described as an '*estetica del simpatico*', which is supposed everywhere to replace the true refinement of taste.

Clearly, for aesthetic theory to have advanced on so slight a basis to such point of obscurity and dogmatism, something very questionable must have been taken for granted. Some may wish to say that the assumption that aesthetic interest is not interest in something as a means is simply a dogma, inspired like so much else by the romantic movement, with its excessive emphasis on creativity and personal expression. One can point to societies and civilizations where the whole idea of art as an end in itself seems without an application. Surely, the prime purpose of what we now call art in ancient Egypt was to create an atmosphere of awe, to cast a sort of spell that would give permanence to the acts and desires of Pharoahs who might otherwise have been forgotten.[6] Is this not an example of a society in which art and the appreciation of art cannot have the structure that the philosopher claims is essential to them? In other words, it can be argued, and to a certain extent persuasively, that the supposed intuition of an autonomous character in aesthetic appreciation is nothing more than the reflection of a transient historical bias in favour of one sort of attitude to art, which has no more right to be classed as *the* mode of aesthetic appreciation than any other.

But this argument is perhaps not as important as it appears. For what is of interest is that we should be able to classify *some* mental activity as aesthetic appreciation, and that we should

[5] Cf. Clive Bell, *Art*.
[6] Cf. Collingwood's diagnosis of this attitude – and its contemporary equivalents – in his study of 'magic art', *The Principles of Art*, pp. 69–77.

be able to analyse it so as to show its differences from and resemblances to, for example, practical and moral attitudes. And whether or not other civilizations would have made the classification in the same way is not strictly relevant to our purpose. For our purpose is to produce a theory that will create some semblance of order among our present ways of talking about, and experiencing, aesthetic objects. We are not analysing a pre-existing and self-sufficient notion of the aesthetic that will enable us to say with any certainty that some other civilization, or some other period of history, appreciated objects aesthetically, but nonetheless in an unfamiliar way. We need some theory before we shall ever be able to gauge the importance of this fact, if it is indeed a fact.

A far more direct diagnosis of the aesthetician's confusion is this: no adequate analysis has been given of what it is to be interested in something as a means, or as it is in itself, for its own sake. We do not know fully what distinction is being invoked. And yet that there *is* a distinction is, I think, something that we do not doubt. Perhaps, then, we should combine our two intuitions, first that appreciation of art is not appreciation of it as a means to any independent end, and secondly that there is in some sense a distinct activity of aesthetic appraisal, and use them to clarify each other. That is, perhaps we should argue that the best way of defining in what way aesthetic appreciation is appreciation of an object 'as it is in itself' is through an analysis of the procedure of aesthetic appraisal.

This suggestion might be supported in the following way: when I evaluate or assess the merits of something, then I evaluate it with respect to some interest that it satisfies. If I am interested in something as a means then my interest is directed to an end towards which the object may contribute. For example, if I am interested in a car in order to travel in comfort to the Highlands, then this purpose is the determining factor of my interest in the car, and I shall assess the car's merits accordingly. I shall judge it to be a good car for my purpose to the extent that it is comfortable, reliable, able to ascend steep hills, and so on. I shall not judge it to be good for my purpose because of its shape or speed, except to the extent that I regard these qualities as themselves contributing something that is integral to my purpose. My purpose defines criteria of relevance, which enable me to set aside those features of the object which are relevant to its assessment from those which are not. And since the features which are relevant to the assessment of the car need not be identifying features (for any purpose distinct from the car itself) it is clear that different cars may yet be identical with regard to their merits as means to my particular end.

But if I have no end or purpose separately identifiable from the object of my interest, then surely there can be no criteria of relevance of this kind, no criteria that will enable me to say that some features of an object will be relevant to its assessment, others will not. So that, if interest in a work of art is not interest in it as a means, it seems to follow that there can be no criteria of relevance that will enable us to say that a work of art's merits depend on this feature rather than that, or which will enable us to produce any formula as to what features a work of art must possess if it is to be wholly successful from the aesthetic point of view. We thus arrive at the views that every feature of a work of art is relevant to our assessment of it, and that there can be no rules for the assessment of works of art. In other words, whatever aesthetic appraisal is, it must involve just that kind of interest in the *uniqueness* of an object which Kant and Croce, in their several ways, attempted to describe.

We seem then to have achieved a partial characterization of the aesthetic attitude. It is a kind of spectator interest, whose object is the uniqueness or individuality of some work of art or other object of aesthetic interest. It issues, therefore, in a particular mode of evaluation of its object, in which the idea of a feature relevant to assessment can have no place. This nest of doctrines in fact originates in the same pair of seemingly undeniable intuitions, and their mutual coherence can only seem to confirm the view that this is what aesthetic appreciation is like. It is scarcely surprising that the doctrines occur more or less unchanged in the writings of several modern aestheticians.[7] The question is how far this theory gives an adequate or complete characterization of a separate realm of mental life, and how far it enables us

[7] See especially Stuart Hampshire, 'Logic and Appreciation', in W. Elton (ed.), *Aesthetics and Language*, and P. F. Strawson, 'Aesthetic Appraisal and Works of Art', in *The Oxford Review*, 1966.

to place art and the experience of art in relation to the other phenomena with which it is normally compared and contrasted.

It is important to separate the question of the uniqueness of the work of art – which, as I have outlined it, involves a theory of aesthetic appreciation – from questions about the identity of the work of art. The uniqueness that is conferred on an object by its criteria of individuation and identity is implied in all our references to it, and if works of art have conditions of identity which confer 'uniqueness', then this simply means that they can change in no respect without ceasing to be the same works of art. Whether or not this is true is, it seems to me, a question of little interest in aesthetics. The question is not whether works of art do have such strong criteria of identity, but rather whether every change in a work of art is necessarily a change in its aesthetic character. If a work of art does change in some respect, then the important question is not how it is to be identified through the change in question (whether it must be identified as the same or as another work of art) but rather how our aesthetic interest will be affected by this change.

The uniqueness of the work of art is not, therefore, a product of restrictions that might be placed, for whatever reason, on the criteria for the identity of works of art. It is rather an outcome of the fact that, in a certain state of mind, which we are referring to as aesthetic appreciation, the object is *appreciated* for its uniqueness: the object is not regarded as replaceable by another that will 'do just as well'. In other words, there need be no special problem about the identity of works of art. We are under no logical obligation to stipulate, for example, that all the features of a work that we appreciate aesthetically must for that reason be defining features.[8] It is to Kant's credit that, unlike many more recent philosophers, he saw that the supposed uniqueness of the aesthetic object could not be objectified as an attribute of it, but must be analysed as a formal element in aesthetic interest.

It might be said that our appreciation of works of art is such as to *impose* the need for a special criterion of identity; for example, we should only identify a painting with a physical object if we really appreciated it as such, otherwise our concept of a

[8] A view that is upheld by Strawson, op. cit., p. 11.

work of art and our concept of an object of aesthetic interest would fall asunder. But this argument seems to be wrong. Against those philosophers who argue that all works of art are essentially 'types', for example, one need only point to examples. Buildings have whatever aesthetic character they have as physical objects: to institute a system of limited reproduction of Borromini's delightful church at the *Quattro Fontane* could only serve to alter its character as an object of appreciation. Hence it could not be our way of appreciating the building that dictates that it should possess the identity of a type and not that of a physical object. Of course, we could imagine a situation – the perfect reproduction of buildings and paintings – where works of art previously identified as physical objects would have to be redescribed as types.[9] But this is simply to imagine a situation in which some physical objects have been so perfectly reproduced as to become mere tokens of universal types, in which case the grounds for making a distinction between building- or painting-identity, say, and physical-object-identity collapse. The conclusion is, I think, that we should identify works of art in the way dictated by the respective media of art. Some works (paintings, sculptures and so on) will be physical objects; others (poems and novels) will be types; others (musical works) may have the more complicated kind of identity conferred by a developed notation. In every case the question of identity and the question of uniqueness are distinct.

We need, then, to discuss aesthetic appraisal independently of its supposed contribution to the identity-conditions of a work of art. Thus there arises the attempt to derive a more useful notion of 'uniqueness' through a consideration of the kinds of reason that can be adduced in support of aesthetic judgements. It might be argued that aesthetic appraisal cannot share the logical structure of moral reasoning. For there cannot be reasons in favour of aesthetic judgements in the sense of descriptions which would always count towards some given conclusion. There cannot be properties that 'confer value' on a work of art. The effect of any property must be determined *a posteriori*, through experience of the case in hand. This is part of what Kant meant when he wrote that the judgement of beauty is free from concepts: it involves no prior classification or description of its object. Criticism is

[9] Cf. Strawson, op. cit., p. 10.

concerned with the merits of the particular case, the work of art in itself, as a unique and unrepeatable performance. In morality, on the other hand, we are concerned with properties that confer moral value on our acts and character; for we wish to guide our conduct in the light of rational principles.

This is an interesting suggestion, which seems to be supported, at first sight, by a recognized truism. Cannot one work of art be of great value and interest partly on account of some feature that, in another work, creates dullness and disorder? (Compare the effect of the repeated diminished harmony in Brahms' *Intermezzo*, No. 6, op. 128, with its effect in the recitatives of *Der Freischütz*, or the effect of the 'drunken soldiery' in Yeats' 'Byzantium' with their effect in the first chapter of *Salammbô*.) On the other hand, this alone can scarcely be regarded as a distinguishing mark of aesthetic reasoning. One action might be morally good and another morally bad, where a single feature contributes to the goodness of the one and to the badness of the other. An action that causes pleasure may be good when the pleasure is deserved, but bad when the pleasure is depraved. Many examples are familiar from moral philosophy. Often the only clear guarantee that we have identified a criterion of value in an action, in the sense of a feature that *always* adds merit, resides in the fact that we have described the feature in its total context. But then we have not described it independently of the action.[10]

It will be replied that there could be features of actions which really *do* count one way in deciding their merit, although these features would not be simple 'first-order features' (such as causing the happiness of someone) but rather 'second-order features', features whose presence can only be discovered by a certain amount of interpretation. These features would be those the value of which is laid down by a moral code (or, on a naturalist view of ethics, the value of which is discovered by a moral code), or which play a decisive part in moral thought. The traditional virtues would naturally belong to this class of features. It makes sense to say (whether or not it is in some sense necessarily true) that it is *always* a reason for the merit of an action that it is courageous, benevolent, honest, noble or kind. Whether an action

[10] See Ruby Meager, 'The Uniqueness of the Work of Art', in C. Barrett (ed.), *Collected Papers on Aesthetics*.

possesses such a feature is not discoverable by direct observation of its structure or consequences. But, none the less these features can be described without giving a complete description of the actions that possess them.

Again, however, the point is not established. For there are also two orders of description applicable to the objects of aesthetic judgement, and it makes perfectly good sense to say that the presence of a property on the second level is always a reason for calling a work of art good. (In so far as it ever makes perfect sense to say that the presence of any feature is *always* a reason, while not a sufficient condition, for describing an object in a certain way.) For example, we describe works of art not only in terms of their metrical or harmonic structure, their slowness, loudness, brightness, or literal meaning, but also in terms of more tentative and context-dependent interpretations, in which we speak of them as tragic, moving, balanced, evocative, sincere, sad, refined, noble, sentimental and so on. This second vocabulary is in some ways similar to the vocabulary of moral virtue, and seems at first sight to play a similar role in aesthetic thought and judgement. So why do we not admit that it is a vocabulary referring to the criteria of value which works of art are supposed not to exhibit? Although it is true that we may have to invoke the whole context before we can determine whether a work of art is sentimental or profound, we can describe these features without giving a total description of the works of art which possess them.

It might be replied that the 'aesthetic features' (such as those just referred to) are named by evaluative words, and so themselves convey evaluations; they do not provide genuine reasons *for* these evaluations.[11] But it is very unclear what is meant by saying that the second-order, aesthetic, descriptions of a work of art are evaluative – clearly it cannot be meant to deny that a work of art can be sad, noble, sincere, or whatever, and yet nonetheless a failure, just as an action can be benevolent, noble and honest without being right. Clearly it is difficult to force any contrast here with second-order descriptions in moral discourse. If there are added arguments for saying that the language of moral virtue is more truly descriptive than its aesthetic counterpart, then not only do they need to be produced, but it would also be very

[11] Cf. Strawson, op. cit., pp. 11 and 13.

difficult to know what interpretation to put on the fact that they could be produced, if it is a fact.

It seems then that it would be wiser to abandon the attempt to make a distinction between aesthetic and moral assessment in terms of the kind of uniqueness attributed by the former. The conclusions offered by the attempt are too vague to be of much use without some independent theory about the nature of aesthetic interest. Clearly aesthetic and moral assessment do differ; for while they each involve the evaluation of objects as ends rather than as means, the connection with ends, in the case of aesthetic assessment, is more immediate. Aesthetic assessment involves the evaluation of a particular object, for its own sake; it must be supported, therefore, by reasons of a certain kind. But the kind of reasons cannot really be described until we have some independent account of how aesthetic and moral assessment arise. For example, if we could describe aesthetic attitudes, and contrast them with moral attitudes, conclusions will immediately follow as to the nature of reasons which will support the one and not the other, or as to the logical nature of the evaluative speech-acts which, on one plausible theory of the nature of 'assessment', will express or convey them.

In answer to this objection it might be argued that aesthetic appreciation is to be characterized in terms of its objects and not in terms of the evaluative procedures that give expression to it. But what are these objects? We find that the preceding discussion contains a possible answer: just as the objects of practical interest are the practical or utilitarian features of a thing, and just as the objects of moral interest are the virtues, vices and moral properties generally of a thing, so the objects of aesthetic interest are the 'aesthetic' qualities of a thing – the features named by the 'second-order' descriptions of which I gave examples above.

This suggestion is, on the face of it, highly persuasive. It gives us an immediate means of characterizing aesthetic interest and appreciation – they are simply interest in, and appreciation of, certain features. Aesthetic judgement is, except in the exceptional case of overall evaluation or assessment, the simple cognitive procedure of judging that an object has certain aesthetic features, and taste is the faculty of being able to discern those features. And it is clear that there are features which do receive special emphasis in the criticism of art – features such as expressiveness, nobility and grandeur. Moreover, these features are associated immediately with the mode of evaluation whose consistency of expression was one of our few intuitions about the nature of aesthetic interest.

This suggestion also makes room for a contrast between aesthetic and practical attitudes. For the 'aesthetic' features commonly referred to are in some sense intrinsic features of an object – that is, they do not belong to it on account of any end which it may serve. A piece of music is not sad because it can be used to evoke sadness, or noble because it can be used to create an atmosphere of authority. This seems to provide some confirmation for the view that an adequate theory of the distinction between what is aesthetic and what is not can be arrived at by listing the features that are the characteristic objects of aesthetic judgement. This is the view that we must now examine.

CHAPTER THREE

Aesthetic Perception

The suggestion that aesthetic interest and evaluation should be defined in terms of the features in which both are grounded is familiar[1] and it is a small step to the idea that these features can be set apart as a roughly independent class. Perhaps the most interesting development of this idea is in the theory of aesthetic perception, a theory which derives from Hutcheson, and which has been one of the mainstays of empiricism for at least two centuries. This is the theory that to appreciate an object aesthetically is to 'perceive' its aesthetic features, aesthetic features being precisely those that it needs aesthetic perception (or 'taste') to discern. It is this theory that I shall now discuss.

In order to avoid confusion I shall distinguish features from properties. By 'feature' I mean whatever is, or seems to be, attributed by a predicate. In other words, if 'X is Y' makes sense, then, whenever X is Y, X possesses the feature of Y-ness. But it does not follow from this that Y-ness is also a property: it is only a *property* if the sentence 'X is Y' has realistic truth conditions (truth conditions in the strong sense explained in Chapter One). In other words, the idea of a feature is grammatical, whereas that of a property has an epistemological content. This distinction is of great importance, and I shall elaborate it in detail in the following chapters. For the present I shall use the term 'feature' as a convenience only: there is a feature for every predicate. Thus it is a feature of a man that he is good, irritating or beautiful, even

---

[1] See, for example, J. O. Urmson, 'What Makes a Situation Aesthetic?', *A.S.S.V.*, 1957.

though, in the realistic sense, goodness, irritatingness and beauty may not be properties at all.

How do we identify aesthetic features? It seems that there is no adequate pre-theoretical answer to this question. Nonetheless, we have the idea that some properties of an aesthetic object can be discerned by anyone with normal eyes, ears and intelligence, whereas others can be discerned only with the additional help of taste, perceptiveness or judgement.[2] This difference corresponds to the distinction we wish to draw, although in order to identify aesthetic features in advance of any theory, we must simply list the predicates that attribute them. Among these predicates we find a great variety. For example, there are predicates whose primary use is in aesthetic judgement, predicates like 'beautiful', 'graceful', 'elegant' and 'ugly'. These terms occur primarily in judgements of aesthetic value. Then there are descriptions referring to the formal or technical accomplishment of a work of art: 'balanced', 'well-made', 'economical', 'rough', 'undisciplined', and so on. Many aesthetic descriptions employ predicates that are normally used to describe the mental and emotional life of human beings. We describe works of art as sad, joyful, melancholy, agitated, erotic, sincere, vulgar, intelligent and mature. Almost any mental predicate can be applied to a work of art and some (e.g. 'sad') can be applied to aesthetic objects generally. Aesthetic descriptions can also refer to the expressive features of works of art. Works of art are often said to express emotion, thought, attitude, character, in fact, anything that can be expressed at all. For example, Watteau's *Embarcation à Cythère* can be said to express the transience of human joys, Shakespeare's *Measure for Measure* to express the essence of Christian charity.

Closely connected with expression terms are the terms known philosophically as 'affective': terms that seem to be used to express or project particular human responses which they also indicate by name – examples include 'moving', 'exciting', 'evocative', 'nauseous', 'tedious', 'enjoyable' and 'adorable'. We must also include among aesthetic descriptions several kinds of comparison. For example, I may describe a writer's style as bloated or masculine, a colour as warm or cold, a piece of music as architectural.

[2] On this point see F. N. Sibley, 'Aesthetic Concepts', *Phil. Rev.*, 1959, and 'Aesthetic and Non-aesthetic', *Phil. Rev.*, 1965.

Examples can be found by the score. When it is said that this use of terms is purely 'figurative' or 'metaphorical' it must not be thought that any problem has been solved. There is a philosophical question about the nature of metaphor and about its distinction, if any, from simile, which is as intransigent as any problem about the nature of aesthetic judgement.

Finally there are various descriptions of a work of art in terms of what it represents, in terms of its truthfulness, or its overall character or genre (whether it is tragic, comic, ironical or what) which cannot easily be fitted into these classes, but which have an important role, despite this, in aesthetic judgement.

This bewildering list of examples must be extended to include any description that can be used (whether or not it normally *is* used) to refer to an aesthetic feature – a feature which it needs 'taste' or 'perceptiveness' to discern, and which can be mentioned (according to the intuition of the last chapter) as part of the reason for an aesthetic assessment. The list is so large that it might seem at first absurd to attempt to use it as a definition of aesthetic judgement. For one thing, since it includes the categories of comparison and metaphor, it will be impossible to avoid the conclusion that any and every object has an aesthetic character of indefinite complexity. But whether or not this is really an objection to the theory is a question that can scarcely be settled in the abstract. For the theory states that we can do no better than to distinguish an aesthetic interest as an interest in the aesthetic features of an object – an interest in the features of objects attributed by descriptions, such as those above, in their aesthetic use. Aesthetic appreciation is the gaining of *knowledge* about these features, by means of 'aesthetic perception', or 'taste'.

This theory need not appear implausible. It is worth mentioning the fact that we very often *do* judge whether a man's interest in an object is primarily aesthetic, on the basis of the descriptions he would be prepared to give of its object. It is not absurd to suppose that these descriptions refer to perceivable properties of the object. For example, someone who condemns the actions of others not as cowardly, brutal, evil or corrupt but rather as tedious, inelegant, depressing or vulgar has a consciousness of them that we might wish to describe as at least partly aesthetic – at any rate, amoral. His aesthetic interest has pervaded the sphere of moral judgement, and this is revealed in the features of actions that most awaken his praise or blame.

This, of course, like all our pre-theoretical intuitions in aesthetics, is open to as many interpretations as there have been theories. Nonetheless, it will show, I hope, that the theory under discussion is far from absurd, and fails, if it does so, for a far deeper reason than its inability to conform to common intuition. The central problem is to discover whether there is any unitary logic characterizing the aesthetic use of terms. Without this unitary logic the concept of aesthetic appreciation, defined *merely* in terms of an open and indefinite class of features, will be an arbitrary and uninteresting notion, with no ultimate ground, and with no special place in the philosophy of mind.

Now Sibley has recently maintained, in defending the theory of aesthetic perception, that there *is* a distinguishing logic of aesthetic description.[3] Although he does not actually use the term 'criterion', it is part of Sibley's view that there are no criteria, in Wittgenstein's sense, for the application of terms in their aesthetic use. Although aesthetic features depend on non-aesthetic features, so that a painting might be delicate, say, *on account of* its pale colours and slender shapes, they are not 'conditioned' (as Sibley puts it) by non-aesthetic features. Sibley's arguments for this conclusion are reminiscent of the Kantian arguments against the possibility of criteria of value in art. He asserts that any description given as a reason for a work's being, say, sad, *could* be given as a reason for some other work's being boring or staid, and any two works could be sad for quite different, and often conflicting, reasons. Therefore, 'reason' in aesthetic judgement cannot mean anything like 'criterion' as I have used it – aesthetic reasons are not truth conditions. Of course, 'reason' does not usually mean 'criterion' in non-aesthetic judgement; it is Sibley's contention that there simply *are* no criteria for aesthetic descriptions.

It is worthwhile mentioning that this point is extremely difficult to prove. It is not the fact of counting one way that makes a reason refer to a criterion (or verification condition) – as is clear in the light of the argument of Chapter One. For example, many predicates that attribute mental states share criteria: one and the

[3] See F. N. Sibley, op. cit.

same feature can be both a criterion of sadness and a criterion of anger. Whether it is a *reason* for any particular judgement can depend only on the context. It might be thought that we could at least establish that there are no sufficient conditions (in terms of non-aesthetic features) for the truth of an aesthetic description. No list of non-aesthetic features can *entail* an aesthetic judgement. But it is open to someone to argue that at least the list of features that constitutes the complete, phenomenal, 'first-order' description of the work of art must entail the presence of whatever aesthetic features it has. For if aesthetic features are truly *dependent* then any other work of art with entirely the same first-order properties and relations must also have the same aesthetic character. Certainly, this gives us no *rule* for the reapplication of an aesthetic term. But this absence of rules is insufficient to define the contrast between aesthetic and non-aesthetic judgement. For once again there seems to be no distinction between aesthetic and certain indubitably non-aesthetic descriptions – for example, certain descriptions of action in terms of mental concepts. Often we can describe or point to a sequence of behaviour that would be sufficient for attributing some mental state (such as sadness) to a man. Hence we have sufficient conditions for saying that the behaviour in question is expressive of sadness: its being so is the basis for our judgement that the man himself is sad. But here, as in the case of aesthetic description, we cannot convert this sufficient condition into a rule that isolates more than the individual case – a recurrence of these actions, or this behaviour, even as the behaviour of another man, would be a recurrence of the same actions or the same behaviour.

We seem, then, to have no conclusive proof for the view that there are no criteria for the application of aesthetic terms. This is partly, I believe, because it would be very hard to imagine what a general proof would look like. Just as no one has yet succeeded in demonstrating that there is a naturalistic fallacy in ethics, or a logical gap between description and evaluation, so no one is likely to succeed in demonstrating that there is a similar gap between non-aesthetic and aesthetic descriptions. For while it may follow from the truth of some theory about the meaning of moral or aesthetic judgements that they are logically independent of ordinary descriptions, the plausibility of the theory hangs on whether such intuitions as we have about meaning and synonymy confirm this lack of any logical relation. And notoriously people's intuitions differ.

The comparison with moral judgements in fact helps us to clarify the notion of an aesthetic feature. It will be quite properly objected that the sharp distinction between aesthetic and non-aesthetic, first-order and second-order, features that has been assumed by the theory is grotesquely absolute, like the comparable distinction in ethics between 'brute' facts and moral values. Just as the naturalist in ethics will argue that the creation of this artificial dichotomy provides the only reason so far given for the dogma that there is a logical gap between description and evaluation, so will the opponent of the idea of an aesthetic feature argue that the seemingly 'unconditioned' character of these features arises purely out of the crude classification of features into exclusive types. It sounds plausible to say that features of a poem such as its length, rhythm and rhyme-scheme cannot be criteria of profundity. But is it so plausible to say that subtlety of rhythm, development of rhyme, the control of thought, are only contingently related to the aesthetic judgement? They seem to stand between the plain 'first-order' features and the aesthetic features which depend on them, as the complexities of 'institutional fact' stand between brute facts and values.[4] We should not therefore expect to find any proof of the logical autonomy of aesthetic description by attempting to show that aesthetic descriptions lack criteria. For this can never be shown. And if it is merely hypothesized, then we need a complete and plausible theory of the meaning of aesthetic judgements that will explain independently everything that needs to be explained about them. It is the failure to provide such a theory of meaning that has prevented the formation of a genuine alternative to ethical naturalism. Simply to insist that aesthetic features are not conditioned by non-aesthetic features is to utter a pointless protest against a likely hypothesis. It is a theory with which we can do nothing.

The kind of argument that is brought against the naturalist in ethics can be brought against the view that there are criteria for aesthetic judgement, but with just as slight a degree of success.

[4] Cf. G. E. M. Anscombe, 'On Brute Facts', *Analysis*, 1958; J. R. Searle, *Speech Acts*, ch. 8.

It could be argued, for example, that someone can acknowledge and accept a complete description of a work of art, show complete understanding of the terms used to attribute an aesthetic character on the basis of this description, and yet still dissent from any particular attribution, no matter how closely he studies the work. But this amounts to no more than the *assertion* that there are no sufficient conditions of aesthetic judgement. It is certainly not a proof, relying as it does on an intuition about what it is to 'understand' an aesthetic judgement that could as easily be denied. Besides, what is meant by a complete description of a work of art? Similarly if someone merely argued that there are no criteria for aesthetic judgement – since a man can dissent from any reason for an attribution of some aesthetic term without thereby showing that he fails to understand the term – this still amounts to no more than an assertion of what may, indeed, be a consistent and tenable position, but which needs to be proved by some other means.

Nonetheless, it may still be true that terms used in aesthetic descriptions have no criteria. But we must bear in mind that this view is at best an hypothesis, which can be made plausible only by what we build on it. The theory of aesthetic perception uses the view as a basis for an account of aesthetic judgement that is reminiscent of the ethical intuitionism that Moore derived from his 'discovery' of the 'naturalistic fallacy' in ethics.[5] Moore concluded that moral features such as goodness must be like colours, simple properties answering to a basic classification of objects in terms of experience. He invented a special faculty – intuition – whereby these 'simple' properties could be discerned. In a similar way, we might argue that aesthetic features are discerned by a single perceptual faculty – 'aesthetic perception' or 'taste'. The one difference is that for the theory of aesthetic perception aesthetic properties are not, strictly speaking, 'simple' properties, but 'tertiary' or 'emergent' properties:[6] they always depend in some way on other properties, although the relation between them and these other properties is not a logical one. As examples of emergent properties we might consider aspects, and Gestalt configurations generally.

[5] G. E. Moore, *Principia Ethica*, ch. 1.
[6] See F. N. Sibley, op. cit.

The idea of an emergent property needs to be closely examined. We are told that emergent properties depend on others in some way, but in no *particular* way: all that can be said about this relation of dependence is that, seeing the first-order properties on which an emergent property depends, someone with the right perceptual capacity (taste, in the case of aesthetic judgement) will come to 'see' the emergent property in the object. This is analytically true (or almost so), for it is really an explanation of what it is to possess this perceptual capacity. The capacity could not be identified in any other way – say, in terms of a sense-organ, or in terms of a particular sensation which would need to be identified itself by reference to some part of the body. The judgements in support of aesthetic descriptions do not really give reasons, but rather aim at a certain 'perception'. Criticism is a matter of judiciously referring to the first-order features that another might have missed, or attached a wrong importance to, and then hoping that the emergent property will become apparent also to him. (I shall argue that in certain important ways this is a correct account of what happens in criticism.) No amount of argument can bring *knowledge* of an aesthetic feature, however; its dependence on other features is not logical. In the last resort one can only look and see if it is there. Nonetheless, aesthetic features are dependent, so that not to have noticed an aesthetic feature might simply be a matter of not having noticed some first-order property on which it depends. It is for this reason that one has to 'see for oneself' in the appreciation of art: if you do not perceive aright, then there is no process of reasoning that can oblige you to change your mind or be counted irrational, even though there *are* reasons, whose validity you must also learn to 'see' in the particular case.

The notion of an emergent property is confused, for the following reason: in the case of aspects (which are one kind of emergent property) different emergent 'properties' can depend on precisely the *same* set of first-order properties. (In the ambiguous figure, the duck aspect and the rabbit aspect are not the *same* aspect, even though they depend on the same observable shapes.) Extending this observation to criticism we come at once to the conclusion that *incompatible* critical judgements can be (even if they perhaps never are) entirely based on the same set of first-order features of a work of art.

The point can readily be illustrated by an example. Consider the following passage from *Paradise Lost*:

> the other shape
> If shape it might be called that shape had none
> Distinguishable, in member joint or limb;
> Or substance might be called that shadow seemed,
> For each seemed either; black he stood as night;
> Fierce as ten furies; terrible as Hell;
> And shook a deadly dart. What seemed his head
> The likeness of a Kingly crown had on. . . .

There is an undeniable obscurity of imagery in this passage, combined with a strict regularity of iambic rhythm. Someone might point to further features – the numerous qualifying descriptions, none of which serve to add any visual detail, other than the final two; the use of rather common phrases such as 'fierce as ten furies', 'black as night', 'deadly dart'; the repetition of the same idea in 'member', 'joint' and 'limb', and so on – and argue that there 'emerges' from these non-aesthetic features a dead and rhetorical aesthetic quality. But it is equally possible to re-describe the passage, mentioning the same set of non-aesthetic features, so that the reader comes to take them in quite another way. It is possible, for example, to argue that the 'common' phrases are used deliberately, in order to prevent the details they refer to from standing out above the obscurity of the overall impression; that the repetition involved in 'member, joint or limb' serves to obliterate what might otherwise have been too tangible and concrete a detail; that the uncertainty and obscurity are carried forward with the same regular and determined iambic rhythm, so that when the imagery at last becomes concrete in the reference to a Kingly crown, this serves only to confirm the terror and confusion latent in what has gone before. It is as though the only detail of the scene that could be grasped is the detail which confers power and majesty on the object of terror. Clearly someone might argue in this way, and eventually persuade the reader to 'see', in the very same first-order features that seemed responsible for a deadness of effect, the proper sublimity which Burke chose this passage as exemplifying.[7]

[7] Edmund Burke, *A Philosophical Enquiry into the Origin of our Ideas of the Sublime and the Beautiful*.

Exactly what has happened in the course of this argument is difficult to assess. But it does suggest that the notion of a merely emergent property whose presence can only be detected by a kind of perception, is confused. For in what sense are the incompatible properties A and B dependent on the first-order properties P, Q and R if P, Q and R do not determine either A or B uniquely? And in what sense can A and B be observable properties if, purely on the basis of someone reasoning about P, Q and R, I come to see A where once I saw B, and if this is supposed to be all there is to the seeing of either?

There is a further argument for the same conclusion which, although less general (applying only to certain terms in their aesthetic use), is more powerful. Consider the application of an emotion term – such as 'sad' – to a work of art (or, for that matter, to an event, or a letter, or anything that cannot literally be in the emotional state of sadness). To understand the word 'sad' is to know how to apply it to people in order to describe their emotional state. The criteria for the application of the term 'sad' concern the gestures, expressions and utterances of people on the basis of which I describe them as sad, and to grasp the concept of sadness is to know how to apply it on the basis of these criteria. When we apply the concept to art, however, it is arguable that these criteria are not, or need not be, present. Does this mean that the term 'sad' is ambiguous?

To say that the term 'sad' in its aesthetic use names a perceptual property which is emergent but which has no criteria is to say in effect that it is ambiguous between its aesthetic and non-aesthetic uses. For the basis of its ascription in each use is not the same. In the one case the term denotes an emergent perceptual property, in the other use it denotes a property determined by established criteria. It follows that a man could understand one use without understanding the other. However, this does not seem to be possible. The use to refer to an emotional state is primary, and anyone who did not understand *this* use of the term 'sad' – did not understand what the emotion of sadness was – would not know what he was talking about in attributing sadness to a work of art.

This point is confirmed by the following consideration: suppose that there is some agreement among adults trained in the appreciation of art as to which works of art are sad. The very idea of an observable property seems to require that, at the very least, such an agreement is possible, if not actual.[8] Suppose, then, that I classify all works of art as sad or not sad: I classify them into two groups, with perhaps a third group in between where the question whether or not they are sad is undecidable. Now suppose also that someone else carries out the same classification, without consulting me, and groups works of art together in exactly the same way as I do myself. And suppose, finally, that both he and I agree in our application of the term 'sad' to people (its use to denote an emotional state). That is, we agree about the normal sense of the term and use it according to the same criteria. Imagine, then, that while I call the two categories 'sad' and 'not sad', he refuses to apply these terms. He says, for example, that it is nonsense to call works of art sad, he does not know what to call the property in virtue of which he has made the classification that he has made, but certainly it would be wrong to call it sadness – works of art cannot have states of mind.[9] Despite this, if the aesthetic feature in question is an observable emergent property, we must say that the man has perceived the sadness of the works of art in question, just as someone who used the term 'hot' to name the property of redness, would count as perceiving the redness of things, provided only that he made the right classification on the basis of his visual experience.

But it is very odd to say that the man in question has seen the sadness of the works of art that he classifies together. He has not seen that what it is they all have in common is *sadness*, one wants to say, for he has not seen the vital connection that exists between these works and the emotional state. It is a strange fact that he has classified these works of art together, a fact which could be a reason for saying that he has seen their sadness but not, *pace* the theory of aesthetic perception, a sufficient reason. For he must in some way make the connection between these works of art and the sadness of people.

It is easy to see that this connection must not be broken. For it could be a reason for saying that Henry is sad that he chooses,

[8] Cf. F. N. Sibley and M. K. Tanner, 'Objectivity and Aesthetics', *A.S.S.V.*, 1968.
[9] Let us suppose also that in saying this our subject is not, like Stravinsky in his many attacks on musical sentimentalism, merely philosophizing.

say, sad works of literature to read aloud to his family, or sad pieces of music to play at the piano. And if the sadness of music and the sadness of men are quite different properties, then Jacques, in *As You Like It*, is simply deceived in thinking that he '... can suck melancholy out of a song As a weasel sucks eggs ...'. Besides, there are many non-aesthetic uses of 'sad' where what is sad is not a person, nor any kind of sentient being: it might be an event. If we say that here too we have a different concept of sadness then a very important connection is broken – that between the sadness of lamentable occurrences and the sadness of people. But if we say that we have one and the same concept of sadness here then we are pressed to admit that we employ the same concept of sadness when referring to the representational arts too. For otherwise Stephen Dedalus's torment at school, which is sad in the way that any living person's torment at school might be sad, would nonetheless have to be sad in a quite different way from that in which the opening part of *The Portrait of the Artist as a Young Man* is sad.

Similarly, if we do not say that a piece of music is sad in a way that marks some kind of relationship between the music and a certain emotional state, the whole point of making the judgement seems to vanish. Unless in saying that the music is sad we are relating it not only to other works of art but also to certain situations outside the context of aesthetic judgement, the point of making the judgement seems to disappear. Suddenly it becomes a *peculiar* fact that we should be interested in the sadness of music, and certain kinds of response to this sadness become quite incomprehensible. And yet it is plain that, if asked to explain what we mean by calling the music sad, we should naturally point to more commonplace manifestations of sadness. It would never be enough to go on referring to parallels with other works. Think of the case of a man who only ascribed sadness to works of art, who showed no ability to employ the concept of sadness in talking of people (including himself), or other sentient beings. We should say that he did not understand what is *meant* in saying that a piece of music is sad.

It seems then that the idea of aesthetic features as merely emergent properties falls to the ground, and with it the concept of aesthetic perception. The theory of aesthetic perception fails –

– as do many other theories – by creating too sharp a divorce between the aesthetic and the non-aesthetic use of terms, so that, ultimately, it leaves itself with no explanation of the meaning of aesthetic judgements.

The creation of this sharp divorce between the meaning of terms in aesthetic judgement and their meaning in other contexts is also characteristic of the tradition in aesthetic thought described in Chapter Two – although for rather different reasons. There are many philosophers in the tradition of idealism who have spoken of the work of art as a special kind of entity, distinct from any material object in which it might be, as it were, incarnate. Works of art cannot be described in the terms appropriate to material objects. Even though they are expressive, say, there is no independent description available of what they express (in terms of attitude, thought or feeling). Thus when we speak of the expressive qualities of a work of art we do not mean to refer to some ordinary property – that of expressing some identifiable feeling – which we could find in other things besides works of art. We are referring to a unique feature of the work of art itself, a feature which can only belong to a work of art, and only to *that* work of art. This way of thinking is characteristic of many aestheticians besides Croce and Collingwood, and the idea of an 'aesthetic property' is perhaps its clearest equivalent in empiricist aesthetics. It is interesting to note that Croce insists explicitly on the fact that terms used in describing the aesthetic quality of works of art are used in a quite distinct sense. To take an example: for Croce the term 'sincerity' is ambiguous, denoting on the one hand the moral virtue of not deceiving one's neighbour, and on the other hand the aesthetic property of 'fullness and truth of expression'.[10] It is the acceptance of this kind of ambiguity, and the view of aesthetic autonomy that goes with it, which leads to the triviality of expressionism.

In the next chapter I shall return to the question how this kind of crucial ambiguity might be avoided, and what are the consequences for the notion of an aesthetic feature if we do try to avoid it. It is clear that, unless we do avoid it, the point and meaning of critical judgements will be extremely difficult to explain. Aesthetic interest will become an entirely autonomous and un-

[10] *Estetica*, p. 60.

related section of human activity, whose significance and value will be impossible to assess. This consequence is unacceptable – but note that it is not simply the consequence of *any* cognitive theory. It is only a consequence of theories like that of aesthetic perception, which construe what we are aware of in aesthetic appreciation (the aesthetic character of an object) as something unrelated to what we are aware of in ordinary moral and practical attention.

On the other hand, there is no doubt that the aesthetic perception theory is led into this paradoxical consequence by its attempt to separate the aesthetic (from the moral, the practical, or whatever) by a simple logical criterion. But without this simple logical criterion, the idea of an aesthetic feature ceases to be of help in the attempt to define the nature of aesthetic interest. It becomes difficult to see how attention to the aesthetic features of something can become the distinctive mark of aesthetic, rather than moral or practical, appreciation. For if a term like 'sad' means the same when applied to a work of art (to describe its aesthetic character) and when applied to a human being (to describe his emotional state), then how can an aesthetic interest be defined as an interest in such features as the sadness of things, when such features are precisely the kinds of thing towards which our ordinary moral and practical interests are directed? Perhaps one can still mark off a group of features which predominate as the objects of aesthetic interest, but without a logical distinction of the kind proposed by the theory of aesthetic perception, there will be no rationale for our marking off *these* features as the objects of a separate attitude. The importance of such a concept of the aesthetic attitude will be totally obscure.

Moreover, once we abandon the theory of aesthetic perception, the notion of an aesthetic feature, as whatever is referred to by an aesthetic description, becomes extremely problematic. For if the word 'sad' cannot be applied to works of art on the basis of criteria other than those governing its normal use, and if it is not, on the other hand, applied to a perceptual property, then in what sense is it applied to a property at all? The property is neither perceptual, nor based in what is perceived. Can we speak of it, therefore, as a genuine property? That is the question that we must go on to answer.

The attempt to explain aesthetic experience in terms of the features towards which it is directed must, then, be abandoned. Whether or not any conclusions can be drawn from a more plausible analysis of aesthetic description remains to be seen. But we have to admit that both attempts at explaining the notion of aesthetic experience so far considered – in terms of the assessment to which it gives rise, and in terms of the features towards which it is directed (the grounds of aesthetic assessment) – are inadequate.

CHAPTER FOUR

Aesthetic Description

Having rejected the idea of aesthetic perception we find ourselves facing a difficulty. For we have admitted the existence of an aesthetic use of terms while rebutting the most natural explanation of it. We must, therefore, say something definite about the logic of aesthetic description.

The principal objection to the idea of an aesthetic property was this: either terms denoting aesthetic properties have the same meaning as they have when used in their normal contexts, in which case, how can we distinguish aesthetic properties as a separate class? Or else they have a different meaning, in which case, what is the point of naming aesthetic properties as we do? We found that terms used in aesthetic description must have their normal meanings. But that implies that we have criteria for sameness and difference of meaning. In view of the scepticism with which such a claim is frequently greeted, it is wise to begin with a few remarks about the notion of ambiguity.[1]

Philosophers of logic pay too little attention to the distinction between ambiguity and extended meaning. This is because they treat the concept of meaning entirely through the categories of syntax and formal semantics, neglecting the connection between meaning and understanding that was emphasized in Chapter One. And yet the notion of meaning is more than the skeleton that is picked bare by logical analysis: it has its life in practice, in the teaching, learning and speaking of words. The theory of meaning, like the theory of truth, requires a pragmatic as well as a formal

[1] The scepticism is of course largely due to Quine. See, for example, *Word and Object*, ch. 4.

basis. Now ambiguity is always to some extent a matter of degree, and it will often be difficult to say whether a new use of some term is independent of the old use or merely an extension of it. But the distinction can be drawn sufficiently clearly for our purpose once we turn to the connection between meaning and understanding. Take the example of 'fair'. The criteria of fairness divide naturally into two groups, which have little or nothing to do with each other, and out of which sufficient conditions for something's being fair cannot be formed by taking some (but not all) criteria from one group and adding to them more criteria from the other group. The two sets of criteria are logically independent in that each provides totally adequate rules for the particular use of 'fair' in question: hence one can fully understand one use without understanding the other. There is, therefore, nothing in the meaning of 'fair' itself that forbids its replacement by two heteromorphic terms. This is not to say that there is no chain of conceptual connections between the two uses. For example, we might trace the transformation of the word 'fair' through the following series: fair skin, fair prospect, fair weather, fair chance, fair question, fair verdict, fair judge. To make such connections is to give (in part) a lexicographical explanation (as opposed to a logical explanation) of why we have the same term.

It is not always true that the several uses of a term are logically independent in this way. For example, take the word 'duck' used of decoy ducks and live ducks: we would not say the the word 'duck' was ambiguous because it can have *these* two uses. Nor would we say that the class of ducks has been extended by the invention of decoy ducks, for the simple reason that a decoy duck is not a duck. Our reason for saying that 'duck' has only one meaning here is that one use is parasitic on the other, and could not be understood independently. It is only if I understand what ducks are that I can understand the application of the term 'duck' to a decoy.

One way of extending the meaning of a term is through analogy, or 'shared features'. To use a term analogically is to use it in the absence of some of its criteria, but in the presence of others (or in the presence of 'symptoms' normally connected with the criteria of the term). But analogy is not the only method of extension. Austin draws attention to what he takes to be Aristotle's notion of paronymy:

> A very simple case indeed is one often mentioned by Aristotle: the adjective 'healthy': when I talk of a healthy body and again of a healthy complexion, of healthy exercise: the word is *not* being used just 'equivocally'. Aristotle would say that it is being used 'paronymously'. In this case there is what we may call a *primary nuclear* sense of 'healthy': the sense in which 'healthy' is used of a healthy body: I call this nuclear because it is 'contained as a part' in the other two senses, which may be set out as 'productive of healthy bodies' and 'resulting from healthy bodies'.[2]

It is clear that a term used 'paronymously' in this sense is not being used ambiguously. A paronymous use is a derivative use, and can be understood only by someone who has first understood the primary employment of the term. Here is a case, then, of a term that can be treated as unambiguous for our present purpose. And the example is close to the one that we have been considering: the term 'sad' applied to works of art. Can we, then, rest here, and construe aesthetic description as a species of paronymy? On this account, aesthetic features would still be observable properties of a work of art, like the healthiness of a young face, or the sadness of a gesture. And the theory of aesthetic perception would be quite superfluous as an explanation of this fact.

Here is a suggestion: I call a gesture sad because it is a symptom of sadness (paronymy). I call the music sad because it resembles such a gesture (analogy). Thus Susanne Langer argues that works of art share certain formal structures with human emotion, and hence come to be named after the emotions that they imitate:

> . . . there are certain aspects of the so-called 'inner life' – physical and mental – which have formal properties *similar to* those of music – patterns of motion and rest, of tension and release, of agreement and disagreement, preparation, fulfilment, excitation, sudden change, etc.[3]

[2] J. L. Austin, 'The Meaning of a Word', in *Philosophical Papers*, 2nd ed., p. 71.
[3] Susanne Langer, *Philosophy in a New Key*, p. 193.

This theory is a descendant of Aristotle's, according to which music acquires its moral and emotional character through the 'imitation' of human behaviour and states of mind.[4]

It is clear, I think, that this theory gives us no indication of the *general* sense of aesthetic descriptions – how can a landscape picture share the formal properties of human feeling? – and in any case leaves us guessing as to why we take the so-called 'sadness' of music so seriously as we do. But we find that other paronymous accounts of the meaning of aesthetic descriptions fail to produce a more satisfying theory. For example, 'It is sad' clearly does not mean 'It makes me sad', any more than 'It is good' means 'I approve of it'. This way of maintaining a connection with the central use of the term 'sad' falls immediately into the paradoxes familiar in the refutation of ethical subjectivism. More importantly, 'It is sad' does not mean 'It makes people sad', or 'It tends to make people sad'. Songs and poems too weak or sentimental to be truly sad have had a saddening effect on many people. (This is why we wish to say that 'taste' is involved in the perception of aesthetic features.[5])

We soon discover, then, that, while there is a range of cases over which analogy and paronymy provide a fairly adequate explanation of aesthetic description, there are also many cases where neither seem appropriate. Now I have given no reason as yet to suppose that there must be only *one* way in which terms are employed aesthetically; it may seem that we have already arrived at a partial account of aesthetic description. But we can hardly rest satisfied with this account, since it seems to fall short at precisely the point where aesthetic description begins to reveal peculiarities of logic, peculiarities which perhaps derive from its connection with the aesthetic point of view.

In this respect it seems more promising to argue that aesthetic descriptions are essentially normative: when I call a piece of music sad this is like calling it exciting or depressing. I am not saying anything about what people do feel, but I *am* saying something about what it would be natural or appropriate to feel.

Now certainly we can speak of sadness as justified, or made appropriate, by its object, and the importance of this fact – that

[4] *Politics*, 1340a ff.
[5] Cf. David Hume, 'Of the Standard of Taste', in *Essays*.

emotions can be made appropriate by their objects – is enormous. But *what* is it that I am saying is appropriate when I call the music sad? We find no immediate answer. The appropriate response is rarely sadness itself: only in special circumstances is anyone saddened by a work of art. Art, as Hegel said, is essentially cheerful. Besides, it seems odd to talk of *the* appropriate response in a case like this.

I shall assume, however, that this sceptical rejoinder can be refuted. I shall assume that we could in principle identify something – an emotion, a response, a feeling, an experience or whatever – that we might wish to say is involved in every appropriate reaction to the sadness of a work of art. Can it be that, in calling a poem sad we are saying that this experience or response is appropriate to it? Plausible though such a theory might initially seem, we can see at once that it must inevitably make room for another, more simple – namely, the theory that aesthetic description does not *assert* that a certain state of mind is justified but rather gives direct expression to the state of mind itself. Hence the function of aesthetic description is not, primarily, descriptive.[6] The normative view has mislocated the speech-act involved when terms are used in an aesthetic sense. It may be that I must have some notion of what it is to justify a response if I am to engage in the activity of criticism as we know it. But it is not necessary to argue that I am therefore *saying* that a response is justified when I call a piece of music or a poem sad. Such a theory leaves us with the task of explaining what it is to regard a response as justified, and this, as we shall see, is a needless complication. Moreover, it fails to explain why we feel no hesitation in proceeding with the aesthetic use of 'sad': it seems the most natural thing in the world to extend the use of the term in this way, and we do it quite unthinkingly. It is conceivable that this extended application of the term should be an established practice among people who at the same time lacked any idea of the justification of responses – for example, they might always agree in their responses, and so never need to defend them. It is surely for this kind of reason that many philosophers think of aesthetic descriptions as lacking truth conditions, in the strong (epistemological) sense – for we

[6] This suggestion has been made by Ruby Meager, 'Aesthetic Concepts', *B.J.A.*, 1970.

can understand them, at least in part, without knowing how they might be justified.

Let us suppose, then, that at least some aesthetic descriptions are not descriptive. All that need be said for the moment to explain this supposition is that aesthetic descriptions are related to certain 'non-cognitive' states of mind in the same intimate fashion that genuine descriptions are related to beliefs. I shall use the term 'expression' as a name for this intimate relation between a sentence and a mental state, and I shall assume that there is a sense in which expression determines meaning, through determining our understanding of a sentence; the supposition is, then, that certain aesthetic descriptions are non-descriptive in that they express not beliefs but rather 'aesthetic experiences'. To understand such an aesthetic description involves realizing that one can assert it or assent to it sincerely only if one has had a certain 'experience', just as one can assert or assent to a normal description only if one has the appropriate belief. We have been asking such questions as 'What is an aesthetic feature?', 'What is aesthetic description?', How do I know that a work of art possesses a certain aesthetic feature?' Clearly, if our supposition is correct, these questions are the wrong ones, since they misconstrue the purpose of aesthetic judgement. We should ask instead what it is to agree to or dissent from an aesthetic description, just as the moral philosopher asks what it is to accept or reject a moral judgement.[7] I shall call the theory of aesthetic description that is grounded in this analogy with moral judgement an 'affective' theory.

The first problem for an affective theory is how to avoid the ambiguity that destroyed the theory of aesthetic perception. How can the term 'sad' preserve the same meaning when transferred from a descriptive to a non-descriptive use? We find an answer to this question once we see that it is not only individual words that acquire extended uses (through analogy, or paronymy, or some other 'figurative' device). Our words as a whole can be used in a new way without a change of meaning. This might occur when I describe a dream: here the normal referential function of my word is, as it were, held in abeyance, but if what I say is to be understood then the words must have their normal meanings.

---

[7] See R. M. Hare, *The Language of Morals*, for an application of this method.

Consider also the following passage from Wittgenstein:

> Given the two ideas 'fat' and 'lean', would you be rather
> inclined to say that Wednesday was fat and Tuesday lean, or
> the other way round? (I incline to choose the former.) Now
> have 'fat' and 'lean' some different meaning here from their
> usual one? – they have a different use. – So ought I really to
> have used different words? Certainly not that. – I want to
> use *these* words (with their familiar meanings) *here*. – Now, I
> say nothing about the causes of this phenomenon. They *might*
> be associations from my childhood. But that is a hypo-
> thesis. Whatever the explanation, – the inclination is there.
>
> Asked 'What do you really mean here by "fat" and "lean?",
> – I could only explain the meanings in the usual way. I could
> *not* point to the examples of Tuesday and Wednesday.[8]

This brings out forcefully, I think, the point that words may be
used with their standard meanings but out of context, not because
they are being used to describe some *de facto* relation with the
central case, but because the point of using these words is
here entirely different. To understand this use of terms is not to
know a new meaning, nor even a paronymous meaning, for the
individual terms. It is rather to 'see the point' of the description.
It is this kind of extended use that most readily eludes the
logician's modes of analysis. For example, suppose that we opt
for a semantic criterion of ambiguity. Thus we decide to call a
predicate ambiguous if it can be incorporated in a semantic theory
at two separate points, marked out by two separate systematic
contributions to the truth conditions of sentences as a whole.[9]
(This criterion would cover the example of 'fair' given earlier.)
Such an analysis could not possibly be used to legislate about the
univocality or otherwise of terms which, in one use, make such
a systematic contribution to truth conditions, while in another use
(such as the one we are considering) making no systematic
contribution at all. We can say no more than that this second use

[8] *Philosophical Investigations*, p. 216.
[9] Such an approach to ambiguity is fruitfully explored in David Wiggins,
'On sentence-sense, word-sense and difference of word-sense', in D. Steinberg and L. Jakobovitz (eds.), *Semantics, an Introductory Reader*, Cambridge,
1971.

is 'extended', and can be understood only by someone who first understands the use from which it derives. Thus we are faced with a sentence whose extended meaning can only be grasped in terms of what it is to understand it, whose peculiarities must be passed over in any syntactic or semantic theory.

Now Wittgenstein's example has much in common with certain kinds of aesthetic description – descriptions of the 'warmth' of a colour scheme, of the 'weight' of certain visual effects (stained glass, for example), of the 'heaviness' of a musical style, of the 'baroque' quality of a literary embellishment. And clearly there is a continuum from this kind of description to the suggestive comparisons of criticism, as exemplified in Baudelaire's description of Chopin's music as 'un brillant oiseau voltigeant sur les horreurs d'un gouffre'.[10] Clearly all these judgements could be *supported* by analogies, but it would be peremptory to suggest that there is nothing more to their meaning than that. They do not *need* an analogical basis, and this fact arises from the peculiar purpose involved in describing an aesthetic object in this way. Thus any explanation that I might give of such a judgement will proceed well beyond observable analogies: in describing a Brahms rhapsody as 'fat' I might point to a fulsome, exaggerated quality in the melodic line, to a 'tone' or 'feeling' in the music, as though the piano were greedily swallowing clusters of notes – and so on.

Although we may often not be able to say (as in Wittgenstein's example) exactly how we are using words when we use them non-descriptively, this need not always be the case. At the beginning of the *Categories*, Aristotle points to a particularly interesting non-standard use of words. This use is exemplified when I gesture to a picture and say 'That is a man'. If we take the 'that' as here referring to the picture, then the predication again seems to indicate an ambiguity. We should of course wish to deny that the term 'that' refers to the picture: one is not predicating 'is a man' of the picture but rather of the thing *in* the picture. But there seems to be no way of distinguishing this species of 'pseudo-predication' on the basis of semantic theory. For we have no means of deciding in advance that a seeming act of predication is really of this kind or not. The only thing that will tell us is a study of the conditions for the acceptance of the judgement –

[10] 'Eugène Delacroix, Obituary Notice.'

what it is to understand it, accept it, or see its point. It is this that determines the non-referential character of the ostensive 'that'. The same goes for aesthetic description. When I say of the music 'This is sad', there is nothing yet to tell us that the predication is genuine, and hence nothing that will determine whether or not some property is attributed by this description to the music.

The comparison of aesthetic features with aspects is a fruitful one.[11] We can already see how neatly and effectively it solves the problems from which this chapter began. First, we find that we can reconstruct the argument of the last chapter to show that aspects, like aesthetic features, cannot be simple properties, even though, like simple properties, they do not have criteria for their presence that can be stated in other terms. Imagine a man who, sorting through a heap of pictures, happens always to put the pictures of ducks to one side. And yet the word 'duck' seems to him to have no application to what he sees when looking at the pictures. If asked to explain his behaviour he might reply that he feels that these pictures belong together, although he does not know why, or else that they look the same in a certain respect (a respect which has nothing to do with ducks, although it does correspond to a certain shape on the canvas). There is, I think, no contradiction in this supposition. It is as implausible to argue that this man has seen the duck-aspect of the pictures as it is to argue that the man who classifies sad songs together, while refusing to describe them as 'sad', has noticed the sadness that belongs to them. We might support this contention once again by referring to the phenomenon – clearly ruled out by the logic of simple properties – of the ambiguous aspect. Suppose an object has the aspect both of a rabbit and of a duck. A man who 'sees' the duck might consciously reproduce all the features that are responsible for this aspect: from which it follows that he reproduces the rabbit as well. Thus we seem to have the situation, which certainly could not arise in the case of a simple property, where a man may infallibly (and not just by chance) reproduce an aspect, by reproducing only *what he sees*, and yet not 'see' the aspect itself.

Secondly, we can demonstrate that the term 'man' *must* have the same meaning when used to describe an aspect and when used to refer to a man. For it is precisely the disposition to apply

[11] See also John Casey, *The Language of Criticism*, ch. 1, pp. 28 ff.

the term 'man' *in its normal sense* to the picture that is our criterion for saying that someone has seen the aspect of the picture. The 'use of words' involved is not the normal use – but that is beside the point.

Thirdly, we see that the 'use of words' in question is not a figurative use: to see an aspect is not to notice an analogy, even though it is no doubt true that, when I see a man in a picture, the lines in the picture bear some resemblance to the shape of a man. This is a point that I shall explore in detail in Chapter Eight.

Finally, we can see how there is an important sense in which aspects are not properties (as indeed Wittgenstein said they were not). For there need be no criteria for the application of a term to an object when that term is used to describe its aspect. Terms used in this sense are terms whose criteria and meaning derive from some other use. And yet it follows from the arguments above that these terms must have the same meaning when describing aspects as they normally have: hence they cannot have *other* criteria for their application in this secondary use. It follows that, in their use to describe aspects, terms need have *no* criteria for their application. Generalized to cover the use of such terms as 'sad' in aesthetic judgement, this argument would provide the needed proof that aesthetic descriptions are divorced from truth conditions in the epistemological sense: aesthetic features are not properties.

It is worthwhile here to forestall an objection that may already have occurred to the reader. I have assumed that if the aspect-description is a description of anything it is a description of the *picture*. But surely, it will be said, the aspect-description is the description of an aspect, which may be 'in' the picture in some sense, but which is not identical with the picture nor with any part of it. Therefore, the aspect-description *is* a genuine description, although what it describes (the aspect) is not a physical thing. But this objection only makes the same point in a different way. For the question was whether aspects are properties of the items which 'possess' them, and the argument seems to establish that they are not. The objection does no more than propose the aspect *itself* as a bearer of properties, which is simply to beg the question. In any case, if we are to say this, then we must be prepared to give criteria of identity for the thing to which the 'properties' of aspects are attributed, and this will prove to be impossible. For if aspects are objects at all, then they belong to the class of 'intentional objects' for which criteria of identity cannot be specified.[12]

In other words, there is a striking formal analogy between the description of the aspect of a thing, and the description of its aesthetic character; indeed, even the theory of aesthetic perception brackets the two together, treating aspects and aesthetic features as alike 'emergent' characteristics of an object.[13] But we have seen that the formal analogy points away from the perceptual theory to the 'affective' theory: it suggests that we should attempt to describe aesthetic description not in terms of a property of its object but in terms of an experience that it expresses. The theory of aesthetic perception takes as its starting-point the intuition that, in matters of aesthetic judgement, you have to see for yourself – another cannot make your aesthetic judgements for you – and it emphasizes the fact that we use a perceptual verb ('to see') in expressing this opinion. But the theory is unable to explain why you also *have to* see for yourself: and the explanation of this is by no means straightforward. If ϕ is a visual property, say, then it is not true that I *have* to see ϕ for myself in order to know that an object possesses it: there are circumstances where the opinion of others can give me a logically conclusive reason for saying that ϕ is there, as indeed a blind man can have knowledge of colours. In aesthetics you have to see for yourself precisely because what you have to 'see' is not a property: your knowledge that an aesthetic feature is 'in' the object is given by the *same* criteria that show that you 'see' it. To see the sadness in the music and to know that the music is sad are one and the same thing. To agree in the judgement that the music is sad is not to agree in a belief, but in something more like a response or an experience; in a mental state that is – unlike belief – logically tied to the immediate circumstances of its arousal. 'The music is sad' is only superficially, therefore, of propositional form: what you know when you know that the music is sad cannot be elucidated by referring to the conditions for a proposition's truth.

We can now state the affective theory more precisely, by borrow-

[12] See G. E. M. Anscombe, 'The Intentionality of Sensation', in R. J. Butler (ed.), *Analytical Philosophy*, series 2.
[13] See F. N. Sibley, op. cit.

ing from R. M. Hare. One of the central ideas behind Hare's theory of prescriptivism[14] was that the meaning of a judgement is related to the conditions for its acceptance: by what it is to accept a judgement of that kind. The hope was that the conditions for the acceptance of moral judgement could be shown to be importantly different from the conditions for the acceptance of ordinary description. The 'intimate connection' that exists between a judgement and a mental state, for which I have until now used the term 'expression', can be redescribed as the relation of a sentence to its acceptance condition.[15] And only if this mental state is a belief can acceptance conditions bring verification conditions in their train. In the case of 'descriptive' uses of language meaning and justification go hand in hand – we find out the meaning of a sentence by finding the conditions for its use, and these conditions will become the truth conditions of the judgement that the sentence is used to express. To justify a judgement is to justify its acceptance: in this case to justify the belief in which acceptance of the judgement consists. But the belief that we justify is the belief in the truth of *that* judgement and can be fully specified in terms of the judgement itself. The truth of the judgement justifies both the belief and the sentence's use.

The affective theory of aesthetic description argues that the acceptance condition of an aesthetic description may not be a belief but may rather be some other mental state which more effectively explains the point of aesthetic description. To agree to an aesthetic description is to 'see its point', and this 'seeing the point' is to be elucidated in terms of some response or experience that has yet to be described. Hence aesthetic descriptions need not have truth conditions in the strong sense, and to justify them may be to justify an experience and not a belief. This does not mean that aesthetic descriptions are merely arbitrary or 'subjective', having no more validity than preferences for certain kinds of food: we must separate the concept of objectivity from that of truth, as I shall later argue.

It is clear that the comparison with aspects does not yet solve the problem of aesthetic description: sadness and fatness are not

[14] See R. M. Hare, op. cit.
[15] I borrow the term 'acceptance condition' from Roy Edgley, *Reason in Theory and Practice*.

obviously aspects of the music in the way that a battle is an aspect of a picture. In order not to beg any questions, therefore, I shall say simply that the acceptance condition of an aesthetic description (of the kind that we have been considering) is an experience, where this is interpreted in the widest possible sense, so as to stand proxy for whatever answer we may finally arrive at. It will only be after considerable detailed analysis that anything more precise will be available to us.

It follows from the fact that the condition for the sincere acceptance of an aesthetic judgement is an experience that an aesthetic judgement can be sincerely made only by someone who experiences its object in the appropriate way. In this case it is perfectly acceptable to describe the judgement, as I did earlier, as an expression of the experience. Aesthetic description and first-order description are contrasted as the expression of experience and the expression of belief. However, there is an important asymmetry in that the aesthetic 'experience', unlike a belief, cannot outlive the presence of its object, in the absence of which it must remain only as a disposition to react in a similar way. Whereas a 'descriptive' judgement can be the expression of its acceptance condition in a very real sense – in that it is accompanied by the fulfilment of that condition on every occasion of its sincere assertion – the aesthetic judgement can be considered as an expression only in the slightly attenuated sense of being a means of *putting over* some state of mind which at the time may exist only in a latent or remembered form.

In conclusion, we must remind ourselves that terms do not have a special kind of meaning when used in aesthetic descriptions, even though terms are being employed differently there. For we have seen that aesthetic uses of terms, like the use of the terms 'fat' and 'lean' in Wittgenstein's example, must often be construed as derivative. The only clear explanation of what the terms mean in their aesthetic use is to be given by referring back to their *ordinary* use. So we can find no clue in the meaning of the term as to how we can justify applying it in aesthetic judgement.

But this does not mean that there is nothing to understanding the aesthetic use of terms besides understanding their ordinary use. There is a difference between the man who uses a term to make an aesthetic judgement and the man who is simply referring to a relationship of similarity.[16] And there is a corresponding difference between the man who knows when a description is intended as an aesthetic judgement (the man who, among other things, recognizes the difference just referred to), and the man who does not. The latter will think that aesthetic judgements are misguided similes. Such a man understands the form of words that is used in making an aesthetic judgement, but does not understand what is being done by the use of this form of words. The man who does not understand aesthetic description is the man who has no familiarity with the experiences that it is used to express.

Our investigation of the logic of aesthetic description has, therefore, turned full circle. Hoping to define the aesthetic states of mind as those which are directed towards a certain group of features, we find that there is no access to the notion of a 'feature' of this kind except through the understanding of aesthetic description. But we discover also that aesthetic description can itself be understood only in terms of the states of mind that it serves to communicate. We must turn, therefore, to an analysis of the so-called 'experiences' that were invoked as criteria for the acceptance of aesthetic judgements. Before beginning this analysis, however, it is necessary to show that it really is possible to account for the meaning of aesthetic descriptions in the way so far attempted. The next chapter will, therefore, consist in a brief digression into the theory of meaning.

[16] This point is well brought out in G. Santayana, *The Sense of Beauty*, pp. 18–19.

CHAPTER FIVE

Non-Descriptive Meaning

The last chapter has left an unsolved problem. It was argued that aesthetic descriptions need not be descriptions: the condition for their acceptance might not be a belief, and hence there is a sense in which at least some aesthetic descriptions lack conditions for their truth. It remains to be shown that this supposition does not conflict with our intuitions about the concept of meaning.

There are two standard approaches in contemporary philosophy to the theory of meaning: through the analysis of speech-acts, and through the study of semantics. The concept of meaning is applicable both to what is done when words are uttered, and to the utterance itself: the two approaches do no more than reflect this inherent complexity in the concept. The theory of speech-acts takes its inspiration from Austin, but has found its firmest theoretical basis in the work of Grice, who analyses what it is for a speaker to mean something in terms of the intentions that underly his utterance.[1] The semantic approach takes its inspiration from Frege, and in fact seems to move away from the theory of meaning to what Quine has called the theory of reference:[2] that is, its main tendency is to replace questions about meaning with questions about truth. To approach the theory of meaning from the point of view of semantic theory leads almost inevitably to a connection between meaning and truth conditions.

In fact, although the two views are often presented as rivals, neither can be dismissed as superfluous. For the speech-act

[1] H. P. Grice, 'Meaning', *Phil. Rev.* 1957, and 'Utterer's Meaning, Sentence-meaning and Word-meaning', in *Foundations of Language*, 1968.
[2] See *From a Logical Point of View*, ch. 7.

theory and the semantic theory seem to be generalized answers to two separate questions. The first tells us how language has meaning, by showing what it is to use and understand linguistic forms in the practice of communication. The second tells us how it is that we can assign a distinct 'meaning' to any sentence. Unlike the speech-act theory, the semantic theory does not give an ultimate answer to the question 'What is it for a sentence to have meaning?' Rather, it aims to offer a recursive answer to the question 'What meaning does any given sentence have?' (where 'sentence' is used in a structural sense, to refer to an ordered sequence of linguistic elements).

We must assume, therefore, that the conclusions of the last chapter will fit into either theory. And we can see at once that, from the point of view of the theory of speech-acts, the idea of 'non-descriptive meaning' presents no genuine difficulty. The essential feature of Grice's theory, for example, is the analysis of meaning-that-*p* in terms of an intention that someone else should believe-that-*p*. The utterance of '*p*' is accepted or agreed to by the man who acquires the right belief.[3] Clearly there is no theoretical difficulty in extending this account to the case where the intention is to get another not to believe something but rather to 'see the point' of what one says, in the way that, in responding appropriately, he will 'see the point' of an aesthetic judgement. Thus Grice's theory can readily incorporate as part of the meaning of an utterance a specification of the mental state which is its acceptance condition, and the condition for its sincere assertion.

It is for this reason that we have relied, until now, on a speech-act analysis of meaning. But in doing so we seem to have evaded the problems that the semantic theory is designed to solve. How do we give an account of the meaning of a given sentence? Surely, on Grice's theory, meanings will be differentiated only in so far as the mental states expressed are differentiated. For example, one identifies what a given descriptive utterance means by identifying the belief expressed by it. But how is this done? How are beliefs differentiated and identified in a language except

[3] Subsequent emendations have brought about a slight change in this principle but it is not a change that affects the point at issue. Cf. Grice, 1968, op. cit.

by reference in turn to the sentences that express them? Reference to belief in a language must employ sentences of *oratio obliqua* or *oratio recta* form: the belief is identified by the sentence in reported speech. But if this is so, it is possible to understand which belief is referred to only when we have some recursive method that will tell us the meaning of the reported sentence. A semantic theory is designed to meet this demand.

It is a remarkable fact that sentences in a language can be used to express indefinitely many thoughts, beliefs, truths or meanings; and yet they are built up from a finite vocabulary. Now no merely syntactical rules will allow us to say when a given sequence of words is meaningful: from the point of view of syntax 'John drank the milk' and 'The milk drank John' are both well-formed. However, we could understand the way in which a language is built up out of words if we could give a theory entailing some generalizable schema of the form (A): *s* means that *p*, where '*s*' is a structural description of a sentence and '*p*' is another sentence which 'gives the meaning' of the sentence '*s*'. Now Davidson has argued persuasively that, if we make clear to ourselves the conditions that a schema of form (A) must satisfy if it is to give an adequate test for a theory of meaning, we find that they are identical with those laid down by Tarski for the schematic definition of the predicate 'T'.[4] This predicate was defined by Tarski so as to be co-extensive with truth in some given language; for the purpose of formal analysis, therefore, the predicate can be regarded as identical with 'true'. In other words, the schema (A) gives way to (B): '*s*' is T if and only if *p*; where '*s*' is replaced by a structural description of a sentence and '*p*' is replaced by that sentence itself. A theory of meaning will be adequate for our language if it provides a recursive characterization of the truth predicate 'T' – i.e. if it entails all sentences of the form (B). But this seems to suggest that we can answer questions about what a given sentence means only by discovering the conditions for its truth. And this accords with the quite independent argument of Chapter One, which implied that the meaning of a declarative sentence (drawn from a certain central class) is discovered by finding a distinction between the circumstances in which it must be agreed

[4] D. Davidson, 'Truth and Meaning', in *Synthese*, 1967; A. Tarski, 'The Concept of Truth in Formalised Languages', in *Logic, Semantics, Mathematics*.

to by anyone who is to count as 'understanding' it, and circumstances in which it may be denied.

It would seem at first sight that the suggestion that there might be sentences without truth conditions must inevitably conflict with the semantic theory: for how could meanings be assigned to such sentences? However, this is not so: the problems that arise in the case of such sentences are difficulties in the analysis of individual predicates, and a semantic theory says nothing about these. Provided these predicates (such as the 'good' of ethics) have the normal syntactical properties, then they will present no obstacle to semantic theory, which is concerned not with questions of individual analysis but rather with questions of 'logical form'. Semantic analysis is directed at linguistic devices which produce more complicated sentences from simple predicate forms. Unless the predicate itself has a logically complex structure (as in the case of attributive terms) the analysis leaves it untouched, and does nothing to uncover or resolve any epistemological difficulties that the predicate creates.

Any problems about the meaning of particular sentences will be smoothed over in the general theory, and the theory will be adequate simply if it entails all sentences of the form ' "*s*" is true if and only if *s*'. In this sense it is quite possible to produce a semantics for ethical sentences, in terms of a theory whose interpretation would present the same philosophical problems as the sentences themselves. In other words, any philosophical reasons for denying truth conditions in some strong sense to ethical sentences formed in the object-language, would simply resurge as reasons in favour of a similar interpretation of the semantic theory that accounts for them. The semantic theory of meaning embodies a notion of 'truth condition' that is in fact entirely formal: it is still an open question whether the notion corresponds in any particular case to the epistemological concept of a truth condition that was explained in Chapter One. It would seem to follow from this that the semantic theory cannot be used to frame the contrast we wish to make, between sentences with truth conditions and sentences without them, not because it denies the distinction but because it is a distinction that must be made in other terms: for example, in terms of the speech-act theory outlined above.

But although it is true that the existence of sentences that are both declarative and non-descriptive presents no genuine obstacle to semantic theory, it is also true that the arguments that lead us to accept the semantic theory as a genuine account of *meaning* present a new problem for our analysis. For these arguments suggest that the meaning of a sentence is given by the conditions for its truth, so that the theory of meaning collapses into the theory of reference in the Fregean sense. Now it is certainly true that the idea of a truth condition employed by the semantic theory is entirely formal. But it was argued in Chapter One that this idea cannot remain merely formal if the theory of meaning is to explain – as it must – our *understanding* of the words we use. The semantic theory seems to demand its complement in epistemology. For it implies that to know the meaning of a sentence is to know what it says. It follows that if we can fill out the semantic theory with some epistemological content, it will explain the meaning of a sentence in terms of the real information that it contains, that is to say, in terms of the state of affairs that determines its truth. The epistemological notion of a truth condition indicates how the semantic theory might be extended to explain the whole concept of meaning. It will show how our understanding of a sentence rests on our knowledge of the links between individual words and the world – our knowledge of what they stand for, or of the properties they express. But this process of giving content to the merely formal idea of a truth condition cannot, in the case of evaluative sentences or aesthetic descriptions, be carried through. For if we accept, say, a prescriptive account of evaluation, then it follows that nothing makes an evaluative sentence true in the real way that a state of affairs makes a descriptive sentence true. Meanings are not assigned to evaluative sentences in the same kind of way.

A speech-act theorist might object that the conveying of information is only one possible speech-act. How, after all, does the semantic theory make sense of such things as questions and commands? But this objection misses the point. For the difficulty arises from the fact that evaluative sentences, like aesthetic descriptions, share the surface structure of information-bearing sentences, and are, therefore, in some sense a semantic anomaly (unlike commands, whose deviant acceptance condition accompanies a distinct grammatical form).

We should bear in mind in this connection that the main purpose of a semantic theory is to explain the way in which the indefinite number of complex sentences in a language can be understood in terms of a finite vocabulary. Once a declarative sentence is included under Tarski's schema various theories are available which might explain its logical behaviour in more complex utterances – for example, the theory of truth functions. The semantic theory shows us how we can understand conditionals, for example, in a way that takes for granted that sentences occurring in conditionals have conditions for their truth. For if to understand 'p' and to understand 'q' is to know their truth conditions, then the understanding of at least the material implication '$p \supset q$' follows immediately from an understanding of its components. The truth condition of the complex sentence is given by a simple function of the truth conditions of its component parts. (This is not to say that 'if' in ordinary language means exactly what '$\supset$' means, though it is an argument for saying that there is a model for the meaning of 'if' that can be incorporated into semantic theory.) But here we have the basis for the most popular objection to the idea of non-descriptive meaning. For how does this explanation of conditionals apply when one or the other of 'p' or 'q' lacks a truth condition in the realistic sense? How do we learn and understand the conditional structure in such cases?

From the point of view of speech-acts, we might put the other side of this objection as follows: if we say of a predicate that it is characteristically used to perform a certain speech-act, defined, let us suppose, by a certain acceptance condition, and that this explains its meaning in assertoric contexts, then this fact ought also to explain its meaning in the protasis of a conditional (for example, in 'If she is good, then she is happy', or in 'If the music is sad, then Alfred will wallow in it'). But how can these terms ('good' and 'sad') be performing their standard speech-acts in this context, where from the very nature of conditional assertions, their acceptance condition cannot be incorporated as a part of the acceptance condition of the sentence as a whole?[5] This seems to suggest that the meaning of a sentence can only be explained semantically, and that acceptance conditions cannot directly influence meaning. In particular they cannot make meaning

[5] J. R. Searle, *Speech Acts*, p. 138.

'non-descriptive', unless they also bring about the kind of deviant grammatical form to which concepts like truth are no longer applicable.

In order to answer this objection we must again make clear the distinction between the formal notion of truth (as expressed in Tarski's predicate 'T'), and the substantial notion investigated by the theory of knowledge. In explaining the function of connectives and other 'complicators' in a language we need, in fact, to invoke only the formal idea of truth. In this sense, any declarative sentence will have a truth condition, purely on account of its position in the language. Because moral and aesthetic judgements have an indicative and assertoric form, then they can be incorporated into a semantic theory along with all other indicative sentences. But once they have been fitted into the language in this way, then it is inevitable that they should borrow the logical transformations of description. This consequence will follow whether or not the assertoric use of moral and aesthetic judgements has truth conditions in the epistemological sense: the real question is not how it is possible for such judgements to fit into the language as quasi-descriptions, but rather what is the point of their doing so. What purpose does it serve that moral and aesthetic judgements have the fully declarative form of ordinary descriptions? How does our understanding of them extend to their use in complex sentences? This is a question for which answers have already been suggested in the case of moral judgements. In Chapter Nine I shall point to various facts that provide an answer for aesthetic judgements too.

The problem about conditionals arises, I think, because it is assumed that the logical basis of conditional argument can be explained piecemeal, for each particular example. Thus it is assumed that, for any proposition of the form 'If $F(a)$ then $G(a)$', it ought to be possible to say *what* is being hypothesized in the protasis. But clearly, if the relation of non-descriptive sentences to the concept of truth has the merely formal character that we have suggested, this question will, for such sentences, have only trivial answers. It is a question that is by-passed in the semantic theory, and which can be answered non-trivially only in terms of some analysis of the relevant predicate 'F'. But nothing prevents this analysis from relying on a specification of the acceptance condition of '$F(a)$' rather than a specification of the state of affairs which determines the truth of '$F(a)$'.

This last point can be brought home by an example. Suppose that a natural language is in use, with a proper division of parts of speech, and a grammar for descriptive utterances that satisfies the normal conditions of adequacy, including the condition that it should be possible to formulate a schema corresponding to (B) above. It will be possible to incorporate into this language new expressions that lack criteria, by referring only to the conditions for the acceptance of sentences, and not to the conditions for their truth. For example, I might introduce the adjective 'nuff' as follows: 'Call a thing "nuff" only if it attracts you'. The acceptance condition of 'X is nuff' is incorporated into this rule: the judgement is accepted by a man who is attracted to X. The rule gives a clear account of what it is to agree or disagree about the nuffness of a thing, and nothing about the rule prevents the word 'nuff' from having a normal position in the language – that of an adjective, tied to sentences of propositional form. Nor does the rule allow 'X is nuff' to collapse into 'I like X', since the acceptance conditions of these two judgements will be entirely different. I can agree to one and not to the other (except in the 'degenerate' case where I utter both myself). There could be no first-person sentence about a mental state that shared the acceptance condition of the sentence 'X is nuff', since to agree in this judgement is to adopt an attitude and not a belief. Nor does this mean that the attitude must be expressed whenever the judgement is made. The acceptance condition makes intelligible the extension of the use of 'nuff' to the expression of opinion at second-hand: I may remark that a man is 'said to be nuff', and so on. Once the acceptance condition is clear such usages become comprehensible in terms of the structure of language as a whole. The mature user of the language may also find that he has a use for the extension of 'nuff' into complex sentences, such as hypotheticals and disjunctions. Wondering whether I shall enjoy a meeting with X I say to myself 'If he is nuff then everything will go very well', and so on. To use the adjective in this way will show as much understanding as the mastery of its assertoric use.

Note that this example begins from a language to which the truth-schema is already applicable. We assume from the start that it is possible to introduce the word 'nuff' in this way, rather as we introduce the word 'nice' into our own way of talking. Given this assumption, then an explanation of the fact that an adjective can suffer certain transformations without change of meaning is simply an explanation of the fact that adjectives have the logical and grammatical place that they have. It is an independent question what speech-act the assertoric use of an adjective performs, and hence an open question whether the adjective has criteria in any stronger sense than simply being incorporated into the language as an adjective.

This might suggest that judgements without truth conditions (in the epistemological sense) must be incorporated into a language piecemeal, on the basis of a prior understanding of the language as a whole. And it might also suggest that, once a judgement is incorporated in this way, it will have a permanent and inevitable tendency to acquire realistic truth conditions, as indeed ethical judgements seem to have. Nonetheless, it also shows that the semantic theory, like the speech-act theory, cannot be used to demonstrate the impossibility of non-descriptive meaning in aesthetic judgement. Moreover, if it is asked how we explain the place of aesthetic judgements in language as a whole, then an explanation is available which completely by-passes all the difficulties that I have, for the sake of completeness, been raising. We need answer only that words like 'sad', 'expressive', 'heavy', 'fat' and so on already have a use outside aesthetic judgement, a use that is governed by truth conditions, which provides an explanation of their place in aesthetic judgement, and which fits without strain into a semantic theory. Since we are supposing that this use is logically prior, and explains the place of the terms in the language as a whole, then we do not have to ask ourselves how we can derive from an analysis of the speech-act of aesthetic judgement the declarative structure of the utterances that express it. The declarative structure is derived from the primary employment of the terms involved.

There are individual judgements, however, that still need to be accounted for. These are the judgements that do not employ terms in an extended sense, and yet which, nonetheless, have the kind of declarative form that the semantic theory stipulates: judgements such as 'Her dress is elegant', 'His style is beautiful',

'The play was moving'. I wish to argue that there is a sense in which many of these judgements also lack truth conditions, and I shall rely on the previous explanation of how such a thing is possible. It is a separate question, however, and one to which I shall return, why the declarative form of these sentences is useful.

PART II
Aesthetic Experience

CHAPTER SIX

Recognition and Response

I have suggested that we should attempt to explain aesthetic judgement in terms of the condition for its acceptance rather than the condition for its truth. Now, there are certain central examples of aesthetic description – those employing emotion terms and terms of comparison – for which it is plausible to suggest that the condition for their acceptance is not a belief but some other mental state, which for the sake of argument I have described as an experience. If it is possible to characterize this experience, and if it is possible to discover certain features in virtue of which we might wish to describe it as aesthetic, then we will have at least begun our task of describing the general conditions of aesthetic interest. In this chapter I shall examine a straightforward theory that attempts to achieve these aims.

For simplicity's sake, let us continue to discuss the example of 'sad' in aesthetic judgement. How do we describe the acceptance of the judgement that a piece of music or a play is sad? I have argued that there are at least two uses of the term 'sad', one in describing a state of mind, the other in expressing a state of mind. But I have also argued, in criticizing the normative view of aesthetic description, that the state of mind described in one use is not in general the same as that expressed in the other. It is not because the music makes me feel sad that I call it sad – 'sad' does not mean 'saddening'. How then do we come to use the one term in these different ways? What explains its new use in aesthetic and quasi-aesthetic description? It is undeniable that we do not have to learn the new use: it is quite natural to acquire it, indeed it is given along with the primary meaning of the term. This fact

alone serves to lay severe restrictions on the 'experience' that we
must attempt to describe.

Here is a first shot at an answer to the question: when I find
a work of art sad, or see it as sad, I am responding to it in some
way like the way that I respond (under certain specifiable conditions) to sadness (to the sadness of a human being). It is because
I respond to each in a similar way that I use the same term of
each, and this response is the condition for the acceptance of the
aesthetic description. To see the work of art as sad is not simply,
and perhaps not even, to see a resemblance between the work and
the phenomena of sadness – not even a 'dynamic' resemblance,
or resemblance of 'logical form'. I use the term 'sad' spontaneously
to describe all those objects that elicit in me responses analogous
to my response to human sadness, and it is this that explains why
I do not have to learn any new meaning for the term 'sad' in
order to be disposed to use it, and understand it, in this extended
sense. In other words, to find a work of art sad is to respond to
it in the way I respond to a man when I am 'touched' by his
sadness.

Such a theory is by no means uncommon – it is implicit both in
certain works of phenomenology, as well as in a great deal of
standard empiricist thought about metaphor.[1] The theory of
'empathy' can be seen as an elaboration of this view of aesthetic
experience, and even Collingwood, in his quasi-idealist aesthetics,
makes room for a version of it, with the distinction between literal
and emotional representation.[2] When a portrait is said to be 'like'
the sitter, what is meant, according to Collingwood, is that the
spectator, looking at the portrait, 'feels as if' he were in the presence of the sitter. Thus representation becomes detached from
resemblance, and approaches the status of expression: 'The
pianoforte accompaniment of Brahms's song *Feldeinsamkeit* does
not make noises in the least degree resembling those heard by a
man lying in deep grass on a summer's day and watching the
clouds drift across the sky; but it does make noises which evoke

[1] Thus we find that thinkers as diverse as Ingarden and I. A. Richards both
subscribe to a form of this theory: see Roman Ingarden, 'Aesthetic Experiences and Aesthetic Object', *Phil. and Phen. Res.*, p. 305; and I. A. Richards,
Practical Criticism, p. 221.
[2] *The Principles of Art*, pp. 52–6.

feelings remarkably like that which a man feels on such an occasion'.[3]

Before considering the objections to this kind of theory it is important to note what it does not say. For a start nothing definite has been said about the nature of the 'response' in question – all that has been implied is that it is not a belief. Despite the traditional account in terms of 'feelings' it is certainly not true that in giving an affective theory of aesthetic description, we are forced to account for the appreciation of art in entirely emotional terms. As yet we do not know to which category of mental state the aesthetic experiences belong. Consequently, it cannot be objected to the affective theory that it is impossible to extend it beyond the example of a term like 'sad' which names a feature that is the proper object of sympathy. I have mentioned Wittgenstein's example of the description of the days of the week as 'fat' or 'lean'. Someone might at once object 'What is the experience of which "fat" is the expression?' How could there be such a thing as an experience of fatness? Here one might have recourse to the traditional empiricist idea of an association. Metaphors do not simply refer to analogies, it might be said, they also convey associations. Thus to show the part played by judgements of comparison in criticism is to show the importance of association in the appreciation of art.[4] The temptation is to say that I am not merely associating fatness and Wednesday in the judgement that I make (although of course this is trivially true); I am also expressing an association of the two ideas. Certainly, if there is anything to my judgement that Wednesday is fat, anything that you could understand in it, other than the mere fact that I am disposed to say this peculiar thing, than it is not to be found in analogies: there are not, and could not be, analogies of sufficient importance. This is not to say that the judgement that Wednesday is fat *describes* associations; rather, that associations may well enter into the 'experience' that constitutes its acceptance.

In other words, emotion terms and comparison terms present

---

[3] Op. cit., p. 56.
[4] Associationist theories are the stock-in-trade of classical criticism of abstract art-forms, as is exemplified, for example, by Addison's essays, 'The Pleasures of the Imagination', in *The Spectator*, 1712, and other works cited in the first chapter of Peter Collins' *Changing Ideals in Modern Architecture*.

exactly the same problem, and if an affective theory is an answer for one of them, it will be an answer for the other too. But how do we give content to this extremely simple theory that to see a work of art as sad is to respond to it in the way one responds to a man when touched by his sadness? Just to refer to a 'response' is inadequate, for this tells us nothing about the particular conditions of *aesthetic* experience and judgement. The example of Wednesday, for instance, is certainly not an aesthetic judgement as it stands. If it is an aesthetic judgement to describe the music of Brahms as fat, then this is because the description is being used to express a response that has an aesthetic character. But what is this response? The affective theory must remain empty until we provide a description of this response – a description independent of the supposed 'aesthetic qualities' of its object. But immediately we encounter certain quasi-idealist objections that seem to imply that this whole enterprise of independent description is the outcome of confusion. In giving a vague description of an aesthetic 'experience' it is possible to set up a plausible affective theory. But if we attempt to say anything more precise then we are immediately involved in certain familiar paradoxes arising from the supposition that the experience of art can be characterized independently of its object.

First there is the following objection. We have spoken of a response to a work of art which is *in itself* the 'recognition' of the sadness of the work. But responses are intentional: they are directed towards their objects, and certain very important features follow from this feature of 'directedness'. In general, we may say that if responses are intentional it is because, unlike mere reflex reactions, they involve an awareness and understanding of their objects. As a result responses must be founded on a certain conception of their object (a conception that may or may not correspond to reality). We might say, without too much distortion of current usage, that this conception defines the 'intentional object' of the response. Hence, in referring to a kind of response, we must also be referring to a kind of awareness that this response involves. In other words, if a response belongs to some kind K, then it must involve thoughts and judgements characteristic of K. It is a necessary truth, therefore, that the objects of responses of kind K are seen under a certain description: they are thought to possess some property or set of properties characteristic of K. We might put this point by saying that the intentional object of this kind of response must possess a certain feature, and we could call this feature, adapting a usage of Kenny's,[5] the 'formal object' of the response. For example, that which is feared is thought to be harmful (so that the intentional object of fear is 'something harmful'). That which is envied is thought to be desirable, that which is despised is thought to be a weakness, that which is regretted is thought to be bad. And so on. In classifying intentional states of mind we find that we are also identifying certain qualities of their intentional objects (that is, certain qualities that their material objects are thought to possess).

Note that the objection is not concerned only with how we classify emotions. It argues further that emotions, and responses in general, acquire formal objects in that they are founded on beliefs or judgements. It is because I think that something is harmful that I am afraid of it, and so on. Thus the formal object seems to result from a belief or judgement on which the mental state is founded. I believe that an object possesses a certain quality of harmfulness, and my fear both grows out of this belief and depends on it. Without this belief my state of mind would not be described as fear but rather as anxiety or dread. The quality of harmfulness is thus bound up with the emotion of fear. Fear might be described as a way of believing something to be harmful.

The defender of the affective theory immediately has to face a dilemma. He wishes to say that I find a piece of music sad if I respond to it in a way that is either the same as, or at least resembles, the way I respond when I am touched by human sadness. Let us call my response to human sadness R. Then plainly R is founded on, grows out of, the belief that its object is sad. Now either this belief is to be considered as partly definitive of R (so that sadness is the formal object of R), or it is not. If it is considered as definitive of R then it must recur whenever R recurs – in particular it must recur when the object of R is not a man but, say, a symphony. From which it would follow that a symphony can be thought to be sad in exactly the way that a man is thought to be sad, so that the 'recognition of sadness' in aesthetic experience is a matter of belief, and sadness is the common quality

[5] *Action, Emotion and Will*, p. 189.

with which we are already familiar. If, on the other hand, the belief is not considered as partly definitive of R – if R can recur without it – then in what sense is it an important fact about R that it is directed towards human sadness, and by what right do we call its recurrence, in another context, the recognition of the *sadness* of its object?

This objection is, it seems to me, extremely powerful. It forces us to retreat from all the traditional theories of the place of feeling in art, and it determines the description of the acceptance condition of aesthetic judgement in a way that most traditional empiricist theories of mind are unable to follow. Only in the context of a theory of imagination – such as I shall suggest in the next chapter – can the solution to this dilemma be found. First, however, we must rebut the suggestion that the intentionality of a mental state arises only through judgement or belief. To suggest that intentionality arises only in this way is to force the totality of mental states into too rigid a mould. While I must believe that the lion I see is harmful in order to be afraid of it, what must I believe about a situation if I am to be amused by it? To say 'something, but nothing definite' is to give no answer at all. It might be said that at least the object of my amusement must be thought to *exist*: but even that is wrong. I can be amused by something entirely imaginary. Indeed, amusement is just one among many states of mind – horror is another – that can exist with entirely imaginary objects. They may exist, that is, as responses to the scenes that a man calls up in his imagination. Such mental states are not, therefore, founded on belief or judgement at all. The activity of imagination is – as I shall argue – essentially contrasted with belief.

Thus we might compare my response to a man whom I think to be sad, with my response to the imagined spectacle of such a man. In imagining the man I certainly 'respond' in some way: that is, my image or thought gives rise to certain states of mind analogous, perhaps, to those aroused by the spectacle of genuine sadness.

The defender of the affective theory must, then, argue that my response to sad music is not founded on belief in the sadness of its object, and hence does not have a formal object of the kind already described. He must show that my response is founded in some other way, as amusement is founded in another way, a way that allows it to exist independently of any belief about the presence or nature of its object. In other words, we must argue that the response in question is founded not on belief but on some other kind of thought, a thought that does not involve the attribution of some quality to an existing thing. Such thoughts are characteristic of imagination, and if we are to describe 'aesthetic' reactions without mentioning any 'formal' object, we must have recourse to the theory of imagination. My experience of a work of art involves a distinctive order of intentionality, derived from imagination and divorced from belief and judgement. Indeed, it may be that the word 'response' is already tendentious as a description of this experience. For it seems to imply something emotional, while it may well be the case that the recognition of sadness in a work of art involves nothing emotional at all.

The objection from intentionality is just one aspect of the protest against the way in which the distinction between belief and non-cognitive states of mind has been formulated: as though the contrast between belief and the aesthetic responses can be made only by appealing to emotion. This is certainly the way that empiricists – when forced to abandon the idea of aesthetic perception – have tended to think about art: as though it summoned up a wealth of feelings that we could readily describe, and as though these feelings were quite unproblematically separable from the awareness and judgement of their object. This goes completely against our deep conviction that art does not so much arouse as control the emotions, converting crude feeling into directed thought.

It is important to realize that the intellectual content of aesthetic experiences may be so pronounced that any talk of 'emotion' seems out of place. Works of art are highly deliberate and complex objects, and considerable understanding may be required if we are to grasp their meaning. Aesthetic experiences must, therefore, include a large element of intellectual understanding, and hence will have a more than contingent connection with verbal expression. One way to show that one sees a work of art under a description (such as 'sad') is to produce the description itself. The verbal expression of an aesthetic experience is, typically, a description that is held to justify the experience, and frequently justification consists in making comparisons – I show that a poem is tender by comparing it with expressions of tenderness. In other words, the verbal expression of aesthetic experience may well consist in a pattern of reasoned justification, rather like the justification of a factual judgement. And the judgement tends to rest on comparisons, like the justification of the judgement that ascribes a property. For example, take the following passage from a Schubert sonata:

I may argue that this passage has an outward-looking, brightening movement, despite the sinking and lassitudinous line of the melody. And I may justify this 'aesthetic' description by making certain comparisons. The bass, for example, leads the harmony onwards, through the unaffirmed keys of F and B flat, and this bold gesture seems to counteract the sinking of the melody on to the mediant of E flat. If someone notices this feature of the bass line, he is more likely to agree to the aesthetic description: the character of the passage will change for him. It is as though, in describing the relationship of the work of art to other things (for example, to the way the boldness of one gesture may counteract the weakness of another), one were trying to show that the work possessed some property in common with those other things. Reference to a 'response' or an 'experience' seems entirely inappropriate, simply because it seems to ignore the evident intellectuality of the aesthetic judgement. What is interesting about aesthetic experience is, as we shall see, not the experience in its entirety, but rather the thought that lies at its heart.

But having got this far, we find yet another argument against the possibility of producing an independent description of an aesthetic experience. This objection points to another logical relation, but not that between a state of mind and its formal object; rather that between a state of mind and its expression. The argument, familiar from Croce and Collingwood, may be given in the following form: a mental state and its expression are not two phenomena, but rather two aspects of a single process. When I say that a work of art expresses a particular feeling, for example, I am not asserting that there is a relation between the work of art and something else. Likewise, when I say that someone understands the particular feeling of a work of art (its particular quality of sadness, say), then there can be no expression of this understanding other than a close attention to, or involvement with, *that* particular work of art. Any other way of identifying the process of understanding would have the consequence that the work of art, which is the expression of this understanding, is only contingently connected with it. Any generalized description of the experience, which would allow us to say that it could be felt towards some other work of art, would not be a description of what it is to grasp or understand the emotional quality of *that* particular work of art, and hence would not be a description of anything that could be called recognizing the work's aesthetic quality.

This objection is very close in spirit to the objection from intentionality, and occurs in many variants. Perhaps the most impressive statement of it is due to Collingwood,[6] who argued that there must be a distinction of kind between art and craft. For art is an end, not a means, and can only be appreciated as an autonomous activity with no rationale external to itself. It does not, for example, refer beyond itself, to objects or states of mind that are separately identifiable. Nor is it an expression of any state of mind that is already identified, since expression in such a case would have an external end, namely, the expression of that identifiable state of mind. In so far as expression occurs in art it is essentially opposed to description: it gives us the particularity and not the generality of states of mind. In a similar way, we may argue that our feelings *towards* art find their principal and central expression in the appreciation of art, and cannot be identified separately. Extended in this way, the objection argues from the necessary connection between emotion and expression to the necessary connection between emotion and object, exactly as the previous

[6] *The Principles of Art*, ch. 2.

objection, and so arrives at a similar conclusion. But its tenor is in fact very different, since it is based on the view that to attempt an independent description of aesthetic appreciation is, in fact, to mistake the whole nature of appreciation. Appreciation is essentially tied to the particular circumstances in which it finds expression. Wittgenstein, rehearsing the objection, argues somewhat as follows: if someone says that a work of art expresses a feeling of a certain kind, then this suggests that we could identify and describe the feeling in question. But if this were so, we could think of some other way of expressing the feeling which would serve just as well. But this would permit an experimental approach to works of art, which is quite different from our present and accepted modes of aesthetic interest: we do not look beyond the music to something that the music is not.[7] In a similar way, to think that the experience of music can be independently described, to think that it is a replica of some other experience, is to give the music itself a purely instrumental role in appreciation.

At the heart of this objection lies a quibble about identity that needs to be exposed.[8] It is quite possible to choose a very strong criterion of identity for mental states, such that no two instances are regarded as instances of the same state unless their expressions are absolutely identical. Thus when I say that the particular feeling expressed by Tchaikovsky's Sixth Symphony is not identical with the particular feeling expressed by the *Kindertotenlieder*, what I say can be construed as an analytic truth. The plausibility of the Crocean argument given above hangs on a sense of the term 'particular' that masks the triviality of this analytic truth. As Wittgenstein points out,[9] the term 'particular' has an intransitive and a transitive use. When I say that the first movement of Tchaikovsky's Sixth Symphony expresses a particular feeling, or that I react towards it in a particular way, then I might be using the term 'particular' intransitively, so as to forbid the question 'What feeling?' or 'What way?' In this sense 'particular' means

[7] Collingwood, op. cit., pp. 29–36; Wittgenstein, *Lectures and Conversations on Aesthetics, Psychology, and Religious Belief*, pp. 28 ff., esp. pp. 34–6, and *Brown Book*, pp. 177–8.
[8] I rely here on Richard Wollheim, *Art and its Objects*, section 48.
[9] *Brown Book*, pp. 158 ff.

something like 'peculiar',[10] and is being used simply to impose on a mental state the strong criterion of identity. On the other hand, when I wish not merely to refer to a mental state but also to describe it, then I might say that it is a particular feeling, or a particular response, in a transitive sense – so as to allow the question 'What feeling (response)?' Here the word 'particular' stands proxy for a generic description that I have not yet produced. That there is also an intransitive sense of 'particular' does not prove that there is no way of describing feelings referred to by means of this intransitive locution; it means only that the speaker does not intend to give any further description. He has identified the feeling he wishes to refer to as the particular feeling expressed by (or felt in response to) Tchaikovsky's Sixth Symphony. This, for him, is its most important feature – it is this particular expression that he wishes to draw attention to.

But while the objection can be circumnavigated in this way, it leaves us with a puzzle. For it is undeniable that in referring to the feelings that are 'expressed' by art, and to the feelings that art 'arouses', we very often do use this intransitive locution. And we do so because of the way in which we appreciate works of art. If we were always describing the feelings aroused in us by works of art then this would be an expression of the fact that we appreciate art as a means for arousing those feelings (as some people value certain drugs). But this goes against the intuition that, in general, we do not appreciate art as a means at all. This is the principal reason why philosophers, from Kant to the present day, have wished to deny that there is a place for *feeling* in our response to art. If we think of art simply as a means of arousing emotion, then the best art is presumably that which arouses the most emotion of the appropriate kind. But it is objected that the use of art as a means of arousing emotion in this sense is a perverted use, and the whole failing of sentimental art is that it employs whatever means are available for the end of feeling. Such art interests us only in our own emotions, and not in their aesthetic object. Surely, it is argued, aesthetic appreciation is not like this? Or if it is, then it is a far less interesting phenomenon than we had imagined. Appreciation, on this account, reduces to intoxication, and the value of art is of no different order from the value of

[10] Cf. Collingwood, op. cit., p. 113, 'this quite peculiar anger'.

certain drugs. The evaluation of art becomes an instrumental procedure, based on the investigation of its causal relation to certain feelings. No work of art will be regarded as having any relation to human psychology higher than that of pornography or journalism.

The objection to the place of an 'experience' or 'response' in appreciation is thus part of a whole tradition of aesthetic thought, beginning with Kant's attack on the place of 'interest', and reaching into the present century with Croce's dismissal of the *estetica del simpatico* and Collingwood's critique of 'magic art'. It goes with a justified contempt for a certain view of aesthetic appreciation (a view encouraged by standard empiricist theories of mind), and exists alongside the attempt to define appreciation as a self-subsistent realm of mental life, whose value, and whose place in human experience, can be independently defined. To think of aesthetic appreciation in terms of particular experiences seems to involve falling into an old fallacy, the fallacy of reducing aesthetic interest to some other and more commonplace exemplar. Combined with this fallacy are many other errors: the confusion of means and ends, of feelings and thoughts, of causes and objects (for on this view what is interesting about a work of art is not its status as the object of a certain feeling, but rather its status as the feeling's cause).[11] And so on.

Once the presuppositions of this objection have been revealed, we find ourselves bound to agree with them. What we must doubt, however, is the conclusion that, therefore, aesthetic experiences simply cannot be independently described. We will answer the objections if we can describe some experience that is essentially bound up with the perception of its object – in the way, perhaps, that the perception of an aspect already involves the perception of the thing that 'contains' it. Aesthetic experiences, I shall argue, are modes of interest in an object perceived, and must be described partly in terms of a perception. In showing this, I shall have gone part of the way towards analysing what it means to say that aesthetic interest is interest in an object for its own sake. For we will be in a position to see how the fact that aesthetic experience can be classified into kinds, and hence referred to, independently of their (material) objects, is, nonethe-

[11] Cf. John Casey, *The Language of Criticism*, chapter IV.

less, compatible with their involving an appreciation of the *particular* objects to which they are directed.

One thing that emerges from this discussion is that there seems to be little point in saying that a work of art expresses a particular feeling, when one intends the term 'particular' intransitively. Similarly, there is little point in saying that a work of art awakens in one a particular response, when one intends the term 'particular' in this way. And for the most part we do use the term in this way when discussing works of art, simply because we wish to draw attention to the object, rather than to any feeling or experience that could be described independently. And it is this 'above all' that suggests that the attempt to describe such an experience is both futile and irrelevant to aesthetics.

The suggestion that I wish to develop – in the face of this objection – is that it is, after all, both possible and interesting to describe the acceptance conditions of certain aesthetic judgements, in such a way as to distinguish them from beliefs. It is certainly true that traditional empiricist theories of mind have made the task of describing such 'experiences' extremely difficult. This is partly because they supposed that the distinction between cognitive and non-cognitive states of mind is intuitive and obvious, and partly because of their Cartesian assumptions about mental states in general – that they can be distinguished by direct 'introspection', independently of any knowledge of their outward expression. We have rejected these assumptions. If we are to elucidate the nature of aesthetic responses, therefore, we should look deeper; in particular we should examine the distinction between cognitive states of mind – such as belief – and non-cognitive states, such as the mental phenomena grouped under the head of imagination. It is to the subject of the imagination, therefore, that we now must turn.

CHAPTER SEVEN

The Imagination I

In proposing a contrast between declarative sentences that express beliefs and declarative sentences that do not, I seem to have implied that beliefs can be identified independently of the sentences that express them. Since it has been argued by several philosophers that the concept of belief can only be explicated in terms of the concept of an utterance or assertion in language, it might seem that my argument collapses, and that the attempt to distinguish types of judgement in terms of the condition for their acceptance is wrong from the start. It is necessary to say something in reply to this objection if the contrast that I wish to develop between belief and imagination is to have the intended force.

The argument has it that one cannot attribute beliefs to a creature unless one can say something about *what* he believes: if *X* believes something it must be possible to decide, for some *p*, that *X* believes that *p*. Now if we list the number of beliefs that there are, we find that we do nothing but list declarative sentences: there is no way of counting beliefs except by counting assertible sentences. Or, if we do say that two sentences may express the same belief, then the only criterion of this would be their identity of meaning. Sentences and their meanings seem to provide the only sure access to the concept of belief, and this argues a connection between belief and language of a remarkable kind. It seems natural to conclude that, without a language, no creature could express any definite belief (say the belief that *p* rather than the belief that *q*). No merely animal behaviour can express the essential definiteness of belief, a definiteness that must be described in terms of the correspondence between belief and language. To have beliefs, it is argued, a creature must display the ability to assent to a sentence, or to use a sentence as a premise in theoretical or practical reasoning.[1]

If this argument has force, then perhaps there is something wrong with the idea that only *some* declarative sentences express beliefs. And it is certainly true that in ordinary parlance we make no distinction between declaratives that do and declaratives that do not express belief. We talk quite freely of moral beliefs, for example, and there are no restrictions other than grammatical ones on which sentences can occur after the construction '*X* believes that. . . .' or '*X* thinks that . . .'. Indeed, it is arguable that the logic of these constructions must itself be explained in terms of the logic of '*X* says that . . .', and not *vice versa*.[2] It may be that we could still reconstruct a distinction between those sentences that do, and those that do not, express beliefs, in terms of some philosophical theory. (The theory, for example, that while most indicative sentences in a natural language have truth conditions in a strong sense, there is a minority of sentences that acquire meaning in some other way.) But such a theory renders the idea of an 'acceptance condition' redundant: it will no longer be useful to explain the meaning of a sentence in terms of the condition for its acceptance.

How, then, can the difference between belief and other 'modes of acceptance' be described? In fact, if we examine the argument we find that it has certain extremely paradoxical consequences. For if we really could argue from the premise that beliefs are identified in language only by referring to declarative sentences to the conclusion that beliefs are in some way dependent on language for their very existence, then we ought to be able to construct a similar argument for the language-dependence of any other kind of entity that is identified in a similar way. But this we cannot do, for among such entities we find not only beliefs, but also bits of information, truths, facts, and even states of affairs themselves. To argue for the language-dependence of *all* such

[1] Cf. B. Aune, *Knowledge, Mind and Nature*, pp. 213 ff.
[2] Cf. D. Davidson, 'On Saying That', in D. Davidson and J. Hintikka (eds.), *Words and Objections*.

entities is to give way to idealism in its most paradoxical form.

This should lead us to reject such an approach to the concept of belief. Consider the parallel concept of 'information'. It is commonly assumed in scientific circles (whether rightly or wrongly) that this concept can be used in the description and explanation of the behaviour of machines; and yet it shows just the same kind of relation to language and meaning as does the concept of belief. Information is identified in language with just the same constructions of indirect speech that are used to identify beliefs. We speak of the information that . . ., where the gap is filled by a sentence which conveys the precise piece of information that we wish to consider. It is often thought to be true, nonetheless, that the concept of information can be applied to the behaviour of a machine: a guided missile, say. Such a machine may be said to receive and respond to the information that a metallic object is moving ten miles above it at a speed of five hundred miles an hour. It does not matter whether this use of the concept of information is a stretched or extended use. For here we have a sentence in indirect speech, for which no immediate substitute is available, and which is thought to offer a plausible and verifiable explanation of the machine's behaviour. Whether it is the best kind of explanation is another matter: it is certainly the simplest. And no air of paradox attaches to the fact that here explanation rests on a construction in indirect speech. Why should not the same be true, therefore, of the sentences that identify beliefs? We can see the concept of belief as giving a particular kind of explanation of human and animal behaviour (explanation by 'reason' rather than by 'cause'). If the concept of belief is introduced in this way then it by no means follows that a creature that has beliefs must also have a language in which these beliefs may achieve 'direct' expression.

The parallel with the theoretical concept of information leads us to draw certain useful conclusions. First, one could imagine a machine (a computer, say) being given a formula that, while grammatically well-formed, conveys to it no 'information' (say, because it contains an undefined term). And one can imagine the computer being programmed to react to such sentences in one of two definite ways – corresponding to our acceptance or rejection of a non-descriptive sentence. In other words, the analogy of non-descriptive meaning could be reconstructed in the theory of information. Secondly, we find that, if there is a basic application of the concept of belief in the explanation of behaviour (on analogy with the concept of information), then beliefs will be given by precisely those sentences that are connected with truth conditions in the strong (epistemological) sense. For in explaining animal behaviour in terms of belief, one is relating the animal's responses to states of affairs of which it is in some way aware: observable states of affairs that can be directly located in the external world (cf. the relation of the missile to its target). Hence these basic beliefs will be given by truth conditions in the strong sense. Admittedly a language-using creature can also have general and theoretical beliefs which are made available to him by language. But we call the assent to general and theoretical sentences *belief* because of the logical connection with central examples.

This suggests that while it may normally be necessary, in referring to beliefs, to mention the declarative sentences that express them, the mental state of believing something can be explained in terms of its expression independently of language. Exactly what form this explanation will take is another matter, and one quite beyond the scope of the present discussion: but at least we can see how it might lead us back to the kind of strong, philosophical idea of a truth condition from which our investigations began.

It is undeniable, however, that all our ways of referring to belief in language are parasitic on our ways of referring to sentences and meanings – which is only to be expected. In order to discuss belief in the abstract, therefore, it is best to approach it indirectly, through the idea of an assertion in language, as Geach and Aune, for example, have found it necessary to do.[3] But if we do approach belief in this way, then we soon discover a means of distinguishing belief from other modes of thought; for not everything that is said is also asserted. We find that we can distinguish two types of utterance, first the case where sentences are being used to say something, and secondly the case – as in elocution – where sentences are being treated more as patterns of sound than as verbal symbols. And among the examples of things said we can again distinguish between asserted and unasserted occurrences.

[3] P. T. Geach, *Mental Acts*, sections 22–3, and B. Aune, op. cit.

For example, '*p*' occurs unasserted in 'Suppose that *p*', 'It is possible that *p*', '*p* implies *q*', and so on. This is not a distinction of grammar, for sentences that occur unasserted may preserve their assertoric form. Indeed it may often be difficult to tell with which kind of occurrence we have to deal: we may have to relate a sentence to its entire context. For example, someone may embark on a narrative in the following way: 'Suppose that *p*; then *q*, after which *r*, *etc.* . . . .'. It may be impossible to discover the unasserted character of any sentence in this sequence without relating it back to the initial supposition from which the story flows. (The situation is even more complicated in the case of storytelling as commonly practiced; for, except when told to a child, the initial suppositions remain unspoken).

Relying on these broad distinctions, we might say that there is such a thing as entertaining the proposition that *p* unasserted, and we might describe this as a mental act analogous to the overt act of saying '*p*' unasserted, in the way that Geach has argued that judging that *p* is a mental act analogous to the overt act of asserting '*p*'. Now, believing and judging are different concepts, although the former is a necessary condition of the latter. Believing, unlike judging, is dispositional or quasi-dispositional: it is not a mental occurrence of the same instantaneous variety. But this should not worry us unduly, since everything that we need to say about the contrast between belief and other modes of thought can be expressed in terms of the contrast between judgement and other kinds of mental act. Clearly there are modes of thought that involve not the assertion of '*p*', but the more elusive ability simply to hold the proposition that *p* before one's mind, to entertain *p* as a possibility, or as a supposition. Indeed much of our more complex thought processes – imagination, for one – are of this kind, and we know exactly what it is to say '*p*' unasserted. Moreover, it is a celebrated conclusion of Frege's that assertedness cannot be part of the meaning of a sentence.[4] '*p*' must mean the same in its asserted and in its unasserted use. In Frege's terminology, every declarative sentence has an assertible content in common to its asserted and unasserted uses. This content is

[4] G. Frege, 'Sense and Reference', in P. T. Geach and M. Black (eds.), *Philosophical Writings of Gottlob Frege*. See also P. T. Geach, 'Assertion', *Phil. Rev.*, 1965.

'before the mind' when one entertains the proposition that p, whether or not one also believes that p.

So far this seems obvious enough. If there are mental acts of judging, then there are also similar acts of 'entertaining' that are divorced from judgement. In these acts propositions come before one's mind, and it seems to be a necessary consequence of the way in which this idea of an unasserted thought has been introduced that what is before one's mind in entertaining p is precisely what is asserted in asserting p, and hence precisely what is believed in believing p. Thus when we imagine something, or tell a story, while being indifferent to its truth, the content of our thought is the content of a belief; but the thought process itself is independent of this belief.

Entertaining a proposition unasserted, like judgement, involves the idea of a proposition being 'before the mind', an idea that has so far been explained through analogy with the overt act of speech. Indeed we find that the basis in behaviour for attributing mental acts of this kind presupposes that the agent is a language user. We could not make sense of the attribution of such thoughts to animals: they are the peculiar property of rational beings, and, unlike beliefs, require the dimension of verbal behaviour if they are to be expressed at all. As we shall see, this fact has important consequences in the description of imaginative and perceptual experience.

So far we have contrasted belief (and its associated act of judgement) with only one other kind of thought – the entertaining of a proposition unasserted. This is as yet an insufficient basis for a theory of aesthetic description that will meet the requirements of the preceding chapter. For we need an account of some mode of thought that is directed at, and aroused in response to, its object, in the manner of aesthetic experience. And the mere entertaining of a proposition about an object is scarcely yet a genuine response to it. However, we find that we are also in a position to describe other species of thought in terms of the idea of entertaining a proposition. For example, we can already give a partial elucidation of the concept of 'thinking *of* . . .'. To think of X may involve entertaining thoughts about X, that is, it is to have before one's mind propositions whose subject-matter is X. When one thinks of X it is not necessary that one's thoughts about X should also be beliefs about X. Indeed, one can think of things that are entirely fictional or imaginary. 'Thinking of' is, in this sense, indifferent to truth.[5]

Now the first attempt at a solution to the problem of aesthetic responses might be through a consideration of the concept 'To think of X as Y', a mode of thought that is distinct from belief, and yet closely related to 'seeing as'. In the process of thinking of my friend I may think of him as, say, an army officer, or a composer; and I may come to the conclusion that while he would do very well as the one, he has no aptitude for the other. Here again, the propositions entertained are not necessarily asserted: I may think of X as Y while knowing that it is untrue – even impossible – that X is Y. In no sense need I, in having this thought, assert to myself that X is Y. We might say that to think of X as Y at least involves the entertaining of the proposition 'X is Y'. However, this is clearly not all there is to this species of thought. In at least one sense of 'to think of X as Y' the entertaining of this proposition is not sufficient for having the thought. If I say that I think of the Chairman as an elephant, say, then clearly I am saying something about a mental disposition of mine: it is not sufficient for the truth of this pronouncement that I should entertain the proposition 'The Chairman is an elephant' on one occasion. Nor is it sufficient that I should have a disposition to entertain this proposition if I always immediately reject it. The idea must strike me as in some way right or appropriate if it is really to be a descrip-

---

[5] It may seem that I have made a mistake in assimilating thought about a fictitious object to the category of thought that is 'unasserted'. Surely, when I say 'Banquo was murdered' I am asserting something: the peculiarity of my utterance lies in the fact that the term 'Banquo' does not refer to anybody real. What I say, it might be argued, is deficient in the dimension of reference, not in the dimension of assertion. But we must distinguish two uses of the term 'reference'. In one of these, it denotes a property of a linguistic expression, a property which belongs to that expression whether or not it is ever used to assert anything, and which can be analysed independently of the idea of assertion. In the other use, the term denotes a property of a speech-act, of what is done when words are uttered. It is this latter use which is relevant here. In saying 'Banquo was murdered' I do not refer to a man called Banquo, since I entertain unasserted the existential proposition that secures the reference (in the first sense) of the term 'Banquo'. I have supposed the existence of a man called Banquo – and that man, I am saying, was murdered. In other words, the failure of reference in the speech-act can be analysed in terms of the failure to assert (either explicitly or implicitly) a sentence whose truth is a necessary condition for the truth of 'Banquo was murdered'.

tion of the way I think of the Chairman. This is not to say that the thought has an 'asserted' character: for clearly it would be a total misrepresentation of my thought process to say that I am under the impression that the Chairman is (literally) an elephant. In other words, in thinking of X as Y, I very often think of X, and think of the description 'Y' as particularly appropriate (for whatever reason) to X. This is a mode of rational acceptance of the proposition 'X is Y' that is, nonetheless, not a belief, even though it shares many of the properties of belief, including the character of a disposition rather than an act.

Now superficially it might seem that it is precisely this kind of thought that is involved in the acceptance of at least some aesthetic judgements – for example the judgement that a Schubert song is sad, or that a Gainsborough portrait is tender. And, in fact, we might wish to argue that it is precisely this kind of thought that is involved in the exercise of imagination generally: imagination is essentially thought that is unasserted, while being entertained as 'appropriate' to its subject matter. And aesthetic experience, as one of the phenomena of imagination, shares the structure that this particular kind of thought dictates.

Unfortunately, this conclusion is far too hasty. We will find that it both simplifies the concept of imagination in an unacceptable manner, and also fails to locate the precise way in which an aesthetic experience is directed at its object. This point is best appreciated by approaching the topic of imagination independently. We shall find that the relation of imaginative thoughts to their object is considerably more subtle than is implied by the above account.

The first question that comes to mind in attempting to analyse a concept as complex as that of imagination is this – 'Is there one concept or many?' It is easy to say many and leave it at that. When we consider all the separate phenomena that have been discussed under this title it seems unlikely that any series of links could be discovered between them. But in that case why do we use the same term ('imagination') to denote *more* than one concept? I shall argue that there are links of an important kind between the various phenomena grouped under the heading of imagination, and that, in effect, there is only one concept expressed in the use of this term. The phenomena that need to be discussed are:

forming an image ('picturing'); imagining in its various forms (imagining that . . . imagining what it would be like if . . ., imagining what it is like to . . .: some of these constructions are propositional, some not; some relate to knowledge that . . . some to knowledge by acquaintance); doing something with imagination, (imagination as adverbial rather than predicative); using imagination to see something; seeing an aspect. The last of these is rarely described as 'imagination', and hence presents a superficial difficulty. However, it will be one of my conclusions that there is at least one sense of the expression 'seeing as' in which it denotes an activity of the imagination rather than an activity of judgement.

We can investigate how the separate uses of 'imagine' and its cognates connect in various ways, but evidently we do not simply want a map of usage. We must see how to account for certain phenomena in the context of a coherent philosophy of mind. We must discover the truth conditions of certain things that we say about people, and show how they relate to the truth conditions of more fundamental propositions in the description of mind, such as propositions employing the concepts of belief, sensation and desire. The phenomena of the imagination seem to lie strangely detached from the analytical philosopher's list of mental notions, and although at least one empiricist (Hume) gave to the imagination a central place in the theory of knowledge, there has been little attempt to analyse the concept within the framework of an empiricist philosophy of mind. It is not unfair to suggest that this failure is of a piece with the present lack of any systematic aesthetics in the empiricist tradition. No such lack can be discovered in idealist philosophy, and it is common for idealists to devote some part of their writings on aesthetics to the imagination, from which they derive the continuity of aesthetic and non-aesthetic experience.[6]

Where does our investigation begin? Modern philosophers have tended to broach the topic through the notion of an image, as though the presence of images were the distinguishing feature of all acts of imagination. One of the main objects of the discussion has been to refute the traditional dualist and empiricist notion of imagery, which conceives of the image as a private mental picture formed like a copy of a sense-impression, only

[6] See, for example, Collingwood, *The Principles of Art*, bk. II.

slightly more faded, as it were. This notion has been refuted on three grounds: it fails to distinguish imagery from sensation (Ryle, Sartre); it does not account for the intentionality of imagery (Husserl, Sartre); it makes the image into a private object about which nothing can be said (Ryle, Wittgenstein).[7] Each of these arguments is conclusive, but none of them give any basis for a positive theory of imagination. We do not learn what an image is, nor do we learn how imagery relates to imagining, imagination, memory, perception and belief. All that emerges is (i) the need to connect imagery with thought, (ii) the need to give public criteria for the truth of the proposition that a man has an image of something (or 'pictures' something). Ryle's view of imagery, as a species of pretending, meets these two requirements. But for a variety of reasons it fails to provide an answer to the problem.[8] In much of what follows I shall lean heavily on arguments of Wittgenstein's, from *Zettel*, especially sections 621–655, and from the *Philosophical Investigations*, pt. II, xi.

Can we make any general remarks about the notions listed above that will serve as a starting point for a more positive theory of imagination? Only, I think, of the most primitive kind. We can begin by separating two strands in the use of 'imagine' and its cognates, a predicative and an adverbial strand. On the one hand, we talk of '*X* imagining *Y*', '*X* seeing *Y* as *Z*', '*X* forming an image of *Y*', '*X* imagining that *p*, what it would be life if *p*' and so on, all of which predicate an activity of *X*. On the other hand, we talk of *X* doing something with imagination, or imaginatively, using his imagination in the performance of some task (whether it be fulfilling a practical aim, or acquiring some particular piece of knowledge) – in this sense imagination qualifies a further activity, identified separately. The predicative activities are all mental acts, whereas the activities performed with imagination need not be. This is exactly like thinking: thinking is a mental activity; doing something thoughtfully is often not. This might lead us to suppose that the mental activity is prior – although Ryle derives the oppo-

[7] G. Ryle, *The Concept of Mind*, ch. VIII; J-P. Sartre, *L'imaginaire*; E. Husserl, *Ideas*, ch. 3. (There is also an account of Husserl's views in the final chapter of Sartre, *L'imagination*.)

[8] See Hidé Ishiguro, 'Imagination', in B. Williams and A. Montefiore (eds.), *British Analytical Philosophy*.

site conclusion, partly because he seems to think that purely predicative mental concepts open the way to Cartesian dualism.

What does it mean to say of someone that he has (or forms) an image of something? We need a positive account of imagery, but where do we find it? The account given by Sartre, like that of Husserl, from which it takes its inspiration, remains on the level of pure phenomenology – it is a study in depth of the first-person case, independently of the third-person criteria which must be invoked to give the meaning of any psychological term. As the remarks in Chapter One imply, we must not attempt to answer the question 'What is an image?' by looking inwards. The knowledge we have of our own images is immediate, based on nothing; it therefore rests on no *features* of images whereby we recognize them for what they are. Mere 'observation' of our images will tell us nothing about them: the only facts about images are facts about the third-person case. Although there are what might be called 'phenomenological' descriptions of such things as images, they are not properly speaking descriptions – they do not convey information about images in the way that a description of a table conveys information about a table. To understand such descriptions is not to recognize features in experience to which they might apply: it is simply to see how they might be appropriate, or how they might *convey* what cannot be truly described. Such descriptions are metaphors, which may be phrased in a technical language designed for the purpose (Husserl), and therefore incomprehensible, or which may be expressed in the literary language characteristic of Sartre (who compares the image to a magic incantation designed to re-capture an absent thing), and hence pleasant but uninformative.[9] If we wish to know what an image is, we must ask, 'What is it about another that enables us to say of him that he has images?'

There is a feature of both imagery and imagining which serves to distinguish them from many mental states. This is the feature of subjection to the will.[10] This does not mean that 'picturing' or

[9] Sartre, *L'imaginaire*, p. 239.
[10] The feature is difficult to define precisely, and has been variously described by philosophers throughout the ages – see, for example Aristotle, *De Anima*, 427b; Aquinas, *Summa Theologiae*, 1a, 2ae, 56, 5; Locke, *Essay*, II, xxx; and more recently Sartre and Wittgenstein (op. cit.).

imagining are always or nearly always voluntary. Nor does it mean that other mental states – such as sensation, perception and belief – cannot be induced by an effort of will. It means that the request to imagine or form an image of something makes sense. Someone can assent to it directly. There is nothing else he has to do first in order to comply with this kind of request. He can call up an image, and if images are sometimes involuntary, and sometimes impossible to banish or summon, this is entirely contingent, and not of their essence. It is impossible to imagine someone, aware of the evidence which conclusively proves that *p*, for example, choosing first to believe *p*, and then not, at will. Nor is it possible to imagine someone choosing first to see what is before his eyes and then not. What one can imagine is someone choosing to avoid the evidence for *p*, or choosing to close his eyes. But here he is doing something else in order not to acquire the belief or the perception in question. The voluntariness attaches not to the belief or perception themselves, but to the actions that bring them about. The order to believe, or to see, does not in itself make sense.

This might be doubted. Surely when I say that someone has imagined that something, the propositional construction I employ is meant to identify a belief (which I imply to be false). Does not imagining, therefore, sometimes involve belief? If belief is not subject to the will how can imagination be subject to the will? Here we must contrast two different uses of the term 'imagine', one to refer to a mental act, the other to pass judgement on another's beliefs. When I say 'Imagine that *p*', I am not asking you to believe falsely that *p*. Obeying this order does not involve believing something, but rather entertaining propositions unasserted. I shall take it, then, that the use of the term 'imagine' to pass judgement on another's beliefs is derivative. In this use 'imagine' means simply 'believe falsely', and plainly no interesting theory of imagination could be founded on such a usage. A similar derivative use of 'imagine' occurs in reporting a certain kind of speculative belief. For example: 'Where do you think John is?' – 'I imagine (that) he is in the library'.

The contrast with belief is in fact rather difficult to draw, for a further reason. There *is* sense to the request 'Believe *p*' in certain contexts. It gets sense from its surroundings, when these contribute an independent plausibility to *p*, thus making it possible to

'obey' the order. That is 'Believe *p*' is not so much an order as a
way of vouching for the truth of *p*. This is the case in most examples of the form, 'Believe you me, *p*'. Orders to believe are
ways of giving one's word to the truth of a proposition and hence
of adding to the belief the antecedent plausibility derived from
one's own truthfulness. In the absence of these special circumstances, however, the order to believe does not make sense. It
might be said that there are, nevertheless, circumstances in which
I might believe a proposition by *choice* – for example, when I know
no reason against believing it, and wish it to be true. For example,
I might choose to trust someone, and this commits me to believing
what he says. When I say to someone 'Tell me what happened –
I will believe you', what I say is not unlike an expression of intention. It carries the suggestion that belief is at least sometimes
subject to the will. On the other hand, there are further features
of the relation between belief and the will which serve to distinguish imagination and belief. For example, I cannot choose one
moment to believe *p*, and the next moment not to believe *p*, and
so on, without having discovered some further evidence against
p. Whereas I can imagine something one minute, and then cease to
imagine it, and so on, irrespective of any other circumstance.
For imagination is something I engage in, whereas belief is not.
Thus the absurdity of the White Queen's remark: 'sometimes I
have believed as many as six impossible things before breakfast'.
And thus the absurdity of believing something for a practical,
rather than a theoretical, reason (which is the paradox involved in
Pascal's wager).[11]

We might summarize this difference as follows: whereas the
order 'Imagine the following: . . .' makes sense, the order 'Believe
the following: . . .' does not, except in very special circumstances.
And this is a logical point, reflecting a categorical difference
between imagination and belief. The contrast with perception,
sensation and desire is much clearer. I cannot, for example, order
you to have a pain in your finger, although I can order you to do
something that will ensure that you have such a pain, and so on.[12]
Again it might seem that this difference is only contingent: it

[11] For further arguments see Roy Edgley, *Reason in Theory and Practice*,
pp. 60 ff.
[12] L. Wittgenstein, *Zettel*, section 52.

just so happens that I cannot acquire pains in this way. But, in, fact we find that the difference is more fundamental than this. If we attempt to describe the case of someone obeying the order to have a pain in his finger, we seem constrained to describe him as doing something else, such as thinking about it, as a result of which he suffers the pain. The mental act is the thought, while the pain is only its causal consequence.

Images, like imagination generally, share this feature of subjection to the will. Forming an image is something I can do: it is not always something I suffer or undergo. Likewise I can sensibly ask someone to imagine a scene, or to imagine what it would be like if p, and so on. In this respect imagination is like unasserted thought. Indeed, we can often substitute for 'imagine' and its cognates, 'think' and its cognates ('Think what it would be like if p', and so on), and this might lead us to suspect that in general imagination was nothing more than a species of thought.

Later I shall show that this is too simple an approach: imagination may, and often does, involve imagery, and imagery is not *just* a kind of thought. However, we might wish to argue that imagery is a separate phenomenon: it is not only in imagining that we have images; there are memory images as well. It should be possible, therefore, to treat imagination and imagery apart, since neither is a necessary feature of the other. We might then wish to say that imagination just *is* a species of thought. In fact, we say that a man imagines X (or what it would be like if p) to the extent that he can give an account of X (or p), provided certain further conditions are fulfilled. These further conditions are difficult to specify in detail, but a rough analysis might proceed as follows:

(1) Imagination involves thought which is unasserted, and hence which goes beyond what is believed. Thus a man is not said to be imagining X (or what it would be like if p), if he produces his account on the basis of what he already knows – say, because X is before him and he is studying it, because p is true and he is observing the consequences of its truth; because he has been told, or remembers, the account he now produces, because he has evidence, which in conjunction with knowledge he already has, will enable him to deduce or predict his account of X or p. In

other words imagination goes beyond what is given in ordinary prediction and belief. This is not to say that one cannot believe that X is as one imagines it to be. But one cannot imagine X to be as one knows or has good reason to think it to be. In imagination one is engaging in speculation, and one is not typically aiming at a definite assertion as to how things are. In imagination, therefore, one goes beyond what is strictly given.

(2) Not any way of going beyond the 'given' will count as imagining X, or what it would be like if p. Imagining is a special case of 'thinking of x as y.' It has two objects: the primary object (the X or p that has to be imagined), and the secondary object, which is *how X or p is described*. Imagination is not simply producing descriptions of an object which one is unprepared to assert. It involves thinking of these descriptions as appropriate in some way to the primary object. Imagination is a rational activity. The man who imagines is trying to produce an account of something, and is, therefore, trying to relate his thoughts to their subject-matter: he is constructing a narrative, and to do this it is not sufficient merely to go beyond what he is already 'given'. It is necessary that he should attempt to bring what he says or thinks into relation with the subject: his thoughts must be entertained because of their 'appropriateness'.

Because of this rationality inherent in the activity it is natural that 'why'-questions should be in place when someone gives an imagined description of an object or state of affairs. We can explain, therefore, why there should be a partly normative idea of imagination: we often distinguish among the activities of the imagination between those which are really *imagination* and those which are mere fantasy or whim. This is not a genuine distinction between imagination and something else, but it is an instance of a derivative use of 'imagine': it marks a distinction based on our own sense of what is appropriate in describing an absent thing.

What is it to judge a description to be appropriate to a certain object? This is a deep question, and one fundamental to aesthetics, about which I shall have a certain amount to say at a later stage. Clearly, we cannot reduce this notion to the more commonplace one of judging something to be likely. When one imagines what X would be like one often abandons the normal categories of causal thought, and invents a story which one thinks of as peculiarly appropriate to X, even though one may know it to be unlikely or false. When Flaubert set himself to imagine what it would be like for someone of a vain and romantic disposition to live married to a country doctor in provincial France, he did not tell a story about the likely consequences of such a marriage. He chose the details of his story in the light of what he thought to be most revealing and expressive of the provincial state of mind, whether or not such details were in any way likely to occur. To take a more striking example, Lewis Carroll imagined what it would be like to live behind the looking glass, by carefully choosing illogicalities that create the semblance of a coherent story. Similarly, I may imagine what it would be like for my friend to meet the Queen, and thereby arrive at a story that fits his character, and that exploits the amusing possibilities, without paying the least regard to plausibility or truth. In imagining, propositions are entertained for a reason, and the reason is to be found in the subject matter and nowhere else. This is all that we need say here about the concept of the 'appropriate'.

The element of rationality introduced by this feature must not lead us to confound imagination with belief, even though there is, as we saw, a use of 'imagine that' where it does simply denote belief. When I tell a story what I say counts as an expression of imagination whether or not I believe it. The rationality of imagination is not the rationality of belief (although it might in certain cases include the rationality of belief); it is rather a species of practical reason. When I ask someone 'Why?' in the midst of his account of an imagined object, he replies by giving reasons why he said that thing, not reasons why he believed (asserted) it.

It follows from this account that we might often want to compare two exercises of the imagination by saying that one showed more imagination than the other. By which we mean that it went further beyond the obvious (condition (1)), while not departing from the appropriate (condition (2)), and hence not degenerating into mere fantasy or whim. Imagination admits of degrees. It may indeed be difficult to define the vanishing point of imagination where mere literal-mindedness sets in.

It is in terms of this last consideration that we might attempt to define the adverbial sense of imagination. Doing something imaginatively means doing it thoughtfully, where one's thought is not guided by the normal processes of theoretical reasoning, but goes instead beyond the obvious in some more or less creative way. In doing X imaginatively one does more than X, and this additional element is one's own invention, added because it seems appropriate to X. It goes without saying that there is a normative sense of the adverbial construction: some actions may be judged to be truly imaginative, while others might be thought of as whimsical or foolish. On this basis we can see how the concept of the imaginative becomes extended to apply to a plan, an hypothesis, a work of art or a person. All these uses, even those where something cognitive is implied, can be derived without too much distortion from the above conditions.

But even if we say that the two conditions given above do define the central core of the concept of imagination, and do show how imagination differs from other thought-processes, we still have not explained what is meant by imagery, nor have we accounted for the place of imagery in imagination as a whole. It is here that we find the idea of a thought acquiring an altogether new and more subtle connotation. For there are certain strong reasons for saying that an image is a kind of thought of something – my image of my mother is my thought of her as she looks. This is supported by the following considerations: First, an image is always an image *of* something – imagery has the intentionality characteristic of thought, and this is brought out by the fact that one can only imagine what one can also think of. Secondly, imagery, like thought, is an object of immediate knowledge. I know immediately, on no basis and incorrigibly, the nature of my own images and thoughts.[13] (These two properties, with certain

[13] The notion of 'incorrigibility' employed here perhaps needs some explanation. One may have an image, and later revise one's description of it (just as one may revise one's description of a dream). For example, one may realize that one's initial description failed to capture all that had been suggested to one's imagination; or one may reinterpret one's experience in the light of superior knowledge, and so come to understand it differently (cf. the interpretation of dreams). But while such revision is possible, it does not imply that one can in fact be *mistaken* about one's images in the sense of thinking them to have (non-relational) properties which they do not have. Revision is a matter of redescribing the relations between experiences, thereby enriching their content.

modifications in the case of the first, are also properties of sensory experiences or sense-impressions.) Thirdly, imagery is subject to the will, in the way that thought is subject to the will. (Which is not to say that imagery is necessarily as responsive to the will as thought is.) Finally, images and thoughts are identified in a similar way, and ascribed on a similar basis. Thus the principal criteria for saying that a person is having an image, or picturing something, are verbal – they consist largely in descriptions he would be prepared to offer of an absent or non-existent thing. That is, to think that X had an image of Y involves thinking that, had X been asked what was in his mind, he would have produced descriptions purporting to be descriptions of Y (of the *look* of Y, say), or he would have referred in some way to Y. A (visual) image is like a thought of the way something looks, and to identify *what* image X is having involves reference to criteria that would equally identify a thought. We can imagine criteria other than verbal ones – for example, a man might express his image by drawing or pointing to a picture – but the criteria always seem to apply equally to both images and thoughts.

These four features seem to place imagery firmly in the category of thought, and hence create an immediate distinction between images and such things as dreams and after-images. The justification for regarding such category divisions as all-important will be apparent shortly. But it needs to be said immediately that to conclude that imagery just is a species of thought is to ignore two very important features of imagery, in addition to those mentioned, which it is extremely odd to consider as general properties of thought – the features of intensity and exact duration. These features are in fact characteristic of sensations and sense-impressions, and seem to show that imagery, like sensory-experience, lies across the boundary between thought and sensation. First, then, images can be more or less vivid or intense, while remaining constant in respect of detail. My image of Mary might be so vivid that I almost see her standing beside me. It is a characteristic expression of visual imagery that one should screw up, or even close, one's eyes, as though subjecting oneself to an impression, and the impression may be strong, or not so strong when it finally comes. Thus we speak of images as 'fading' – a description that is not applicable to thought. Needless to say, this phenomenon has nothing to do with the supposed 'degrees of belief' that are mentioned be such writers as Price.[14] When I believe something I may indeed be more or less convinced of it, but this variation has nothing to do with the relative vividness characteristic of imagery and sensation.

Secondly, there is the feature of precise duration. An image, like a sensation, comes into existence at a precise moment and lasts unchanged for a precise length of time: it is a mental process that can be precisely located in the stream of events. We say such things as 'I had a vivid image of Mary, lasting some considerable time, and then suddenly I thought of something else and it went away'. We might compare images in this respect with their nearest equivalent among thoughts: the thought of the look (sound, smell etc.) of something. Suppose I begin to think of the way my grandmother looked. I say to myself: 'Let me think . . . she usually wore blue, her hair was grey, she had a funny way of peering down her nose', and so on. Did my thought of the way she looked begin when I said 'Let me think'? Or just after? Or on completion of the first proposition? Or, suppose it took me time to formulate a thought, was I thinking of the way she looked during this time? Clearly none of these questions need have an answer, and if we *do* choose to give an answer then our choice is not dictated by the nature of the thought itself. It might be said that we should compare imagery with entertaining a proposition, since this is a kind of thought that does have determinate temporal boundaries: if a proposition is before my mind over a length of time, then there is a precise point when this process begins, and it lasts unchanged until the precise point at which it ceases. But again the matter is not susceptible of such an easy legislation. Suppose I am entertaining the proposition that my wife is at church, and while doing so I look out of the window and notice the brown colour of a man's hat against the leaves of a tree: is my thought *interrupted* by the perception, or does it last through the perception unchanged? This question only admits of an answer in exceptional cases – for example, when I have the experience (after observing the hat) of being recalled to my former train of thought. In general, in discussing thought, we have no use for the idea of a single unchanging mental process

[14] H. H. Price, *Belief*, Lecture VI.

that has a precise beginning and an exact duration. If we *do* try to think of entertaining a proposition in this way then we find that we are thinking of the case where one forms an image of the words which hovers briefly before the inner eye or ear.

This distinction between imagery and thought is borne out by the fact that people express images very much in the way that they express experiences. If I ask you to form an image of your mother you may well concentrate for a moment and then, after some time, say 'Now I have got it: it's as though I could see her.' Similarly, the particular form of words 'Now it has gone, now it has come back', which is the expression of an experience, has no place in the report of thinking. On the other hand, it is certainly in place in reporting an image, since I can think of an object even while being conscious that the image is fading. This seems to suggest that while thought is a necessary part of imagery, it cannot be the whole of it. Indeed all our ways of referring to images seem to suggest an element of experience over and above the constitutive thought. Thus I can know what image I had even when I cannot recall, or recapture, the image itself. Plainly for this to be true imagery must be distinct from thought. For only in a very special sense could I ever be said to know what thought I had while at the same time being conscious that it had faded beyond recall. In remembering what the thought was, I have the thought again.

The argument so far is deficient in one very important respect. I have explained the experiential component of imagery in terms of the first-person case alone. The concept of thought has been related securely to its public expression, whereas the concept of an image has been differentiated by features whose significance is so far almost wholly private. (Indeed, certain philosophers have spoken as though this were the essential difference between imagery and thought, Frege, for example,[15] and Collingwood.[16]) If this is the only explanation of imagery that we can give, then clearly we will have given the concept no sure grounding. Not only will it be impossible for me to convince another that there are or could be such things as images; I will even be uncertain that I am entitled to attribute such things to myself.

[15] G. Frege, extract in Geach and Black, op. cit., p. 79.
[16] R. G. Collingwood, op. cit., pp. 157–8.

Fortunately, we can point to a further feature of imagery, a feature that partly explains the two just mentioned, and which can itself be described in terms of the verbal expression of imagery. When a man refers to an image that he has, he describes it in terms of a genuine experience, the publicly observable form of which is familiar to us all: he will describe his visual image of X in terms that are equally appropriate to the experience of seeing X. He will imply that having an image of X is in some way like seeing X; if he does not acknowledge this, then we say that he has not understood the concept of an image. We might put this point by saying that there is an analogy between the two processes of imagery and sensory experience. The analogy is, however, 'irreducible'.[17] That is to say, a man will be unable to indicate in *what* way his image is 'like' a particular sensory experience, although he will feel that to describe his image in terms of a sensory experience is appropriate, and indeed inevitable. A consequence of this connection between imagery and its verbal expression is that it will be impossible to attribute visual imagery to a blind man, or auditory images to one who is deaf. This is a logical truth, not a contingent fact. Thus we can see how the connection between imagery and its public expression will explain the formal (conceptual) properties of imagery. This, crudely, is the principal advantage of third-person analysis over the methods of phenomenology.

We must now say something about the connection between imagery and imagination. At first sight it may seem that there is no special connection, since imagery does not occur only when one imagines, nor always then. We can divide images into two kinds: those where what is pictured is something that has already been seen, heard etc. (imagery as part of memory); and those where what is pictured has not in fact been experienced (imagery as part of imagination). This second kind of imagery – forming an image of something that has never been 'given' in experience – clearly involves the features of imagination, as these have been described. But is there no more to the connection between imagery and imagination than this? We can soon see that there is. For one thing, forming an image is one of the principal ways of imagining

---

[17] P. T. Geach, *Mental Acts*, section 23; 'irreducible' is not Geach's word, although it is a word that is naturally suggested by his approach.

– this explains, I think, why we use the same word to describe the two activities. Moreover, there is a kind of imagining that essentially involves the distinguishing characteristics of imagery. This is the kind of imagining involved in conjuring an experience, as when I undergo an experience in imagination, or imagine the sound, taste, sight or smell of something.

It is useful to recall Russell's distinction between knowledge by acquaintance and knowledge by description.[18] To know what an experience is like is to be possessed of a wholly different kind of knowledge from that involved in knowing what a (material) *object* of experience is like. In knowing what an object is like I can recall certain of its features: I know how to describe it. In knowing what an experience is like, I do not have this kind of familiarity with 'features' of the experience, although I am familiar with the experience itself. Knowledge of an experience by acquaintance means having had the experience and being able to call it to mind. Similarly, we may contrast imagining what an object is like with imagining what an experience is like: the latter involves the ability to form an image which 'matches' the experience, whereas the former involves the contrasting ability to describe an absent or non-existent thing. Thus 'imagining what it is like to . . .', like 'knowing what it is like to . . .', has an experiential component. Imagery – when it is not a species of remembering – is related to 'knowledge by acquaintance' in the way that imagination generally is related to belief.

Imagery is expressed, then, in such reports as 'I can imagine what it feels like to die in battle', or 'I can (cannot) imagine the taste of rum mixed with HP sauce'. It is not sufficient for the truth of such reports that one should be merely thinking of the taste of rum and HP sauce, or whatever. 'Imagining what it's like' refers to the particular experience involved in 'knowing what it's like'. Plainly, thinking of the taste of rum and HP sauce is not yet imagining the taste of rum and HP sauce, since 'thinking of' extends no further than the ability to give an account of an object. Imagining the taste of rum and HP sauce involves the two further properties of duration and intensity referred to above. Olfactory and gustatory images are particularly instructive in this respect. For while visual appearances can be described in terms of visual

[18] Bertrand Russell, *Mysticism and Logic*, pp. 152 ff.

features of an object – and hence can be as it were re-created through description – the same is not generally true of tastes and smells. It is, therefore, more obviously the case here that the request to imagine what a taste or smell is like is a request to form an image.

Here we can see one of the dangers inherent in a phenomenological approach to the problem of imagery. For the phenomenologist what I have called knowledge by acquaintance is already a kind of private knowledge by description: it involves an awareness of *features* of an experience that must be identified introspectively. Images may, therefore, share these features with their original experiences, and so come to be described in a similar way. To reject the phenomenological approach involves insisting that there is nothing more to knowing what it's like to break a bone than being able to recall the particular experience. In a similar way there is nothing more to be said about imagining what it's like to break a bone than that it is an image, irreducibly analogous to the experience of breaking a bone. The point of imagining what an experience is like is not given by the ability to describe the experience. Any description is necessarily the kind of description that could be applied and learned with reference to the third-person case; so it will not relate to 'knowing what it's like' in the quite special sense in which knowing what it's like means having experienced it.

CHAPTER EIGHT

The Imagination II

Among the things that need imagination for their achievement are some kinds of 'seeing': it takes imagination to see from the circumstances that one's friend is unhappy or hurt. This sense of imagination as a kind of 'perception' or 'perceptiveness' has two aspects, and it is perhaps the failure to distinguish the two that is responsible for the Romantic idea (typified by Coleridge) that imagination is the prime source of knowledge. One aspect is given by propositional constructions of the form: 'It takes imagination to see that X is sad' – (A). The other aspect is given by a special metaphorical sense of 'see': 'It takes imagination to see the sadness in X's face (even when one knows independently that X is sad), in the music, in the life at Hill Farm, and so on' – (B). (B) relates to 'seeing as', or noticing an aspect; (A) relates to forming an hypothesis. Only (A) may be counted as fully cognitive, that is, as referring to a species of judgement (a judgement that goes sufficiently beyond the evidence to count as an expression of imagination). (B) does not, or at any rate need not, refer to a species of judgement, strictly speaking; for here what one 'sees' one 'sees' without, in any straightforward sense, believing it to be there. It is not seeing *that* X's face is the face of a sad man (for example), or *that* the music is the kind of music that would be produced by a sad person (for example), or *that* living at Hill Farm tends to make people sad (for example), that constitutes this kind of seeing, although making these judgements may help to put us in a position to 'see' the sadness that is there.

We cannot explain this sense of 'see' as 'see imaginatively', and hence relate the element of imagination to the adverbial sense. For seeing, in the normal sense, is not the kind of thing that *can* be done imaginatively. It is not a voluntary activity, and is not within the control of thought. To add imagination to seeing is to change it from seeing to 'seeing'. We have a new activity of the imagination that cannot be explained in the terms we have already employed. It remains to discover how this new activity should be described.

The activity has already been referred to as aspect perception, or 'seeing as'. But there are at least two activities that might be described in this way, one related to imagining, the other closer to imagery. It is the second of these that I wish to discuss, although I shall shortly make one or two remarks about the first as well. The points that I wish to make arise (in the main) out of Wittgenstein's discussion of the ambiguous figure.[1] But it must not be thought that I shall be treating every problem that this figure raises, nor every idea that Wittgenstein derives from it. The problem of the ambiguous figure lies at the intersection of many different areas of philosophy, and if I use it as a point of departure for the discussion of a particular kind of sensory experience it is not because this is the only – or even the principal – use to which the figure may be put.

When I see the figure as a duck it is not merely that I notice a resemblance between the figure and a duck: I could do this while seeing it as a rabbit. Besides, resemblance is a symmetrical relation – if *a* resembles *b* then *b* resembles *a*. Hence in noticing a resemblance between *a* and *b* I notice also a resemblance between *b* and *a*. But of course if I see a portrait of the Queen as the Queen I do not for that reason see the Queen as her portrait. Nor can the experience of seeing an aspect be reduced to that of noticing a likeness of appearance, for the same reason. Moreover, there are certain very important considerations that I shall touch on, both later in this chapter and in Chapter Thirteen, for saying that aspects and appearances do not belong to the same logical category. (Compare noticing the resemblance between two faces, and then suddenly 'seeing the likeness': there is a quite peculiar experience involved in this whose expression can be one of surprise.) In other words 'seeing an aspect' cannot be analysed in

[1] *Philosophical Investigation*, pt. II, section xi.

terms of 'seeing that': it does not reduce to a set of beliefs about its object, not even a set of perceptual beliefs.[2]

The problem that I wish to discuss is this: to which mental category does the experience of 'seeing as' belong? First of all, we cannot reduce 'seeing as' to anything like a simple sensation: 'seeing as' shares with imagery the property of being internally related to thought. In seeing the figure as a duck we, as it were, think of it as a duck. For example, we think of the shape and appearance of ducks, and think of this particular duck as quacking, say. In fact 'seeing as' is like thought in just the way that imagery is like thought. First, it has intentionality – there is always something that we see *in* the figure when we see an aspect. Secondly the aspect, like a thought, is an object of immediate knowledge – when I 'see' an aspect I know immediately and incorrigibly the aspect that I see.[3] (It goes without saying that when I see something, in the normal sense of 'see', I do not have this kind of knowledge of what I see.) Thirdly, the principal criteria on the basis of which we attribute the capacity to 'see as' are verbal. One criterion for seeing X as Y is to be found in the false descriptions that the subject is disposed to apply (unasserted) to X. This is not the only kind of criterion. But, once again, any criterion of 'seeing as' seems to reflect a similar criterion of thought. A child before a picture may show signs of amusement or fear, and these certainly show that he has 'seen' the aspect that is there. But in interpreting his behaviour as emotional in this way we have already characterized it as an expression of thought. Moreover, it is a thought that is in some sense unasserted, as we shall see. This is an important point, since it has the consequence that animals, who lack a language, and hence have only beliefs and no other kind of thought, cannot see aspects, just as they cannot form images. A dog may take a picture *for* a man, but he cannot in any other sense than this, of delusion or mistaken belief, see the picture *as* a man.

Finally, 'seeing as', like imagery, and like unasserted thought in general, is subject to the will. Which is to say that it makes sense to order someone to see a figure in a certain way. Moreover, once a

---

[2] These considerations are by now fairly familiar: see, for example, Richard Wollheim, *Art and its Objects*, sections 11–14.

[3] But see p. 100 fn. 13.

man has grasped the several aspects of an ambiguous figure, he may see it in almost any of the possible ways at will. Once again it is necessary to remember that the meaningfulness of the command to see X as Y does not mean that it is always – or even usually – possible to obey it. Indeed obedience is even more difficult here than in the case of imagery, which is what one would expect. For what one can see in X (or 'see X as') is strictly limited by the observable nature of X itself. The object presents a visible frame, as it were, into which one's image must fit. Moreover, there is a whole area of 'seeing as' where the order to see an aspect is entirely out of place, and must be replaced by the request to try to see the aspect. It is this area that bears the closest affinities to aesthetic experience.

'Seeing as', like imagery, contains further features which are more truly sensuous, and not characteristic of thought in general. Once again there is the property of precise duration: it is possible to 'clock' the perception of an aspect in the way that it is possible to 'clock' a sensation. For example, I may see the ambiguous figure as a duck, and then suddenly find that it has changed, until, precisely ten seconds later, it changes again. This feature of precise duration makes it possible to locate the phenomenon of 'seeing as' in time in a way that it is not possible to locate the phenomenon of 'interpretation' generally.

But this one property of precise duration does not constitute a complete account of the sensuous element in 'seeing as'. As in the case of imagery, we can point to the conceptual (internal) relation with seeing. We might say that there is something like an irreducible analogy between the two processes of 'seeing' and 'seeing as', which is to say that it is part of the concept of 'seeing as' that the process should be referred to and expressed in the language of seeing (of visual experience). When a man describes his experience in seeing an aspect, he must say something like 'It is as though I were seeing a duck'. And once again it is impossible to say in *what* way the seeing of an aspect is like the seeing of the thing itself. As Wittgenstein puts it, the resemblance is manifested only in the expressions that a man is inclined to use in describing his experiences, not in something he uses those expressions to say.[4] The two experiences do not have introspectible

[4] *Zettel*, section 630.

('phenomenal') features which they share, any more than do the experiences of seeing red and seeing pink (which are also irreducibly similar). This enables us to attribute to 'seeing as' a formal feature that also belongs to perceptual experience – the feature of 'having parts'. When I see the figure as a duck then the aspect is, as it were, spread out over a visual field. Geach has already pointed out that this is the kind of feature that serves to distinguish sensory experience from thought.[5]

However, there is a sensuous feature of imagery that it is difficult to attribute to 'seeing as' – the feature of vividness or intensity. In this sense it might be argued that the analogy with imagery is incomplete. If I notice the duck aspect of the figure then I may be more or less struck by it, and I may see it in more or less detail. But this is not yet to say that my experience may be more or less vivid or intense in the manner of an image. Is it then impossible to attribute this formal property of vividness to 'seeing as'? I think not, although it is difficult to demonstrate that 'seeing as' is the kind of mental process to which such a dimension must belong. But perhaps it will help to study the similar case of ordinary visual experience, whose relation to sensation has also been a matter of considerable dispute. It is an undeniable fact that certain things stand out to a greater or less extent in our visual field, and this property is not necessarily to be attributed to their clarity, interest or illumination. In a similar way a detail in a picture may stand out from the rest: indeed it is possible to have the sense of some detail suddenly 'coming at' one, and then receding once more into the background. In default of analysis it is natural to hypothesize that this feature of 'seeing as' (and of seeing) is the feature that corresponds to the dimension of vividness that is common to imagery and sensation. But I do not wish to dwell on this point, nor to attempt a non-phenomenological analysis of the feature in question. It should by now be sufficiently clear that 'seeing as' bears a relation to both thought and sensation that is strikingly similar to that of imagery.

A digression into phenomenology will bring out this relation between 'seeing as' and imagery in another way. For example, there is the following peculiar characteristic involved in description of images. Suppose that I have an image of a sail, and someone

[5] *Mental Acts*, p. 128.

asks me what it is like; I may point to an A written in this way – ♪ – and say 'It is a triangular sail, bellying out in a peculiar way, like this'.[6] Only if someone sees a quite specific aspect of the figure I point to will he understand what I wish to say about my image. Always in identifying a visual image, I must refer to physical objects. But here I wish also to show what my image is like, in the sense in which really to *know* what it is like is to have the image oneself. It is significant, therefore, that this knowledge can be achieved through the perception of an aspect. A similar illustration of the phenomenal proximity of imagery to 'seeing as' is provided by an example from Miss Ishiguro.[7] Suppose I see a photograph of a man, and suppose that as I look at it the photograph gradually fades away, even though I am, nonetheless, able to go on seeing it as a man as less and less of the features remain. It seems that I must in some way 'supplement' the disappearing features with an image. At the point of attenuation, when I am left with nothing to 'see as', there remains the image of the man. And this image is the image of precisely the man whom I had previously seen in the picture. It seems then that in this gradual change from seeing the photograph as a man to merely imagining the man without the photograph something remained the same.

It seems, then, that the strange mixture of the sensory and the intellectual characteristic of images is present also in 'seeing as'. The very same phenomena recur here in a different form: in 'seeing as' it is as though I imagined an object and simultaneously saw it in something else; in imagery it is as though I imagined an object and then my imagination came alive in quasi-sensory form. Moreover, the element of thought involved in 'seeing as' lies clearly in the field of imagination: it is thought that goes beyond what is believed or inwardly asserted, and beyond what is strictly given in perception. Hence it is thought that is subject to the condition of 'appropriateness'. My seeing an aspect raises the question of the appropriateness of what I see *in* the object to the object in which I see it. 'Seeing as' is rational, and the normative distinction between true imagination and whimsy can be applied to it. Aspect perception may change in the light of reason. I can

[6] I owe this example to Professor G. E. M. Anscombe.
[7] 'Imagination', *A.S.S.V.*, 1967.

be stopped from seeing a picture as a rabbit by being shown that it is meant to be taken as a duck, or that the mood of the picture can only be understood if it is taken in that way. To take a more interesting case: I can see some of the bathers in Cézanne's picture (National Gallery) as either moving or at rest, and my understanding of the picture governs the aspect that I choose. Reasoning in terms of appropriateness can equally be applied to images. If I am asked to describe my image of Brutus I may give a description which another might find unjustified or fanciful; he would attempt to persuade me to imagine Brutus differently.

On this basis we might conclude that, in fact, there is only one concept of imagination, which covers all the activities I have attempted to describe. Imagination is a species of thought, involving distinctive features that recur even when the thought is as it were 'embodied' in an experience, as in imagery and 'seeing as'. We might say that it is a characteristic of imagination that it is liable to this kind of embodiment in experience.

Our description of 'seeing as' stopped short at the comparison with images. In fact the locution 'seeing as' has a wider use than this comparison suggests. There seems to be a continuum between the kind of case exemplified by the ambiguous figure, where my imagination becomes part of my seeing, hearing, or whatever, and other examples where I simply imagine something in an object (the sadness in the music, the Mozartian style in Verlaine). As the thought process involved in 'seeing as' becomes more complex it becomes ever more difficult to have the particular experience of seeing (or hearing) an aspect, even though one is still, as it were, bringing the thought and the perception together in imagination. That there is this strange transference of imagination to experience might be one source of the idea that aspects are properties – for in many ways they bear a logical analogy to 'simple' properties, such as colours – and hence one source of the idea that in aesthetic appreciation one is really *seeing* properties of a work of art.

We must now attempt to describe in more detail the kinds of thought process that go by the name of 'seeing as', and which underlie the experience of aspect perception. In order to do this we must first make clear in what way the experience of 'seeing as' relates to ordinary perception. Several philosophers have argued that all seeing is or involves 'seeing as'.[8] Why is it then that we call 'seeing as' a branch of imagination when imagination, we argued, always goes beyond the content of present sensory experience? What does this distinction between ordinary perception and imaginative perception amount to if the latter is always involved in the former?

Here is an argument for saying that 'seeing as' *is* always involved in ordinary perception: it is often possible to find a trick of thought that will enable us to experience a change of aspect or dawning of an aspect, even while looking at something that we straightforwardly *see*. I can make the tree that I am seeing change into a man with waving arms. If I can get this peculiar experience of a change of aspect, then there must have been something from which the aspect changed: the tree must have already presented an aspect to me in my ordinary seeing of it.

But does this argument really prove very much? That we have this peculiar experience of change does not establish the point. Involved in ordinary sensory experience there is a belief (or tendency to believe) in the existence of an object. Indeed, it has been argued that there is, from the mental point of view, nothing more to sensory experience than this.[9] Whether or not this identification of sensory experience and perceptual belief is warranted we must concede that there is at least a close logical connection between the two,[10] just as there is a close logical connection between imagery and unasserted thought. In other words, sensory experience, unlike 'seeing as', is internally related to belief: hence, unlike 'seeing as', it is not subject to the will.

Now, in the case we are imagining, we are asked to believe that our ordinary perception of the tree involves the recognition of an aspect. This would involve saying that all perceiving of the tree involves not only the belief in an object, but also something analogous to entertaining a thought about the object (thinking of

---

[8] See, for example, R. Chisholm, *Perceiving, a Philosophical Study*, ch. I; P. F. Strawson, 'Imagination and Perception', in L. Foster and J. W. Swanson (eds.), *Experience and Theory*. B. N. Fleming, 'Recognising and Seeing As', *Phil. Rev.*, 1957.

[9] See D. M. Armstrong, *Perception and the Physical World*.

[10] For example we might argue that, necessarily, in the normal case, visual experience accompanies visual belief, and that visual experiences are classified by reference to beliefs.

it). The consequence must be that animals, who can have beliefs but no other kind of thought, cannot see. Such a consequence is, I think, unacceptable. Of course, human beings often will entertain propositions about what they see, but this is not an essential part of seeing. What is essential to seeing is the thought (or belief) *that* there is an object (answering to some description). This thought is not subject to the will, and it can give rise to no embodiment in an aspect, in the sense of this term discussed so far. The particular experience which goes with it is the sense-impression, which is no more voluntary than the thought itself. Now it is undeniable that in some Kantian sense, beliefs, and the visual experiences that depend on them, go beyond experience, and hence that our report of a sensory experience already contains more than the mere register of a visual sensation. But this does not affect the present issue, since it only serves to confirm that sensory experience is not, as it stands, one of the phenomena of imagination, since it lacks the essential relation to unasserted thought. Perceptual experience involves genuine interpretation, or judgement, and that is what the locution 'seeing as' might be used to refer to in this context. But in this case 'seeing as' means, in general, no more than 'taking for'.

What happens, then, when the 'change of aspect' takes place? We can describe this quite simply: I imagine myself not believing that the tree exists, and instead I think of the tree *as* something else. Suddenly the imaginative thought may become embodied in an image, which I 'see in' the tree. There is no change of aspect, only the dawning of an aspect where previously there was none.

One cause of the view that all seeing involves 'seeing as' lies in the vagueness of the locution 'to see X as Y', which I have been using until now as a purely technical term. Sometimes the locution means 'to take X for Y', in which case it is of course understandable that philosophers have argued that all seeing involves 'seeing as'. For perception always involves beliefs about the external world, and to say that someone took X for Y is to say, with certain minor qualifications, that he believed X to be Y, and that he came to believe this as a direct result of sensory experience. Again, the locution 'seeing X as Y' might be used to report a likeness of appearance, and not all likeness of appearance involves the perception of an aspect. This is a matter that I shall explore further in Chapter Thirteen.

However, this vagueness in the notion of 'seeing as' extends beyond the fact that it is sometimes used to refer to perceptual beliefs. Indeed the particular phenomenon so far described under this heading is not even typical of all aesthetic experience, as we shall see. It is clear from the start that 'seeing as' can be used to refer to attitudes and emotions, and this use tends to occur intertwined with the perceptual use. When I say of someone that he sees his mother as the most perfect of God's creatures, or that he sees social failure as more humiliating than the loss of private affections, or that he sees his neighbour as hateful, I am referring to his emotions and attitudes.

Furthermore, the locution 'seeing as' is associated with certain modes of what we might call interpretation – this in two ways. First, there are such cases as the interpretation of motives, of fine points of history, and so on; cases where judgement is necessarily tentative or uncertain, and where imaginative hypotheses are more in place than dogmatic assertions. For example, I may say 'Whereas John saw his behaviour as jealous, I saw it as motivated by a nervous concern for his wife's state of health'. What characterizes these cases – and distinguishes them from 'seeing as' in the perceptual sense – is the fact that here 'seeing as' aims at truth. It involves a tentative judgement. It is not possible for both John and myself to be right, and in this sense the phenomenon of a 'double aspect' cannot arise.

Secondly, there is a rather more subtle kind of 'seeing as', which cannot be said to aim at truth, so much as at coherence. This is emphasized in particular by memory judgements, where, for example, the truth of the matter is either long established, or beyond the reach of further knowledge, but where it may still be necessary to form some kind of 'picture' of past experience. Indeed, everyone forms in this way a 'picture' of his past existence, and in so far as more than one picture may be compatible with the totality of his knowledge, a phenomenon somewhat analogous to the double aspect can arise. For example, a man's vision of his childhood in old age may become totally transformed. Events that were confused, chaotic or trivial at the time form into more coherent patterns under the influence of ideas acquired in later life. Some such process can occur in psychoanalysis (an activity that Wittgenstein explicitly compared with aesthetic judgement); but it is by no means a recent discovery. Consider, for example, the famous opening sentence of the *Vita Nuova*: 'In quella parte del libro della mia memoria, dinanzi alla quale poco si potrebbe leggere, si trova una rubrica, la quale dice: *incipit Vita Nova*.' Clearly such a rubric could only be the result of later reflection: and yet it has become, as it were, part of the remembered experience itself. The picture that Dante has formed of his childhood experience has – by drawing it into relation with later events – given to the experience a character that no child could have discovered in it.

Finally, we should note that the phrase 'seeing X as Y' may be used simply as a substitute for 'thinking of X as Y'. In effect then, 'seeing as' has two dimensions: one of thought, and one of experience. As thought it might refer either to a variety of quasi-interpretative attitudes, or to the imaginative thinking of an object as something that it is not. This second kind of thought process seems to underly the experience of 'seeing as', which we might be tempted to describe as the sensory 'embodiment' of just this thought.

Now it might be asked 'What does it matter if there should be no 'experience' of seeing as? Is the thought process itself not enough?' In fact it does matter. For when we examine the phenomenon we must conclude that it is impossible to treat the sensory aspect of 'seeing as' as a mere optional addition to an underlying core of thought. For we cannot, in fact, give a fully independent account of a thought process to which the sensory experience of 'seeing as' is related in this simple way. All we can do is describe thought processes – such as the quasi-interpretative attitudes mentioned above – that are in some way analogous to 'seeing as'. In other words, it is wrong to think that, when a man sees a picture as a cow then it is first that he thinks of it as a cow (where this thought is of the unasserted kind discussed at the beginning of the previous chapter), and then (or perhaps simultaneously) that this imaginative thought becomes embodied in an experience, so that he also sees the picture as he imagines it. For it is clear that, in the experiential sense of 'seeing as', the thought cannot be isolated from the experience and described independently.

Suppose that I am looking at a picture and see it as a man. It does not seem unnatural to say that I am also thinking of something – whether it be the picture, or the figure – as a man. But it could hardly be maintained that I have before my mind a proposition of the form 'This picture (or this configuration of lines) is a man'. If I entertain a proposition then it is the proposition that *this*, namely, *the thing in the picture*, is a man. But in that case, the thought that I have must be described in terms of the aspect that I 'see' and not vice versa. Again, if I entertain the proposition that this (whatever it is) is some man, then which particular man do I have in mind? Surely once more the only answer is *this* man, or the man who looks like *this* – pointing to the picture.

In other words, the attempt to give an independent description of the thought involved in the seeing of an aspect cannot be carried through. Moreover, this result is hardly surprising. For when we look at 'seeing as' from outside, from the point of view of its expression, we find that it is impossible to identify any object that is thought of as something else. For if there are thoughts characteristically expressed in 'seeing as' they are not thoughts about the (material) object – the picture that is seen. It would be natural to express one's perception of an aspect in the terms 'It is a man!', but not in the terms 'The picture is a man!' The question '*What* is a man?' then makes no sense. For the 'it' in 'It is a man' cannot be construed referentially[11] – on the contrary, it stands proxy for an intentional object of sight, and hence marks a position that is referentially opaque. It follows that the attempt to describe the component of thought in 'seeing as' in terms of 'thinking of X as Y' is illegitimate. It is for this reason that we might prefer to speak not of seeing X as Y, but rather of seeing Y in X.

What, then, becomes of our previous conclusion that 'seeing as', like imagery, is a species of thought? I think that we can still abide by this conclusion. But we must remember that there need not be a thought which both fully specifies the intellectual content of 'seeing X as Y', and which can be itself described independently of this experience. 'Seeing as', like imagery, was assimilated to thought because it shared the formal and exterior characteristics that are definitive of thought. But this does not mean that we

[11] E. Bedford, 'Seeing Paintings', *A.S.S.V.*, 1966.

must be able to split up the mental process of seeing a picture as a man into two components – a thought and an experience – even though there are thoughts which clearly influence the way the picture is seen, and even though we may well have the sense that it is precisely these thoughts that we see, as it were, embodied in the picture.

This becomes clearer as we turn our attention once more to the case of seeing. When I see a man I have a visual experience, and intimately connected with this experience there is a perceptual belief. Now there are powerful arguments – as I have already mentioned – for saying that the experience and the belief are internally related. The experience of seeing a man carries with it – in the normal case – the belief in the presence of a man. But can we specify this belief in detail? Again we find a difficulty, not wholly unlike the difficulty we experienced in trying to describe the thought process involved in 'seeing as'. To say that the belief is 'There is a man', is scarcely to do justice to the complexity of perceptual experience, just as we scarcely do justice to the complexity of 'seeing as' if we describe the thought component of seeing a picture as a man in the terms 'There is a man'. The man appears in each case enmeshed in a complex of visual features. We see a tall man, in a red coat, with pink hands and an arrogant expression. But it would be unwise to think that we have any means of completing this description. We do not seem to be able to capture the content of what is seen in the form of a proposition that is, as it were, simultaneously believed. For if we attempt to describe in full what it is that we believe above the man that we see, then we must have recourse to the fact that he has a certain appearance: we believe that he looks a certain way. But now, of course, we have identified the belief in terms of the way the man looks, and so have not described it independently of the visual experience.

The quest for a total and independent specification of the thought involved in 'seeing as' is as out of place as the request for a total and independent specification of the belief involved in visual experience. But it is clear that this is no more an argument for saying that 'seeing as' is not a mode of thought than it is for saying that visual experience is not (in some sense) a mode of belief. We must say that the thought involved in 'seeing as' is in some measure *sui generis*: it has an irreducibly sensuous character. However, its relation to other modes of thought (in particular to the mode: 'thinking of X as Y') can be delineated, and this can, as we have seen, shed light on its essentially 'unasserted' character. In conclusion, we might say that the relation between 'seeing as' and perception mirrors the relation between imagination and belief. 'Seeing as' is like an 'unasserted' visual experience: it is the embodiment of a thought which, if 'asserted', would amount to a genuine perception, just as imagination, if 'asserted', amounts to genuine belief. This point is very important, since, as we shall see, the 'unasserted' nature of 'seeing as' dictates the structure of aesthetic experience.

We have developed what I hope is an adequate theory of imagination, and we must now use it to describe the aspects of aesthetic experience that have until now proved so elusive. This I shall do in the next chapter, before moving on to an account of the conditions of aesthetic experience in general. In conclusion, it may be wondered how the above account of imagination squares with certain prevalent views – for example the view that 'seeing as' involves the organization of experience through a concept, and that 'seeing as' is somehow a basic ingredient in all perception. These doctrines are combined in the Kantian theory of imagination as the fitting of 'intuitions' into a sensory manifold, according to conceptual rules.[12] What I have said implies a piecemeal account of visual phenomena in terms of the various categories of thought: to this extent it goes against the Kantian view. In Chapters Twelve and Thirteen I shall show in more detail why I think that such a view is mistaken.

[12] This is the view sketched and defended by Strawson in 'Imagination and Perception', op. cit.

CHAPTER NINE

Imagination and Aesthetic Experience

The argument of the last chapter stopped short of describing the precise kind of 'seeing as' that is involved in aesthetic judgement. In fact, not only is there more than one kind; it is also difficult to describe any of the several kinds with adequate precision. However, in this chapter, I wish to illustrate some of the more important connections between aspect perception and aesthetic judgement, basing my remarks on the theories just expounded.

Let us return to our principal example – the sadness of music. Normally we do not doubt that the recognition of this sadness involves something like an experience – you have to hear the sadness in the music. And the use of this locution seems to suggest that the case is not so very far removed from the examples of 'seeing as' discussed in the last chapter. But if this is so, we ought to be able to give at least a partial description of the thought that is 'embodied' in the experience. Can this be done? Clearly, it must be done if the objections of Chapter Six – objections from which this analysis of imagination began – are to be answered. For we have yet to show that there is a core of thought on which aesthetic experiences are founded, and that this core of thought is genuinely distinguishable from belief.

In fact, it is easy to see that, in a great many ways, 'hearing the sadness in the music' is formally analogous to 'seeing the man in the picture', and this might lead us to suspect that the thought involved must belong to the same unasserted category. To see this, we have but to resume the features of 'seeing as' that this particular auditory experience shares. For we soon discover that 'hearing the sadness' has all the thought-like characteristics possessed by 'seeing as'. For example, its principal expression is verbal, and consists in descriptions that the subject wishes to apply to the music. And these descriptions have an unasserted character. Indeed, if he is to count as understanding them, the subject must show that he does not mean them literally. Moreover, it makes sense (at least in some contexts) to order someone to try to hear the music as sad, rather than as, say, languorous or tender. (And again this point is not affected by the impossibility, in any case, of actually obeying the order.) Normally, of course, one does not *order* people to try to hear music in a certain way; rather one attempts to persuade them. One says 'Hear it as sad, and then it will make more sense to you'.

I think we can see that the structure of thought involved in our example of aesthetic judgement is not that of the quasi-interpretative 'seeing as' discussed at the end of the last chapter – although there is a sense in which it is legitimate to talk of aesthetic description as a kind of 'interpretation' of a work of art. For in this case 'interpretation' is not primarily cognitive: it does not aim at literal truth. Nor can we say that the prime import of the judgement that a piece of music is sad is simply to 'bring the music under a concept ("sadness")'. For, given that 'sadness' is not a concept under which the music could literally fall, this description of aesthetic judgement is empty. Nor, again, can we say that the prime purpose of the judgement (to return to the theme of Chapter Four) is to indicate analogies. To say this is to confuse meaning and justification in an area where we have every reason for saying that the two concepts – which can only co-exist in the notion of a truth condition – fall apart. In fact, the comparison with aspects is all that we have to fall back on if we wish to illuminate the conditions for the acceptance of this kind of aesthetic judgement.

Just as two aspects can be seen in the same first-order features of a figure, so can two rival 'interpretations' of a work of art find support in identical descriptions of it. And, in fact, the same phenomenon of a double-aspect may arise in aesthetic judgement. While there are ways of dismissing some 'interpretations' as whimsical or unilluminating, more than one interpretation may be equally helpful. As an example it is useful this time to take a passage of music, for it is with music that the problem of aesthetic description is at its most acute. Take the slow movement of

Schubert's penultimate piano sonata, in A major. This begins with a melancholy theme in the minor key. Suppose a critic, in discussing this work, wished to describe the particular quality of this opening passage, to show the extent to which poignancy is qualified by irony, and so on, as might be necessary to convey a full understanding of the passage.

Schubert: A major Sonata, 2nd movement. (*Andantino*)

It would be normal to begin with a kind of analogical catalogue of elements, hoping to bring out the contribution of each to the overall effect. Suppose, for example, that we were to argue in the following manner: 'The melody begins on the minor third: it has that character of being "pulled down", of drooping towards the tonic, which results from the tonic being sounded simultaneously in the bass. The left hand is simple and bare, providing no more than a skeleton of octaves and fifths, which leave to the melody the principle task of expression. When the melody falls a semitone, however, the bass falls with it, resulting in an unstable harmony (first inversion) that necessitates an upward move. It might be said of this fall, on account of its heaviness (the bass falling with it) and its inevitability (it began on the minor third) that there is something lassitudinous about it. And yet, at the same time, because of the unstable harmony in which it results, necessitating an upward move, it gives the impression of a strength that returns through the melancholy movement, pushing it onward . . .'. To argue in this way is to pick out certain salient features, so describing them that they seem to contribute to the emotional quality with which the melody began. (It is as though the melody were 'imitating' a state of mind.) For example, there is the sudden rise of the melody into the relative major, from which point it gains strength to rise again – though on to the minor sixth and a dissonant harmony (dominant minor ninth – see the asterisk in the example) that drags it, through a series of faltering notes, back on to the tonic from where it begins again. It is interesting to examine the transformation of the theme as it is repeated in a new context, almost without change, over a bass equally bare and unornamented, in the relative major. (It is a great part of Schubert's genius that he could discover these melodies which, while beautiful and subtle in themselves, suffer such transformations with hardly a changed note – cf. *par excellence* the slow movement of the last sonata. Thus a theme seldom wears its character on its face, but must be understood through layers of careful irony.) A new strain of tenderness is introduced by this transformation, which remains when the minor key reasserts itself, adding dignity to the conclusion.

Producing some such analogical description has the effect of uniting the first-order features of the work under a particular 'interpretation'; in which case it is not difficult to see that, since any detail can be made to upset the interpretation, every detail is to that extent answerable to it, and can play a determining role in deciding on the correct interpretation of the piece. Likewise, to decide on the emotional value of any one part of the work it is never possible to dismiss other parts as irrelevant. The significance of 'Un Amour de Swann' only emerges in its sequel, and to characterize the emotion expressed in a novel which, taken alone, can only strike the reader as vacuous, we must refer to parts of the total work which come long after the episode of Swann's love is forgotten.

Now, it is plain that such analogical interpretations as the one I have given are subject to the kind of reasoning that produces double aspects. One man can see a work of art as tragic, another as ironical (*Death in Venice*, say), both be able to justify their judgements to each other, and both refer to the same first-order features in doing so. It is clear that the phenomena of the double-aspect can be translated into the realm of critical 'interpretation' substantially unchanged. Indeed, emotional ambiguity has often been prized, as an artistic virtue. Troubadours would deliberately obscure their poems so that it was impossible to decide whether the love they expressed was religious or sensual. One mark of a successful troubadour poem is that the ambiguity should strike the reader as a unity, so that the love expressed seems both religious and profane at once. In this way the poems came to express an ideal, an ideal which animated Provence during the Middle Ages and which reached its culminating expression in Florence at a later time – in the *Vita Nuova* of Dante and the *Donna mi Priega* of his friend Cavalcanti.

As an example, we might choose the falling phrase from the Schubert slow movement (Ex. 2).

Ex. 2

This could equally be described as dance-like or stumbling, as tenderly melancholy or heavily sad. Perhaps one might say that the context decides between the two descriptions, but the context only seems to have weight when considered in the light of some relevant interpretation. Now the question arises 'Where do we stop?', and we see that this question cannot have the kind of answer that would be associated with the quasi-interpretative idea of 'seeing as' discussed in the last chapter. That is, we do not stop when we have arrived at the *right*

answer, when we have shown that the music is, literally, melancholy. For such an answer would not be meaningful. In other words, the judgement is wholly unlike the interpretation of the feelings and emotions of another man, where, however many rival opinions there may be, not more than one of them can be right. In the case of the aesthetic judgement, the phenomenon of a double aspect may endure with just the same degree of tenacity as the double aspect of an ambiguous figure.

Now it may be argued that there are important differences between representation and expression, and that it is on account of these differences wrong to explain the recognition of what we might call 'expressive' features (such as 'sadness') in terms of the recognition of the aspects that embody representation. For it is arguable that whereas an aspect is always of some definite object, what is expressed is always a feature or property.[1] But if this is so, then we should be able to identify some object to which this expressive feature is ascribed. And in fact there *is* such an object in the case we are considering, namely, the music itself. Hence it might seem that the argument that, in the sentence 'It is a man', said of an aspect, the 'it' does not refer to the picture, cannot be extended to cover such expressive features as sadness. For when I say 'It is sad' I am speaking of the music, to which I attribute the aesthetic feature of sadness.

But this argument is scarcely conclusive, and could have weight only if we were to construe the sadness that is attributed to music as a genuine property. I have already argued that this is impossible. Now it is often said that the sadness that we hear in music is in a sense unattributed. That is, it is something that seems to wander detached in the music, and although we can *imagine* a subject for it (the composer, say), it is certainly true that this imagined subject is not, and cannot be, present in the music in the way that he might be present in the aspect of a picture. The question is, does this really matter? In a way it does matter, since we find that it is even more difficult to specify the thought that is 'embodied' in the perception of the music's sadness. The thought 'It is sad' will scarcely suffice, since in this case there is no 'it'. And the thought 'There is sadness' is misleading, to say the least.

[1] N. Goodman, *Languages of Art*. I discuss Goodman's views in detail in Chapter Thirteen and Fourteen.

What we can say, however, is that the experience of hearing the sadness in the music is in some irreducible way analogous to hearing the expression of sadness – say, in another's voice. That is, we can do as we did for 'seeing as', and define the element of thought in terms of the experience. Hearing the sadness in the music then becomes the 'unasserted' auditory perception of sadness. In other words, we can resuscitate the original intuition of 'affective' theories of aesthetic judgement. It is not that the music is analogous to the emotion, but rather that the experience of hearing the music is analogous to the experience of hearing the emotion. Our theory of imagination has, I hope, rescued this contention from the triviality and circularity into which it naturally seems to fall. What is significant is that, if we attempt to explain, by analogy and approximation, the element of thought involved in hearing the music as sad, then we must – as in the case of 'seeing as' – resort to the general category of unasserted thought, and not to the category of judgement or belief.

The affective theory of aesthetic description has, then, been vindicated and substance has been given to the logical analogy between aesthetic perception and aspect perception that was noted in Chapter Four. It goes without saying that we can also show how it is that the term 'sad' has the same meaning when applied to music and when applied to men, just as the term 'duck' has the same meaning when used to describe an aspect and when used to denote a duck. But while the problems that we experienced over the nature of aesthetic description have, I think, now been largely solved, there remains a problem about the nature of aesthetic experience. In Chapter Six I spoke of the acceptance conditions of some aesthetic judgements as 'responses'. In fact, this was in one way misleading, since it seems to suggest that the appreciation of a work of art is something that goes on after the work has been heard or seen. The comparison with aspects implies that there is something like an experience which *accompanies* the hearing or seeing of the work of art, and which is indeed not truly separable from that seeing or hearing. From the point of view of the autonomy of aesthetic experience this is a more satisfactory conclusion. But having isolated the core of thought which defines the experience, we still have to describe the feelings, reactions and so on that might arise out of this thought. For it would seem to follow that these feelings will enter as an important and perhaps even determining feature into aesthetic experience as a whole, and if the perception of aesthetic features has any value it may well be on account of the feelings to which it gives rise.

It is a consequence of the theories of the last chapter that the mental life of the imagination will be quite different from that of judgement or belief. If there are, as has been argued, aesthetic emotions (which can be, as it were, 'seen' in their objects, in the manner of aspects) then these emotions must be founded on imagination and not on judgement. It is, therefore, impossible that they should be identified in a similar way. Our account of aesthetic experience will, therefore, grant to these emotions a measure of the autonomy that has often been claimed for them. But it was pointed out *en passant* in Chapter Six that there is a difficulty inherent in the idea of autonomy. We wish to say that my response to a sad poem, and my response to a sad person are in some way comparable. How else can we explain the importance of the poem's sadness? Yet in the one case the reaction is founded on a belief, and in the other case it is founded on a mere 'unasserted' thought. How, then, can the emotions be comparable, and how can the one be used to identify and make clear the nature of the other? We see that our theory of imagination is after all in danger of doing us a great disservice in destroying the necessary continuity of aesthetic and non-aesthetic experience.

To appreciate the force of the present difficulty it is necessary to remember the intimate connections that exist between emotion and belief, and between emotion and desire. Normally, as the argument about 'formal objects' given in Chapter Six makes clear, an emotion is identified partly in terms of a belief. It follows from the statement that a man is afraid, for example, that he believes that there is or might be something harmful to him. It also follows that he desires to avoid that thing. We might say – simplifying somewhat – that an emotion is, normally, a complex of belief and desire, united in a causal relation. But aesthetic emotions are not founded on belief but rather on the entertaining of propositions unasserted. Before an enraged lion I feel fear, and my fear is of a piece with the awareness of a dangerous object. But before a lion hunt by Rubens or Delacroix I have no such awareness: the propositions that I entertain about the dangerous object are not asserted. How then can my emotions in the two cases be compared? Moreover, without the beliefs characteristic of fear I do not have the desire to avoid what I see: on the contrary, I desire to look at the painting and 'drink in' its horrifying aspect. If neither the belief nor the desire characteristic of fear are present, in what way can I be said to feel anything resembling fear?

The response to the picture can be compared with the response to a real lion hunt in two ways. First, we might compare them on the level of normal, 'factual' emotion, as I have already done. In one case I believe myself to be in the presence of a lion hunt, with all that this entails. Consequently, I desire a successful outcome; I desire that the danger should be removed and the lion's ferocity overcome. In the other case I believe myself to be in the presence of a painted canvas, and I desire to look at it. On this level, comparison of the two emotional states is fruitless. But suppose now that I see the aspect of the painting, and so come to (as it were) imagine just what in the 'normal' case I would also believe. It is now as though I were entertaining unasserted just those propositions that in the other case I would take for true. Why do we not say that I also entertain, along with these propositions, the desires that would also, in the normal circumstance, arise out of them? Why can I not 'entertain' desires? I can imagine my fear (in the sense of 'imagining what it is like' that relates to knowledge by acquaintance). In other words, just as I may recreate in my imagination the thoughts that I would have, so can I recreate the feelings to which these thoughts give rise. (Something comparable to this occurs when one imagines 'what it is like' to die in battle, or to discover oneself heir to a fortune.) In describing the emotion that a man feels towards the aspect of a picture, therefore, we refer to the 'imagined counterpart' of his reaction to the situation depicted. In the only sense that matters we might then say that the emotion he feels in response to the picture is the 'same' as (and classified by reference to) the emotion he would feel towards the depicted situation. For his feeling towards what he sees *in* the picture is, like his perception itself, only 'unasserted'.

This argument does not imply that the subject's emotion before the painted lion hunt has the same intensity as the corresponding 'real' or 'factual' emotion. It is only rarely that works of art aim to excite intense (as opposed to deep or serious) emotion. In this respect the intensity of an aesthetic emotion is a function not of the assertedness of its core of thought, but rather of the degree of 'imaginative involvement' that is experienced, and this in its turn depends on the realism of the presentation. An enactment of a gun battle on the cinema screen is more horrifying than a medieval painting of a martyrdom, where the bloody event is indicated through conventions the function of which is didactic rather than pictorial. Nonetheless, the spectator's thought is in each case 'unasserted'. It is a purpose of convention in art to overcome emotional involvement. Convention neutralizes fantasy and removes the sterile gratifications which fantasy seeks in art. One might say that convention exerts its control over feeling by replacing an immediate impression with an abstract idea: it is an instrument of the universality of art.

But there is a more important respect in which the aesthetic emotion differs from its equivalent in life. For the difference in thought process seems to imply a difference of identity, and our attempt to overcome this difficulty has an ominously phenomenological sound. We must, then, try to show how someone manifests aesthetic emotion, and how the expression of aesthetic emotion bears on its description. But if there are no beliefs on which such emotions are founded, and no desires embodied in them, how are they expressed at all?

Now if there were no more to aesthetic experience than the kind of unasserted thought that we have analysed, this question would pose no difficulty. For we could readily set about describing the verbal expression of unasserted thought. But this would not satisfy us. For not only is it clearly true that aesthetic experience involves emotion, it is also true that if it did not involve emotion, or something like emotion, we would be unable to indicate its value. Is the expression of aesthetic experience the expression of anything more than a thought?

It is not unusual for someone, on looking at the portrait of a child, say, to remark that it awakens in him a feeling of tenderness. Do we dismiss this remark as metaphor? I think not. For it occurs (typically) in circumstances that forbid us from construing it as the mere expression of a thought. First of all, we must not neglect the fact that a man wishes to describe his feeling in this way – it is an integral part of the experience that *tenderness* should be called to mind. Secondly, the subject will describe the object of his feeling in terms that can themselves be construed as an expression of feeling. It is significant that he describes the painting in a certain tone of voice (not any tone of voice is appropriate to the remark), and that he makes connections with his attitudes and emotions in other circumstances that are important to him. It is for this reason that we have a clear test of the sincerity of his remark in his subsequent behaviour. A man who declares that his tender feelings have been awoken by the child he sees in the picture is at odds with himself when he shows himself unable to feel tenderness towards a real child. Thus, although we are supposing that his remarks betray an emotion in which neither belief nor desire is present, and which does not, therefore, have its characteristic forms of expression in action, but rather in the passive symptoms that remain when all belief and desire have been subtracted, we may still test the sincerity of his remark through his subsequent behaviour. There is a non-contingent connection, therefore, between imagined emotion and the behaviour that, in other circumstances, counts as an expression of the corresponding 'real' emotion. What I feel in the presence of works of art may find its ultimate expression in my behaviour towards my fellows. My 'imagined' feelings can show their effect in the expression of their 'real' counterparts.

It will be objected that all these suggestions point to connections with behaviour that are remote from the aesthetic experience itself. If what I feel before the painted lion hunt is something analogous to fear then it ought to be possible to characterize what I feel at the time in terms appropriate to fear. But suppose we were to characterize fear: we refer to the beliefs, the desires, the 'passive' symptoms such as trembling, sweating and palpitating, and the causal relations that bind all these together. And suppose we propose this (as would be correct) as a complete analysis of fear. Then someone might object that we have yet to explain what fear is *like*: what it feels like to be afraid. Here we can do no more than refer once again to the totality of the symptoms of fear, including its expression in language. And if we subtract from this description those elements that are expressions of the beliefs and desires characteristic of 'real' fear, then there is no reason to think that we have not given a full characterization, in what remains, of the symptoms of 'imagined' fear. But suppose our objector is not satisfied – like Siegfried, he wishes to know what fear is *like*, independently of its expression. In that case either he is asking to be made to feel fear (so that he may 'know what it is like'), or else he is asking a question of pure phenomenology that has no coherent answer. It is no more possible to describe fear independently of its expression, origins and circumstances than it is possible to describe any mental state in terms of pure phenomenology. A phenomenological description is not, in the relevant sense, a description. *A fortiori*, it is no special objection to the notion of a purely 'aesthetic' emotion that we cannot describe it independently of its expression, which is the expression of an emotion that includes neither belief nor desire. Hence the so-called ineffability of aesthetic emotions is a logical consequence of their being mental states at all.

It remains to point out, however, that there is little of interest that can be said about aesthetic emotion, beyond describing the thoughts on which it is based, and referring to its expression in subsequent behaviour, when it is no longer strictly felt. It is through our words and our subsequent behaviour that we show our understanding of an emotion that we have entertained in thought – and it is the same with every case of 'imagining what it is like'. It is not surprising, therefore, that the language in which we discuss works of art – the language of criticism – is primarily descriptive in form, and that it contains few attempts to classify the feelings aroused by art. There are no subtleties in our aesthetic emotions that are not matched and explained by subtleties in the thoughts on which they are founded. This, briefly, is the reason why criticism must be concerned with interpretation and not with the recording of subjective impressions. If we attempt to communicate an aesthetic emotion, then we communicate a thought. An excellent illustration can be found in Shakespeare's description of the feelings of Lucrece before the painting of the sack of Troy. Lucrece's emotion is entirely captured by a sequence of thoughts about imagined objects – there is no need for Shakespeare to say anything else about what she felt.

We must now return to the analysis of aesthetic experience, in the light of this account. We are still far from a solution of the problem from which we began. We have shown that imagination, and emotions founded on imagination, have a part to play in aesthetic appreciation, and are expressed in the judgements to which this appreciation gives rise. But this does not show that imagination and aesthetic experience are co-extensive. Indeed they are not. We have done no more, in solving the problem of aesthetic description, than to describe a single strand in aesthetic experience; we have not characterized aesthetic interest as a whole. But it will be seen that we are now in a position to answer the general question.

CHAPTER TEN

The Aesthetic Attitude

This work began with a discussion of aesthetic judgement. We found that the meaning of a central class of the 'descriptions' involved in aesthetic judgement could be displayed through the conditions for their acceptance. The analysis of these conditions has given us good reason for regarding the imagination as an essential ingredient in aesthetic experience. But if we return to the somewhat random list of aesthetic descriptions given in Chapter Three we see that our theory cannot possibly provide a general explanation of their meaning. Indeed, it would be a difficult task, and one hardly worth the labour, to present a complete account of aesthetic description. Nonetheless, there are certain aesthetic judgements which call out for analysis – the purely aesthetic descriptions (those employing such words as 'beautiful', 'lovely' and 'sublime'), and the descriptions of form. These judgements include all the usual terms of aesthetic praise and dispraise, and their existence was one of the reasons given earlier for saying that there is such a thing as aesthetic interest, and that the aesthetic is a roughly integral realm of human experience. I shall follow the procedure of previous chapters, and attempt to explain the meaning of these descriptions in terms of the states of mind that are conveyed by them. We shall find that this completes our account of aesthetic experience.

I shall begin by considering judgements that employ purely aesthetic terms. Among the terms with a primary aesthetic use we find: 'lovely', 'beautiful', 'elegant', 'ugly', 'pretty' and 'hideous'. These terms are for the most part evaluative, used to express preferences for or against objects of aesthetic interest. I shall argue that there are, in fact, distinctively aesthetic attitudes, which are expressed in the judgements that employ these terms. I shall also argue that it is these attitudes that determine the structure of aesthetic experience. However, my arguments will be far from conclusive, and it is well to point out from the start that I shall be assuming that, where there are 'evaluative' judgements, there are also attitudes that give these judgements their point. This is not a view for which I shall be concerned to argue. Only at the end of the chapter will it be possible to estimate the plausibility of the premises from which it begins.

However, a difficulty arises immediately. It is arguable that the purely aesthetic terms are not evaluative, or not only evaluative. They seem to have a descriptive function also. We feel that there is a distinction between a thing's being elegant and its being beautiful, and that it is not always or necessarily a virtue from the aesthetic point of view to be either. It is meaningful to argue that some of James' stories would be better for being less beautiful, or that the elegance of Satie's music is a vice of style. I. A. Richards attempted to answer this problem in terms of an emotivist theory of aesthetic description:

> . . . we have the special apparatus of the aesthetic or 'projectile' adjectives. We express our feeling by describing the object which excites it as *splendid, glorious, ugly, horrid, lovely, pretty* . . . words which indicate not so much the nature of the object as the character of our feelings towards it. . . . Some of these words . . . may be used together, while others bar one another out. A thing may be both grand and sublime, it can be glorious and beautiful, or gorgeous and ugly; but it can hardly be both pretty and beautiful, it can certainly not be pretty and sublime. These accordances and incompatibilities reflect the organization of our feelings, the relations that hold between them . . .[1]

Richards makes no attempt to describe the separate feelings that are collated with the several 'aesthetic' terms, and one suspects that the task would prove extremely difficult. The terms seem not to indicate distinct feelings but rather to convey something about the character of their objects in virtue of which we like or

[1] *Practical Criticism*, p. 220.

dislike them. If there are distinct feelings involved, then their distinction is acquired through the distinction of their objects, and not vice versa. We must try to make clear how the purely 'aesthetic' terms can also attribute a character to objects, how a supposedly 'evaluative' judgement can, nonetheless convey something definite about the object to which it is applied.

There are certain features of the use of aesthetic terms that are worth considering. First, we should note their frequent occurrence in interjections: it is as common to hear 'How elegant!', 'How beautiful!', 'How ugly!' and 'How sublime!' as it is to hear, for example, 'The Ninth Symphony is beautiful', 'I think she dresses elegantly', 'If it is a beautiful film then I shall go to see it'. Terms of which this is true have, in general, an evaluative use which connects them with the expression of favourable or unfavourable attitudes. Secondly, while it is not odd to say 'It is good to do X, but I do not like doing it', or 'X is a good man, but I take no pleasure in his company', it *is* odd to say similar things in the context of aesthetic judgement. For example, it is odd to say 'I cannot stand the sight of an elegant horse', or 'It is a beautiful novel and I never want to read it again', or 'I like the look of that – it is the most hideous suit I have ever seen'. Only in special circumstances would these locutions make sense at all. This leads us to suspect that aesthetic appreciation involves enjoyment of, or pleasure in, an object. Enjoyment and pleasure occupy a central place in the aesthetic attitude. We might be tempted to think that purely aesthetic descriptions are used primarily as substitutes for interjections, in which pleasure or displeasure find expression. Wittgenstein, for example, argues that it is central to the logic of purely aesthetic terms that they can be learned as interjections.[2] However, we cannot derive an account of the meaning of these terms from that fact alone. It is an *important* fact that a word is used as an adjective, a fact that prevents us from explaining its meaning as that of an interjection. An adjective occurs in sentences that can undergo all the logical transformations of the declarative form. It is, therefore, an odd fact if a word that is learned as an interjection can come to have an adjectival use, a fact that should tell us something important about the attitude or preference connected with it.

[2] Wittgenstein, *Lectures and Conversations on Aesthetics* etc., section 7.

In Chapter Five I showed how it is possible for an adjective to have a non-descriptive meaning. However, I made no attempt to discuss the conditions under which a non-descriptive judgement may possess a *stable* propositional form. I argued that, in the case of such judgements, the propositional (or descriptive) form is in some sense an anomaly. It is to be expected that, under the right kind of stress, it will break down and give way to a statement of personal choice. This is, in fact, what we discover with many judgements that are used to convey 'matters of taste'. For example, the propositional form of the judgement 'Strawberries are nice' may often be dropped in the face of criticism. If asked 'Do you really think so?' there will always be a point at which I shall find it more reasonable to say '*I* like strawberries at least' – a judgement whose acceptance is easier to demand. Now it is an interesting fact that this breakdown of propositional form occurs more readily for some classes of judgement than it does for others. While it is possible to argue that the condition for the acceptance of a moral judgement is, typically, an attitude, we find that it is extremely odd to replace a moral judgement with a subjective statement. We cannot replace '*X* is good' with 'At least *I* approve of *X*', for not only does the second judgement show a partial withdrawal of the commitment expressed in the first, it is even difficult to make sense of it at all. Aesthetic judgements seem to lie somewhere between the two extremes of moral and gustatory judgements. The propositional form of 'The symphony is beautiful' is stable, but it is not so stable as the propositional form of a moral judgement. When questioned it is possible to withdraw to '*I* found it beautiful at least', with a certain loss of face, but without logical absurdity.[3]

In other words, the propositional form of a judgement expressing preference may be more or less stable, depending on the kind of preference expressed. Although the grammatical form of 'Strawberries are nice' allows such transformations as 'If straw-

---

[3] Further arguments for construing gustatory, aesthetic and moral judgements as hierarchically related are to be found in Phillipa Foot, 'Morality and Art', *Proc. Brit. Acad.*, 1970. The distinction between aesthetic and gustatory judgements is well brought out by Stanley Cavell, 'Aesthetic Problems of Modern Philosophy', in Max Black (ed.), *Philosophy in America*. Cavell also makes the connection with Kant's thesis of 'Universality'.

berries are nice then we will buy some', the use of a sentence of this kind seems to presuppose a certain background of understanding and agreement. Neither moral judgements nor aesthetic judgements are like this. They have a further quality that gives point to their propositional form, even in unasserted contexts, in the absence of any pre-established background. This quality is a matter of degree (moral judgements clearly possess it to a greater degree than aesthetic judgements), and I shall attempt to explain it as a property of the attitudes that underly these particular kinds of judgement.

Consider the 'affective' terms: 'moving', 'irritating', 'boring' and so on. These terms are not correctly used by someone in aesthetic judgement if he uses them *simply* to convey the fact that he is moved, irritated or bored by something. A correct use of these terms presupposes that one is not indifferent to the reactions of other people.[4] If I say that a film was boring, then it is not a matter of indifference to me that you were not bored by it. I feel that you should have been bored by it too: either you failed to notice something about the film, or else your response is inappropriate to its object. It follows that, if you ask *why* the film was boring I shall be prepared to look for an answer that could provide you with a reason (and not just a cause) for reacting in a similar way. It is significant that it is not so easy to say (in the face of opposition): 'I don't know why it was boring, but it certainly was', as it is to say: 'I don't know why I was bored, but I certainly was' – the first of these expresses something more than the simple reaction recorded in the second.

This additional element in aesthetic judgement is difficult to define. Kant wrote that 'the judgement of taste exacts agreement from everyone; and a person who describes something as beautiful insists that everyone ought to give the object in question his approval and follow suit in describing it as beautiful'.[5] Kant's instinct was sound; but he chose too strong an expression for it. It is not necessary that one's demands in aesthetic judgement should be so strong as to find expression in an aesthetic 'ought'. We might put the point less strongly by saying that aesthetic attitudes are normative: that is, they involve a sense of their own

[4] Cf. T. L. S. Sprigge, 'The Definition of a Moral Judgment', *Phil.*, 1964.
[5] *Critique of Judgement*, p. 82.

'correctness' or appropriateness to an object.[6] Although I am certain that there is such a property as the normativity of a desire or attitude, I do not think I can define it with any precision. Normativity goes with a search for agreement, but not any search for agreement is normative: I may seek agreement because I feel that it is nicer that way. A normative attitude seeks to found agreement in reason, and not in some chance convergence of opinion. A man with a normative attitude to X feels that others should recognize the qualities that he likes or admires in X, and on this basis come to like X themselves. Explained in this way, normativity is clearly a matter of degree – some attitudes may have it to a greater extent than others – and it is what explains the stability of the propositional form in both ethics and aesthetics. For a propositional form can be used as a means of exchange and persuasion; it is associated with the idea of truth, and so can be used to embody the sense of 'correctness' or 'appropriateness' that is contained in a normative desire.

This normative quality in aesthetic appreciation leads us at once to a similar quality in the activity of criticism itself: criticism is a normative science. After remarking the expressive function of such terms as 'beautiful', 'fine' and so on, Wittgenstein goes on to argue that really these terms have far less prominence in aesthetic judgement than the notions of what is right or correct, what fits, and so on.[7] We say that the bass moves too much, that the door is not the correct height, that it is inappropriate to put oak panelling above an Aubusson carpet, and so on. This normative quality pervades the whole realm of critical discourse. Critics do not seek to establish *how* people respond to works of art: they attempt to create a series of norms, in the light of which some responses to a work of art will seem appropriate, others not. Individual critics do this in different ways. It is characteristic of Leavis, for example, that he will criticize a poem for 'inviting' or 'calling for' a response that involves the reader in certain con-

---

[6] I use the term 'normativity' in place of Kant's 'universality', since the latter might be confused with the more formal property of 'universalisability' discussed by Hare. Aesthetic judgements are normative, but it is arguable that they are not universalisable, since the object of aesthetic interest is a particular, and not a class.

[7] Wittgenstein, *Lectures and Conversations on Aesthetics* etc., op. cit.

fusions of thought or feeling. It is possible to respond fully to such a poem only in a confused way. The *appropriate* response to the poem will, therefore, embody a critical awareness of this confusion of thought; hence it will be impossible to enjoy the poem as it asks to be enjoyed.[8]

I do not propose to analyse what it is to hold a reason to be valid for others. This is a problem for the theory of practical reason, and belongs as much to ethics as to aesthetics. It should already be clear, nonetheless, that as a result of the normativity of aesthetic attitudes, the concept of the 'appropriate' will lie at the heart of all aesthetic judgement. Our feelings and responses towards art will be in part an outcome of our sense of what is appropriate, and this sense will permeate all that we learn from art, and all that we expect to find in it.

It is perhaps best not to consider normativity as a *necessary* condition of the aesthetic attitude. There are cases of primitive but basic appreciation that it would be wrong to exclude from the 'aesthetic', despite their proximity to the less normative preferences of sensuous enjoyment. For example, there is the dislike of clashing colours, and of grating or discordant sounds: these lie at the heart of more complex aesthetic experiences, while being themselves unfounded in any normative judgement. It is true, nonetheless, that the aesthetic attitude has a permanent tendency to *become* normative. Aesthetic interest, like many of our reactions towards people (of which morality is the most systematic) brings with it both a sense of right and wrong and a quest for rational agreement. A man who is displeased at the taste of Valpolicella is simply displeased, whereas a man who is displeased at the sight of his neighbour's room is, typically, aware of something inappropriate or wrong.

How is it that we can make this demand for agreement? We cannot, surely, rest content with the addition of this feature of normativity as though it were an optional extension of the analysis. For many would wish to argue that not only is there no hope of reaching agreement, but also that the demand for it is intrinsically irrational, like the similar demand in matters of (sensuous) taste. In the final chapter I shall, therefore, attempt to

[8] For a philosophical discussion of Leavis's procedure, see John Casey, *The Language of Criticism*, ch. VIII.

give an explanation why aesthetic interest assumes this particular character.

Granted that we do admit normativity as a condition of the aesthetic attitude, the question arises how we distinguish the aesthetic from the moral. Two lines of argument suggest themselves. First we might pursue the idea that aesthetic appreciation, being aimed at enjoyment, involves the contemplation of a particular object, and is not directed at the object purely as a member of a class. Moral appreciation, on the other hand, is essentially directed at a property or class, and this feature brings in its train the logical property of universalisability. But this approach, familiar from the nest of doctrines discussed in Chapter Two, is inconclusive. For the object of aesthetic interest may often be a type, and types – while they are in a sense particulars – share many of the logical properties of universals. It would be better to distinguish aesthetic from moral attitudes by pointing to the absence of sanctions from the former, and their presence in the latter. A man who holds a moral attitude is disposed to certain attitudes against those (whether himself or others) who infringe his moral code. If these attitudes are directed against himself then they will take the form of guilt, remorse, self-hatred and repentance. If they are directed against another, then they will involve blame, indignation, the removal of goodwill and the application of sanctions. This property of moral attitudes – whereby they make themselves felt precisely when they are most disregarded – is one of the central features of morality. It is this above all that distinguishes the acceptance of a moral principle from the acceptance of less rigorous judgements. Acceptance of a moral principle has an added dimension of seriousness: it involves a particular kind of submission and respect for the authority of a moral code.

Now it may be that not every moral assessment *must* involve these 'punitive' attitudes, and it may be also that it would be unhelpful to *define* morality in terms of them. Nonetheless it is not a contingent fact that a moral judgement tends to be accompanied by such attitudes as these. These reactions must be part of the phenomena of morality on any view. I shall assume that no such features need to be involved in aesthetic judgement. This is part of what is meant by saying that moral considerations override aesthetic ones (which is not to say that moral requirements necessarily prevail, only that, unlike most aesthetic requirements, they leave their residue of guilt and indignation when they are ignored). Thus people often defend themselves against blame for their aesthetic outrages by saying 'It's all a matter of taste', reminding us not to give a moral emphasis to the question. Of course, this by no means implies that reasons cannot be given for or against aesthetic judgement, or that there is no such thing as accepting a reason or changing one's opinion over a matter of taste. For aesthetic attitudes are normative, even if they do not involve the kind of sanctions characteristic of morality.

Now of course it is conceivable that someone should elevate matters of aesthetic judgement to a status of supreme and over-riding importance in his life. Such a man will be outraged and indignant at the bad taste of others, and ashamed or angry at his own lapses. But such a case is a rarity: it gives us no grounds for saying that these punitive attitudes are also an essential part of aesthetic judgement. On the contrary, one would be tempted to describe this man simply as one who had given a moral emphasis to matters of aesthetic preference. One can, of course, see how this might come about. It is undeniable (and, perhaps, in some sense, necessary) that a man of educated taste will be guided in his preferences by his lasting intuitions about life, and in this case it is clear that his aesthetic preferences will be an index of his moral feeling. So that often (perhaps always) an aesthetic disagreement between two people masks a genuine moral difference. And it is a small step from condemning another's taste on account of the moral values expressed in it, to regarding lapses of taste as peculiar moral failings. But even in such a case it is wrong to suggest that moral condemnation is based on aesthetic judgement. We must remember that a chief criterion of the moral point of view lies in a man's attitude to his own behaviour. In lapsing from an accepted code a man inevitably feels compunction, perhaps in the form of remorse or guilt. But in the case of a lapse of taste a man cannot feel these things. The 'intentional object' in aesthetic judgement conflicts with the moral emotions. While a man may feel ashamed of his taste, he can hardly feel remorseful about it. To say that he feels remorse is to imply that he regrets not the lapse of taste in itself so much as its effects on other people, as one who regrets being party to the demolition of a building that was widely admired. Such a man may feel remorse in respect of other people, for he has deprived them of something they loved. About his own lack of taste he can only feel regret or shame.

In the absence of punitive attitudes, we discover, then, a point of contrast between aesthetic and moral judgement. In aesthetic interest we are no longer concerned with the enforcement of a code of conduct, but rather with the development of a particular capacity for enjoyment. If we react to the aesthetic heresies of other people it is out of a desire to educate their taste. Education is all that we can rationally hope for; no one can be compelled by the spectacle of common indignation to enjoy what bores or repels him. This brings us back to the considerations of the second chapter – we have a sense that in defining aesthetic appreciation we are defining something separate from, although not wholly independent of, the demands of moral judgement. And in the attempt to clarify this point, it is to concepts such as enjoyment that we turn. But it is precisely here that the discussion becomes obscure; what kind of enjoyment is involved in aesthetic appreciation? The answer – enjoyment of an object *for its own sake* – raises many more difficulties than it solves. What is it to enjoy, appreciate or be interested in something for its own sake? We will be unable to describe aesthetic appreciation if this phrase 'for its own sake' remains obscure. The theory of the uniqueness of the work of art can be seen as an elaborate attempt to explain the meaning of this phrase. But we discovered that it lapsed into obscurity at precisely the most important point, where the distinction between moral and aesthetic judgement was to be drawn. We must, therefore, attempt an independent analysis of the meaning of the expression 'for its own sake'. Only then will our characterization of the aesthetic attitude be complete.

We might attempt to clarify the notion by considering the kind of answer that is given to the question 'Why are you interested in that?' It seems that, if someone asks me why I am interested in what the workmen are doing outside then he can tell from my answer whether my interest is in their actions, for their own sake, or whether my interest goes beyond what I see. For example, I might reply that I was wondering what the workmen were doing – in which case we conclude that I was seeking knowledge from

what I saw, and that my interest in what I saw was consequent
on a desire for knowledge. Similar answers are: 'I wanted to see
how many of them there are', 'I can't stand the noise', 'I don't
think they ought to be working at this time of day', 'It relaxes
me to see other people working', 'I was not interested' (a rejection
of the question), 'I didn't know I was looking at them', and so on.
In all these cases the answers reflect an attitude to the actions of
the workmen that is either cognitive (involving an interest in
knowledge) or else part of an attitude which goes beyond the
desire simply to look at what is going on (a desire for the noise to
stop, the desire for relaxation, the normative attitude expressed in
the judgement that they ought not to be working). But there is a
particular kind of answer to the 'why'-question which is not like
these at all. This is the kind of answer in which, instead of referring to some interest I might have in what I see, I simply describe
what I see. For example, I might say 'Because the workman standing there looks very big against the light, and he moves his arms
in a strange way'. Again, if I am curious simply because I want to
know *why* he moves his arms in that way, then my interest is
once more explicable in terms of a desire for knowledge: there is
a further answer I could give to the 'why'-question which is not
simply a description of what I see. The kind of answer to the
question that I wish to indicate is the answer which consists
solely in descriptions of the object of interest, where these descriptions are not given because they serve to explain how this object
is related to other desires or interests that I have. They are given
simply as descriptions of the object. If asked to give further reasons
for my interest I might refer to the thoughtful way in which the
workmen are digging, the abrupt sound of their conversation on
the evening air, their bulky shapes, and so on; all these answers
seem to suggest that my interest in the scene is an interest in it
for its own sake. Further descriptions might depart from the
pattern of those given so far, ceasing to be descriptions of first-
order features, and acquiring a distinctly 'aesthetic' character.
I might refer to the 'atmosphere' of the scene, the 'balance' of the
human figures; I could think of what I see as 'poignant', 'wintery'
or whatever: these descriptions are still cogent answers to the
'why'-question, and they still have the form of descriptions of the
object independently of any relation it may have to further desires

and interests of mine. But they now serve to clarify my own reaction to the scene, and they begin to show, also, an element in my appreciation of it that we might want to describe as 'aesthetic'.

Now it may be wondered how far this approach to the problem is satisfactory. For it is unclear what is being said when we analyse the notion of interest in an object for its own sake as an interest for which the question 'Why?' has a certain kind of answer. Someone may still ask the question which we have been attempting all along to answer, namely, '*What* is it about the interest in question that requires 'why'-questions to be answered in such a way?' However, if there is a basis in the interest itself for the fact that it is related to a certain kind of reason-giving, then we will have to go very deep to find it. The basis is not to be found in the notion of desire. For although it seems plausible at first to say that an interest in a scene for its own sake can be explained entirely in terms of a desire to go on observing it, there could be all sorts of reasons why such a desire exists. I might desire to go on looking at a dark thicket because it rests my eyes, or because I have an impression that there is someone hiding in it. If it is replied that what was really meant was the desire to go on looking at the thicket for no other reason, then this simply brings us back to the point from which we started. What does this phrase 'for no other reason' signify?

It might be suggested, nonetheless, that there is another way of elucidating the notion of 'interest in a thing for its own sake' in terms of desire. For it might be said that every desire is a desire *for* something, and that, while one often desires a thing because it is a means to something else it cannot be the case that all desires are of this nature. Ultimately there are things that I just want, and it is in application to these things that such phrases as 'for its own sake', 'for no other reason', and so on, make sense. And if we were asked to say in what the distinction between desiring as a means and desiring as an end consists we could perhaps have recourse to the Thomist theory that the first, unlike the second, is finite and bounded: if there is something *for* which I desire, say, money, then it follows that I only desire the amount of money which will secure that thing. Whereas if I desire money for its own sake, then I desire it 'infinitely': there is no amount of money that will satisfy my desire, even though my desire may as a matter of fact cease after the acquisition of a certain sum.[9] Thus we might say that to be interested in a thing for its own sake is simply to desire to observe it, where there is no point at which this desire to observe can be said to be *satisfied* (although it may at some point cease).

There are certain considerations that should persuade us that this is not the notion of 'for its own sake' that we are trying to describe. We attribute desires not only to human beings but also to animals, but we do not attribute to animals the kind of interest in an object for its own sake, or for no other reason, that is characteristic of aesthetic appreciation. There are reasons for this, and perhaps the most important is the following: most of the desires that we attribute to animals fall under the notion of appetite. We ascribe to animals general appetites for certain kinds of satisfaction – appetites for food, shelter, procreation, safety and so on – and any desires that animals have for particular objects we assimilate to these ineradicable dispositions from which animal reactions spring. The lion's desire to pursue a deer is part of its appetite for food and so on. Set against these appetites is the kind of curiosity that can exist in their absence, the desire for the knowledge that is necessary for the pursuit of anything at all. Even when it is not exactly right to speak of an appetite governing some animal desire – we do not speak of an appetite which governs the desire to escape from danger – there is, nonetheless, an appetitive structure in common to all animal desires. The object of an appetite or similar desire falls under a general specification, as the satisfaction or violation of a need. The object of hunger satisfies (or is thought to satisfy) the need for nourishment, the object of fear violates (or is thought to violate) the need for safety and so on. In other words, we seem to be able to account for the objects of animal desire in terms of the concept of need. Those more complex cases where the idea of a need does not seem sufficient – the case of the dog who is trained to eat only when ordered to do so – can be accounted for in terms of such secondary concepts as that of inhibition.

Why, then, do we find it odd to say that an animal desires safety or plenitude for their own sakes? I think we can see that these descriptions of animal motivation serve no useful purpose. The desire for food, and the desire to escape danger, are not

[9] Aquinas, *Summa Theologiae*, Ia 2ae 30, 4.

directed at plenitude or safety for their own sakes at all, even if these are the ends to which the desires for safety and plenitude point. The phrase 'for its own sake' seems to serve the added function of showing how the end of action is *conceived*. One does not want to satisfy hunger because of some conception of what the satisfaction of hunger is: it is not thoughts or beliefs about the state of plenitude that draw us to it. Hence the question 'Why does one want to satisfy hunger?' has (in general) no interesting answer. To reply 'In order to keep alive' is simply to refer to the need from which this impulse springs, whereas a proper answer to the 'why'-question should consist in an elaboration of the intentional object of desire: it should give the 'description under which' something is wanted, and hence give a reason for the desire and not just an explanation or a cause. The desire for food has no reason in this sense, whereas to want something 'for its own sake' *is* to want it for a reason. 'For its own sake' is a 'description under which' an object may be desired. In other words, we must distinguish the case of wanting something when there is no reason for wanting it (when, for example, one's desire is based in a need) and wanting something *for no other reason*, where one's desire is, nonetheless, based on a conception of the thing one wants.

If we do not make this distinction then we find ourselves entertaining the curious theory that there is an aesthetic need that underlies our interest in art. There is a basic appetite that we satisfy in looking at pictures, and this explains why, when we look at them, there is no reason for our doing so which is not to be given in terms of further descriptions of the pictures themselves.[10] If this theory is absurd it is because it entirely fails to capture what we mean when we say that our interest in a picture is an interest in the picture 'for its own sake', or 'for no other reason'. It is essential to the concept of a need that a need can be satisfied by indefinitely many objects, the objects of an appetite that springs from need can replace each other and still satisfy the same desire. But it is a commonplace that we cannot substitute pictures for one another saying 'This one will do just as well', for we have no description of *what* can be done just as well by either picture. The desire to look at Mantegna's *Crucifixion* cannot be satisfied by the

[10] This theory seems to be implicit in John Dewey, *Art as Experience*, chs. 1 and 2.

sight of *La Liseuse*. To make sense of the idea of aesthetic interest we would, therefore, have to suppose a separate appetite for each of its objects. But in that case the notion of an appetite or need would be entirely redundant.

It should be clear by now that one thing that distinguishes the interest in a picture for its own sake from the desires arising out of animal appetite, is that the former interest involves a thought. We can generalize this result: the interest in a picture for its own sake is distinct from a desire (however explained) to go on looking at the picture in that the former, unlike the latter, essentially involves a thought of its object. The cow who merely stares at a landscape (with or without curiosity) is doing something less than the man who stares out of interest in the landscape, and yet 'for no other reason'. The man is thinking of the landscape, and at the same time thinking of it through his perception: he is thinking of what he sees. Thus we may define an interest in an object X for its own sake as a desire to go on hearing, looking at, or in some other way having experience of X, where there is no reason for this desire in terms of any other desire or appetite that the experience of X may fulfil, and where the desire arises out of, and is accompanied by, the thought of X. This definition is not quite perfect. We need to exclude those cases where the thought of X and the experience of X are not brought into proper relation (as when someone does not know that he is looking at X, even though this is what he is thinking of). However, such cases are already to a large measure excluded by ruling that the desire to continue looking at X should be *founded* on the thought of X, in that the thought should provide one with the reason for one's desire: it is because it is X that one is looking at it, and 'for no other reason'.

This definition successfully explains the applicability of a particular sense of the 'why'-question. For the expression of the thought of an object involves describing the object. Hence, if I am interested in X for its own sake, then I shall respond to the question 'Why are you interested in X?' with the expression of the thought that provides the reason for my continued interest – in other words, I shall respond with a description of X.

It may be asked what an interest of this kind is like. At this stage, the best way of replying to such a question is through examples. For in one sense we have said all that is to be said:

we have given an account of the thoughts and desires that are involved in aesthetic interest. We could attempt to follow Wittgenstein's procedure, and refer to the primitive forms of aesthetic enjoyment: the child's enjoyment of stories and pictures, the primitive society's interest in fiction. The latter enables us to visualize rather strikingly the distinction between aesthetic enjoyment and other attitudes – such as curiosity. It also gives some content to Sartre's comparison between aesthetic enjoyment and magic incantation. The tribe who listen to a messenger speaking of some event in a near-by village are moved by a desire for knowledge. They are impatient for the messenger to finish his story, and only then does their reaction express how they have taken it. Contrast this situation with that of a tribe assembled to hear a legend: now their most important reactions *accompany* the hearing of the story. They smile with pleasure; they are 'all agog'. Their sympathies vary with the thought of the story: they weep at what is sad, rejoice at what is agreeable. It is as though the story had made something present: it no longer points beyond itself to an absent thing which is the object of interest. The tribe may experience a desire to join themselves to the events of the story, and this desire may be manifested in ritual dance or re-enactment.

Magic incantation – the summoning up of an absent thing by ritual – is an activity in which imagination and belief are inextricably mingled. It is partly for this reason that we might wish to say that it is not a manifestation of aesthetic interest: thought and belief are not sufficiently separate. Moreover, unlike aesthetic activity, it is often engaged in for a purpose: to gain power, or to summon up the dead. But we can usefully compare the creation and understanding of artistic forms with incantation; it is as though the element of belief (and hence the delusion of a practical function) had been refined away in aesthetic interest, leaving a residue of thought and feeling properly described as interest in an activity for its own sake alone.

Collingwood criticized 'Magic Art' because of its purposive aspect: to appreciate it as it is intended is not to appreciate it aesthetically. In this he was only partly right. The appreciation of magic art is a confused affair, in which belief and enjoyment are inextricably mixed, the one qualifying the other, so that

enjoyment is intensely serious, and belief only partly so. Collingwood also criticized what he called 'Amusement Art', art which is
designed purely to entertain, at whatever cost. An interest in such
art, Collingwood thought, is interest in it only as a means for
arousing amusement, and not for its own sake.[11] But this view of
Collingwood's involves an interesting fallacy, characteristic of
much writing on aesthetics in the Kantian tradition. In the right
circumstances, amusement can form part of an aesthetic reaction.
The element of normativity is, of course, lacking in general from
amusement, but the remaining features of appreciation – at least
as we have enumerated them so far – may be present. Amusement
is not only a species of enjoyment, it is also founded on the
thought of its object. Except in the sophisticated case where one is
simply amused at the thought of a certain thing (real or imaginary),
amusement is also a response to an observed situation. In amusement, therefore, one's perception of an object exists in conjunction
with a thought of it; and one's desire to look or listen is founded
on this thought. Thus we might describe amusement as a mode of
attention to an object for its own sake.[12] Like many other
reactions amusement *constitutes* the appreciation of its object.
Hence it cannot be true that an interest in what is amusing about
an object is interest in that object *for the sake of* amusement.
Amusement is a central and important case of interest in an object
for its own sake. And the same is true of aesthetic responses in
general: in particular, of the emotions founded on imaginative
perception that were described in the last chapter. In other words,
pace Croce and Collingwood, the aesthetic of sympathy does not
commit us to the heteronomy of aesthetic interest.

Amusement provides us, in fact, with a telling picture of the
kind of enjoyment that is involved in the primitive forms of
aesthetic appreciation. We can contrast a child's enjoyment of the
picture of a funny face with his interest in a picture of his grandmother (shown in response to the question: 'What did Granny
look like?'). In the first case the child will not characteristically ask
whom the picture is of, or whether anyone looked like that. If he
relates it to his ordinary experience it will be indirectly. The remark 'That's Johnny' (his little brother) will be taken as express-

[11] *The Principles of Art*, ch. IV.
[12] Cf. B. A. O. Williams, 'Pleasure and Belief', *A.S.S.V.*, 1959.

ing a particular reaction to the picture and not a belief about its representational status. The second case is different in these respects; it will further involve the feature that, once curiosity has been satisfied, interest in the picture will wane. Or if it does not wane (for there are children who will seize on photographs of deceased relatives and study them endlessly) then we begin to describe the interest differently: the child has come to see something beautiful or moving in the picture.

Before developing this point further we must return to the problem from which this chapter began. We still have to explain the meaning of judgements of beauty and judgements of form in terms of the theory of appreciation we have given so far. The problem about judgements of beauty was, roughly, this: if we explain these judgements as expressions of 'aesthetic approval', i.e. as expressions of a pro-attitude with the structure indicated above, we must also explain why there are so many different judgements employing purely aesthetic terms. For example, we do not think of ourselves as able to substitute 'elegant' for 'beautiful' in all of its occurrences, without considerable loss of meaning. In learning the meaning of such words as 'elegant', 'beautiful', 'fine' and so on, we learn that not everything that is elegant is also fine, beautiful, exquisite or lovely. These terms have distinct connotations – we learn to apply them in different situations, and a person who praised elegance above all else would show different *taste* from another who only appreciated beauty. But to have different taste from another is to appreciate different objects. It would seem, then, that terms like 'elegant' and 'beautiful' refer to distinct properties of things. The theory that these terms gain their separate meanings from the several elements in a complex pattern of responses, as I. A. Richards supposed, is surely quite implausible. One could make a comparison with concepts in ethics. A man may be praised morally for his honesty, courage or benevolence. As a result terms like 'honesty' may become part of the vocabulary of moral appraisal, and may, therefore, seem to be standardly used to express moral attitudes. However, their principal use is, in fact, in the description of human character; the attitudes are merely conveyed by their use, as a matter of conversational association.

But, in fact, there is another way of regarding the use of purely aesthetic terms that will be more in keeping with the tenor of our investigations. It is possible, as Wittgenstein remarked, that these terms are learned as interjections. If this is so, then their transformation into adjectives ought to be accompanied by a nondescriptive meaning: in learning their use as interjections we should at the same time be learning how to manage their adjectival form. But because of this propositional form, the aesthetic adjectives carry a suggestion of genuine description. Moreover, the learning of each term is connected with a distinct set of objects, even though it is learned as an expression of aesthetic appraisal. Hence each term will acquire a separate realm where it may be appropriately applied, and from this realm certain classes of object will naturally be excluded. Loud music will not be elegant, tragedies will not be dainty, humorous poetry will not be sublime. A term like 'elegant' might be taught in the context of aesthetic reactions to clothes, style, mathematical proofs, examples where in general there seems to be question of a fitting exploitation of rules. The term 'lovely' might be taught in another context, say, that of the appreciation of faces, gestures, characters, examples of things that can be loved or admired. The term 'exquisite' is taught in the context of the aesthetic appreciation of a refined and subtle exercise of skill or craftmanship, as in ornamental carving, or classical ballet.

In other words, it is not necessary to assume that a term like 'elegant' has descriptive meaning, even though it indicates that the speaker's appreciation of an object is directed towards features of a certain general but specifiable kind. The use of the term 'elegant' does not tell us which of these features are present: it only indicates the area in which the appreciated features can be found. If it is asked why we have these separate terms of aesthetic appraisal, then it could be said that aesthetic appreciation, since it involves the 'free' thought of its object,[13] will have a different character as its objects differ. My appreciation of what is tragic is a quite different 'experience' from my appreciation of comedy, and my appreciation of refined and civilized things is in one sense utterly unlike my appreciation of what is violent and destructive. Each object of appreciation will be related in thought to its own

[13] I use the Kantian term 'free' to indicate that the thoughts involved in appreciation need not be 'asserted'.

particular area of real experience, and this will determine our response to it. We need a flexible vocabulary of aesthetic appraisal, therefore, if we are to indicate the way in which we appreciate any given object. In a sense Richards was right in saying that the complex vocabulary of aesthetic terms reflects 'the organization of our feelings'. The character of aesthetic appreciation will be entirely dictated by its object: for appreciation is a reflective state of mind, in which belief and action are both to a large extent suspended. In attempting to clarify our feelings towards art we find it necessary to employ terms that also classify the objects of aesthetic experience into different kinds, terms such as 'beautiful' and 'sublime', which have been traditionally conceived as marking a fundamental division in aesthetic interest.

This brings us to the problem of formal features. We notice that many of the terms used in aesthetic description are used extremely loosely: indeed, this is to be expected. For in giving an aesthetic description we are trying to indicate how an object is to be appreciated. For this we need an extensive and partly metaphorical vocabulary. Often we wish to describe what it is about an object that sustains our interest, without referring to imaginative thoughts or feelings that we see embodied in it. Thus we speak of the object as pleasing, satisfying, restful. . . . Gradually the list of these terms will extend to include terms denoting formal features, such as 'balanced', 'controlled', 'harmonious', 'unified', 'whole'. It is not certain whether these are metaphors or literal descriptions, and it does not matter a great deal which they are; for their function is only to *indicate* how it is possible to find in the object the kind of satisfaction that is characteristic of aesthetic enjoyment. They stand proxy for more detailed descriptions which we may not be able to formulate. In many cases – in particular in those of abstract music or architecture – the detailed and technical descriptions are the only interesting things to be said. We use these 'formal' terms to direct someone's attention to the satisfying features of the aesthetic object. There is something ineffable about the capacity of an object to satisfy us in this way, and the vague but extensive vocabulary of formal terms is simply one indication of this fact.

In conclusion, let us return to the discussion of the aesthetic attitude where it was left off. I have characterized this attitude in terms of three conditions: (i) the aesthetic attitude aims at enjoyment of (and satisfaction with) an object; (ii) it involves an attention to that object 'for its own sake'; (iii) it is normative, involving a sense of what is right or appropriate. But it seems that I have avoided the much-canvassed sensuous aspect of aesthetic appreciation. Philosophers who have wished to emphasize this sensuous quality have tended to stress the arts of painting and music, where what is pleasing is the sound or look of something. But to base one's theory of aesthetic interest on these cases alone is to risk making nonsense of the appreciation of literature. Indeed, any attempt to *define* aesthetic appreciation in sensuous terms will fail to explain the arts of poetry and narrative. If there is something inherently sensuous in aesthetic appreciation, then this should follow from the conditions already given – conditions which by no means exclude literature from the sphere of aesthetic interest. It is not something that we should assume from the start. In Chapter Twelve I shall attempt to show that our appreciation of literature must be based in certain perceptual experiences, and that, in this sense, it has a partly sensuous origin. But this is a conclusion that follows from our definition of the aesthetic attitude together with certain assumptions about the nature of literature: the sensuous element cannot be located more directly than this.

On the other hand, we find that, in the case of the visual arts at least, the analysis given leads immediately to a connection with perceptual experience, and, therefore, explains in part why the connection of the aesthetic and the sensuous has so often seemed inevitable. The principal manifestation of aesthetic interest is attention to an object, which, since it cannot go beyond the object in the manner of practical or theoretical judgement, must come to rest in the perception of the object itself. To take an example: I may admire the character of Marcus Aurelius, and as a result be pleased when I come across his bust in an Italian town hall. I begin to look at the bust and study the features of the Emperor's face, thinking of the character that once animated them. There is a point when it would be natural to say that my interest in the bust has become aesthetic, the point, namely, when the nobility of character becomes part of the appearance of the bust. The bust acquires a noble aspect, and my attention ceases to stray beyond what I see to the thoughts that are inspired by it, but comes to rest in the perception itself. My admiration of Aurelius has become part of my desire to look at this particular thing, in that the object of my admiration is now exemplified in the appearance of the bust.

But we see at once that our conditions lead not only to a connection with sense, in this case, but also to a general connection with imagination. In aesthetic appreciation we might say that the perception of an object is brought into relation with a thought of the object. But we discovered previously that it is possible for the thought of absent objects to be brought into a direct and inseparable relation with a perception: this is one of the main activities of imagination. It seems a natural consequence, therefore, that an aesthetic attitude towards a present object will lead to the thoughts and emotions characteristic of imagination. Imagination is simply one way of thinking of, and attending to, a present object (by thinking of it, or perceiving it, in terms of something absent). In aesthetic appreciation, we might say, the object serves as a focal point on which many different thoughts and feelings are brought to bear. Our account of imagination enables us to see how we may avoid the empiricist fallacy of associationism, which one idealist has described as 'the attempt to explain general connections of content by the chance conjunction of particular experiences'.[14] For we can give meaning to the suggestion that the thoughts and feelings that are aroused by art can, nonetheless, become part of our experience of it. They enter as an inalienable element into the experience itself, and transform it without diverting it from its original object. There is no need to have recourse to the vague idea of 'fusion' to explain this fact.

The sensuous element in the appreciation of literature is far less easy to locate. It is arguable, none the less, that there must be a sensuous element: for my interest in a work of literature is by no means an interest in its paraphrase: it cannot, therefore, be an interest merely in what the poem or novel *says*. But there are problems even for this relatively innocuous conclusion, as

[14] B. Bosanquet, 'On the Nature of Aesthetic Emotion', in *Science and Philosophy*, p. 400.

Chapter Twelve will show. The difficulty is that our conditions for the aesthetic attitude do not imply that there is any one way in which appreciation must be sensuous: they do not imply, for example, that the object of aesthetic interest must be the sound, look, taste or smell of something. Indeed, if they implied anything so strong as that they would be open to a powerful objection. For it seems that only the senses of sound and sight *can* be involved in aesthetic appreciation; hence it is not simply the fact of being senses that equips them for this role. Hegel argued that the senses of taste and smell cannot embody sufficient of the intellect to be involved in the appreciation of art.[15] In this he was repeating Aquinas[16] who argued that we cannot speak of beautiful tastes and smells, since the perception of beauty, being contemplative, is only associated with the more cognitive senses, namely sight and hearing. The strangeness of the claret-lover's vocabulary, and of Des Esseintes' symphony of smells, might persuade us of this point. Certainly, when the pleasures of the more cognitive senses approach the purely sensuous level characteristic of taste and smell we tend to regard them as no longer aesthetic – for example, we do not think of the desire for background music in a restaurant as an aesthetic impulse. It is extremely interesting if the important part of aesthetic interest – the imaginative involvement that is its principal value – should be absent or attenuated in the case of taste or smell. But it is difficult to give a fully satisfying explanation of why this is so. One explanation might be simply that the pleasures of taste and smell involve the consumption, and not merely the contemplation, of an object. But this is not the only thing to be said. There is a sense in which the impressions of sight and hearing are more 'structured' than those of taste and smell: we are able to discern an enormous number of features of an object on the basis of just one visual or auditory impression. As a result, visual and auditory impressions have the character of being 'spread' over 'fields'. Taste and smell, however, convey nothing beyond themselves: to recognize the taste of something is to recognize only one feature of it. Thus tastes and smells are in a strange way more evocative than sights and sounds: they convey so little in themselves that in the attempt to attach meaning to

[15] *Introduction to the Philosophy of Fine Art*, tr. Bosanquet, pp. 108–9.
[16] *Summa Theologiae*, Ia 2ae 27, 1.

them one must import a reminiscence of their total surroundings (cf. Proust's *madeleine*).

In describing a notion of aesthetic experience that gives a clear and central place to the imagination we have in fact provided ourselves with a philosophical basis from which to explore the nature and value of art. And through allowing such a central place to imagination and thought we are able to develop a view of aesthetics that harmonizes more nearly with the insights that philosophers in the Idealist tradition, from Kant to Collingwood, have produced. In fact, the theory that seems to have emerged from the empiricist premises from which we started is strikingly similar to that of Kant, who summarized his position as follows:

> (1) The beautiful pleases *immediately* . . . (2) It pleases *apart from all interest* . . . (3) The *freedom* of the imagination (consequently of our faculty in respect of its sensibility) is, in estimating the beautiful, represented as in accord with the understanding's conformity to law . . . (4) The subjective principle of the estimate of the beautiful is represented as *universal*, i.e. valid for every man, but as incognizable by means of any concept . . .[17]

(1) corresponds to two of the features we have described: enjoyment of an object, and the connection with sensory experience; (2) corresponds to our analysis of the phrase 'for its own sake'; and (4) to the condition of normativity. Now it is not unnatural to regard Kant's third condition as reflecting the feature of aesthetic interest that we have brought in under the cover of imagination. Imagination, for Kant, is a faculty that is free (i.e. independent of belief), and yet at the same time bound by the laws of understanding (i.e. rational). But to establish this point would take us into the realms of Kantian scholarship: at least the analogy is there.

[17] *Critique of Judgement*, pp. 224–5.

PART III
The Experience of Art

CHAPTER ELEVEN

The Identity of Art

In the last chapter I gave certain conditions for the aesthetic attitude. It may be asked, are these conditions all necessary, together sufficient, for the aesthetic attitude? And it may be wondered how we might answer such a question. We could perhaps say that the presence of all the features is necessary and sufficient for an attitude's being a central example of aesthetic interest; or alternatively, we could say that no one of the conditions is individually necessary but that together they are sufficient. Finally, we might suggest that these features should be treated simply as criteria, in Wittgenstein's sense, of the aesthetic attitude, and leave the question of necessary and sufficient conditions to be settled as the need should arise. Our language leaves us free to choose whichever formulation we require: but this does not mean that our choice of these conditions – or 'criteria' – is arbitrary. Here we must remind ourselves of a point that was made in passing in Chapter Two: there is no fully articulated concept of the aesthetic in ordinary language. The philosopher's only criterion of success is that his analysis should conform to certain rather fragile 'intuitions', and that it should permit him to make sense of our experience of art. We can reassure ourselves that our analysis answers well enough to the basic intuitions from which we began. It enables us to explain why there should be a diverse but stable vocabulary of aesthetic appraisal, and why there should be an activity of aesthetic 'description' associated with it. It also yields a clear distinction between aesthetic and practical attitudes, and enables us to see how the aesthetic is both distinct from, and yet intimately related to, the moral. Finally, it characterizes aesthetic appreciation as a rational activity, founded on thought, and falling within the province of practical reason. Hence we can begin to explain its privileged and irreplaceable position in human experience.

However, it remains to be seen whether our theory can be applied to that realm of aesthetic interest which has always proved incomprehensible to the empiricist philosophy of mind – the appreciation of art. How can we explain the primacy of art in aesthetic experience? This question must be answered by any theory that seems to imply, as our theory seems to imply, that it is only a contingent truth that the principal objects of aesthetic interest are works of art. The opposite view is certainly more attractive. It has been argued on several sides that it is art and art alone that is the source of our ideas of beauty, and that if nature sometimes seems beautiful to us it is only because it echoes something that we first learn to appreciate in art. As a manifestation of the human spirit, art must have a significance wholly unlike that of any natural thing. Indeed, we describe a landscape as beautiful only if it shows the kind of relationship to human endeavour that is characteristic of an artefact. The Highlands of Scotland have little beauty, although they may once have been called sublime. If we were to describe a beautiful landscape we might choose, for example, some valley in Provence, in which the terraced olive groves and pan-tiled roofs suggest in their outlines and contours the form of a particular way of life. The landscape becomes beautiful because it begins to represent or express a human experience.

This Hegelian argument has a certain charm, and imposes on us the task of examining the experience of art, with a view to discovering how far it can be accommodated by our theory. But no sooner do we turn from the simple case of aesthetic interest in a natural thing (such as a horse, a landscape or a flower) than we find ourselves beset by serious difficulties. In Chapter Two I mentioned a problem that has interested many philosophers, the problem of the identity of the work of art. I argued against the view that the uniqueness of the aesthetic object can be specified in terms of its criterion of identity. A criterion of identity governs all our references to a particular thing, and cannot be considered as the product of any one way of regarding it. There is no reason for saying that the particularity of aesthetic interest necessitates a special criterion for the individuation of its object, any more than that the moral point of view determines the identity criteria of human acts.

This argument seemed to imply that a discussion of the nature and identity of art is not a necessary preliminary to any theory of aesthetic interest, and in a sense this implication has been sustained in ensuing chapters. However, no sooner do we attempt to apply our theory to the experience of art than the question of the nature of art poses itself once again, this time in a more serious form. In general we might have grounds to be sceptical of the approach to aesthetics that has been defended up until now. For suppose that our fundamental assumption is correct, and that there is indeed such a thing as aesthetic interest – a distinct state of mind characterized by certain general features. Then surely it would be odd if it proved to be merely contingent that the principal objects of this attitude themselves belong to a certain class (the class of works of art). At least we need some explanation of this fact, and we will find that our explanation will compel us to supplement our theory in ways inimical to traditional empiricism. We might say that it is a feature of the *intentionality* of aesthetic attitudes that they are primarily directed towards works of art. By this I mean that the thoughts and feelings involved in aesthetic interest can acquire a full elaboration only if the aesthetic object possesses just those features which are characteristic of art.

But there is another way in which our analysis needs completion. For we can see at once that our interest in a particular work of art is under-characterized by saying that it is interest in the work of art 'for its own sake'. For we have not indicated how the word 'it' should here be understood. If someone were to ask me how he should appreciate a particular aesthetic object, and I were to reply 'for its own sake', then he might legitimately complain that I had given no answer to his question. For he needed to be told under what description (as an example of what kind of thing) the object should first be seen.

This point can be illustrated by an example. Suppose that I attend the performance of a Noh play, ignorant of the conventions of Japanese theatre, and with only an inadequate grasp of the language. Here I may appreciate the play as a ballet, or as a sequence of sounds and movements, and yet have no sense of its aesthetic character as a play: I may not even know that it is a play. If my better-informed companion tells me that it must really be taken as a play, then my interest changes, and I begin to attend to quite different features of what I see, even though I am in both cases interested in what I see 'for its own sake'. Ironically, I may describe my experience in the following way: 'I was not treating it as a play; I took a merely aesthetic interest in what I saw.'[1]

In other words, appreciation stands in need of a description of its object. This fact determines our analysis of the 'uniqueness' of the aesthetic object in such a way as to raise again the question of the identity of the work of art. For to say that I appreciate what I see and hear (the performance of a Noh play) for its own sake is to give no indication of the intentional object of my interest. 'What I see' is, considered materially, many things: a group of masked figures chanting and dancing on the stage, a set of movements executed by those figures, a representation of a dialogue between a man and his wife's ghost, two Japanese actors earning their keep; and so on. We might say that I could have a purely aesthetic interest in any of these things, but in order to have this interest, I must have some conception of what I am seeing. It follows that, if I am to appreciate this object as a play, then I must be familiar with the concept of a play. I must know which features belong to this object as a play, and which do not, and this is no simple matter. The Noh theatre, for example, involves conventions which require considerable knowledge if two plays which are, in fact, entirely different are not to be treated as the same. For two plays might differ only in that, while one consists of a dialogue between a man and his wife, the other consists of the same dialogue between a man and the ghost of his wife, the only observable difference lying in movement, dress and intonation. In order to make the right aesthetic discriminations, and indeed in order to be interested in either play for its own sake at all, I must know sufficient about plays to realize that their identity is determined in part by the identity of what is represented, which is,

---

[1] Cf. 'It is therefore quite unnecessary for the spectator to read the words, because he need only appreciate the intrinsic beauty of the actors' movements and the rhythm of the accompanying music', Toyoichiro Nogami, *Japanese Noh Plays*, Tokyo, 1954, p. 31.

in turn, determined by an intention, which is, in its turn, dependent upon a system of conventions and traditional effects. Aesthetic interest will, therefore, depend for its full expression on a complex knowledge of particular human institutions, the institutions of art, and the character of aesthetic appreciation cannot be fully described until we have discovered what is brought to it by art.

There are several conclusions to be drawn from this argument. For one thing, we can see that the question of the identity of the work of art is not, after all, completely irrelevant to aesthetics. It is an arbitrary and uninteresting matter how we specify the identity criterion of any work of art. But it is not arbitrary that this criterion should be chosen from a given range of features. Thus while it matters not a jot whether we call the Folio and Quarto versions of *Hamlet* one or two plays, it does matter if we say that *Hamlet* is constituted by the gestures and movements of a given set of actors (for example), rather than by a particular *action*, involving the representation of things said and done.

We may also conclude that there is something self-defeating in Kant's insistence that at least some forms of aesthetic appreciation are 'free from concepts', in the sense of being dependent on no previous classification of their objects as members of a class. Of course, it is true that the description under which I see the object of aesthetic interest determines no relevant features (features uniquely relevant to the aesthetic point of view). And this is an important point, one consequence of which is that the term 'beautiful' cannot be construed as a 'logically attributive' adjective,[2] an adjective whose content is more or less fixed for specific kinds of things, but which is otherwise indeterminate. Thus when I say that X is beautiful the question 'Beautiful as a what?' does not immediately arise. But this was not Kant's point. He wished to say that aesthetic appreciation does not depend for its existence on any classification of its object. And it is clear that, if he thought that, he was certainly wrong. Kant himself seemed to be half aware of the difficulty in making a distinction between 'free beauty' (the appreciation of which requires no concept) and 'dependent beauty'.[3] As examples of the latter kind of beauty he did indeed refer principally to works of art. But his discussion

[2] Cf. P. T. Geach, 'Good and Evil', in *Analysis*, 1956.
[3] *Critique of Judgement*, section 16.

indicates that the beauty of a play is considered dependent not because appreciation depends on seeing the aesthetic object as a play, but rather because it depends on seeing the play as a representation.

But while Kant's distinction must in this way fall short of answering the present difficulty, it is of interest in another way. For it shows a connection between our problem and another that will occupy indirectly much of the discussion of ensuing chapters. Kant saw that he must give some answer to the question: 'How can I appreciate a work of art for its own sake while at the same time appreciating it as a representation of another thing?' It is only when we concede that the object of appreciation is seen under a description that we find an answer to this question. For we may appreciate a play for its own sake whilst also appreciating it *as a representation*: indeed, there is no other way of understanding it. On the other hand, the difficulty that Kant hints at has seemed so great that some philosophers have dismissed representation altogether, as an offence against the autonomy of art. And in answer to the parallel difficulty created by the concept of expression it has often been argued that what is expressed by a work of art cannot be identified except in terms of the work of art itself, so that interest in expression is not interest in something beyond the aesthetic object.

In what follows I shall show how the experience of representation and expression forms part of our experience of art: appreciation of representation and expression are simply special cases of aesthetic interest. This is certainly how we treat them in practice. Thus we are apt to distinguish expression from association partly in terms of the potentially aesthetic character of the former. This comes out in the language appropriate to the recognition of each. To describe expression is to attribute an aesthetic feature to a work of art: I say that the work is melancholy, or that it expresses melancholy. To describe association is not to attribute a feature in this sense: I say rather that the work of art *makes me think of* something. Clearly, then, we regard expression as a feature integral to the nature of art, something that we experience *in* the work and not by means of it. To appreciate a work of art as expression is not to appreciate it simply as a means of access to the thing expressed.

Similarly, interest in representation is a special case of aesthetic interest: the experience of representation forms part of our experience of art. Representation is misconstrued if it is taken as a means for stimulating or satisfying curiosity about the world, and for this reason, if for no other, photography and journalism are inimical to art. As we shall see, the capacities involved in the appreciation of representation and expression cannot be compared with the thirsts for fortuitous knowledge and for facile sentiment that are sometimes directed at art.

CHAPTER TWELVE
Understanding Art

We have been led to conclude that the appreciation of art is partly determined by a conception of its object. This leaves the way open to theories of aesthetic interest very different from ours. In particular, it might be argued that once we have acquired the complex body of knowledge involved in understanding art it will no longer be possible to treat art simply as the object of a particular experience – certainly not as the object of an experience that might equally be occasioned by a landscape or a flower. On the contrary, art is more like a language, a mode of presentation of human ideas, and it is significant only on account of the ideas or experiences which it expresses. Appreciation of art involves understanding a system of signs, and this understanding is a cognitive capacity, rather than a capacity for any kind of feeling or experience.

It seems, then, that the experience of art, unlike the experience of natural beauty, involves understanding. A man may understand, or fail to understand, the *Four Quartets*, or Rodin's *Danaë* but he can scarcely understand or fail to understand the hills of Catalonia, even when he finds them beautiful or ugly. Understanding seems to be a prerequisite to the full experience of art, and this has suggested to many philosophers that art is not so much an object of aesthetic 'experience' as an instrument of knowledge. In particular, art has the power to represent reality and to express emotion, and it is in understanding these specifically artistic properties that we come to appreciate art. In the present chapter I shall pass over the problems of representation and of expression. Instead I shall try to demonstrate – through the example of music

– that the notion of 'understanding art' is by no means as straightforward as the cognitive theory of aesthetic appreciation seems to imply.

How does the notion of understanding come to be applied to music? One suggestion is that music is like a language, and needs to be understood in the way that a language is understood. This view appeals to the modern philosopher: it disposes entirely of the idea that understanding a piece of music is to be analysed in terms of some experience that accompanies hearing. To picture understanding as an 'experience' is to give an inchoate description of language.[1] The comparison of music with language leads, however, to no useful theory of musical appreciation. Although music is like language in containing what might be called a syntax – rules for the combination of meaningful parts into potentially meaningful wholes – it is unlike language in being intrinsically 'uninterpreted'. In language syntax is subservient to semantics and can be explained in terms of semantics. Music, on the other hand, has no semantics: there is nothing (besides itself) that music means. There are meaningful pieces of music and meaningless pieces, but the difference between them is not to be found in any meaning which the one has and the other lacks. Language is bound by truth, and by the requirements of truthful expression. Hence it must have an underlying semantic structure, dictating the grammatical transformations that are permitted in ordinary speech. In particular, language is absolutely bound by logic: without logic the dimension of truth and reference would fall away. But there are no rules that *bind* music, in the way that language is bound by those rules that make possible a semantic interpretation. What makes a musical phrase 'meaningful', as we say, is not the conformity to rule. On the contrary, this kind of 'meaningfulness', like the meaningfulness of a gesture, is not something that could ever be captured by rules. It is, therefore, not the kind of meaningfulness that derives from reference and predication.

It might be suggested that music is more like pure mathematics, in that it can be understood as an uninterpreted system of symbols, united only by internal rules. But while this analogy is useful as a counter to theories that see 'understanding' only in semantic

[1] Cf. Wittgenstein, *Zettel*, sections 155–76.

terms, it remains no more than an analogy. The central element in mathematical understanding is the ability to see that one formula follows from another, and this ability is quite unlike the ability to see that one note or chord in music 'follows from' its predecessor. It is an essential feature of the logical relationship of 'follows from' (deducibility) that if *q* follows from *p* then it *always* follows from *p*, so that it is never wrong from the mathematical point of view, although it may be inappropriate, to put down *q* after *p*. The parallel with music breaks down at this point. It was right to follow a G major chord with its dominant seventh at the opening of *Eine Kleine Nachtmusik*, but it would certainly have been wrong to have done so at every point throughout the work. Someone who did not understand this – who wanted to hear the seventh chord of D after every G major chord – would simply not understand what he was hearing. Similarly, understanding a mathematical proof is inductive. If I see that each step follows from the preceding step, then I see that the conclusion follows from the premises. But I can see how each separate chord in a piece of music is an apt sequence to the one preceding, and yet hear the whole sequence as nonsense. (This often happens when listening to Hindemith.) My understanding of a passage in music is not consequent on my understanding of its parts.

Finally, we cannot assume that understanding music is in the normal sense a technical achievement. One man may have an understanding and love of music while being entirely ignorant of theory, while another, well-versed in harmony and counterpoint, may show so few preferences, and so little taste for music, that we would be loath to describe him as understanding what he hears. Music, for him, is like an abstract game, the point of which is purely structural. Musical understanding essentially involves the ability to form preferences, and the capacity sometimes to enjoy what one hears. I no more understand a piece of music by being able to give a complete description of it than I understand a joke by being able to repeat it word for word, without the faintest flicker of a smile. The question that we must attempt to answer, therefore, is this: What is it about understanding music that leads us to connect understanding with the ability to form preferences of a certain kind?

It is important to note that we cannot speak of animals as

understanding music. For example, we do not say that birds understand music, or that they understand the sequences that they 'sing', even though it is possible for a human being (Messiaen, say) to understand birdsong as music. The bird's 'musical behaviour' simply fails to reach the right kind of complexity. It is perhaps for this reason that we say that a bird can have neither melody nor expression. For example, a bird cannot develop his song: he can only repeat it, as a musical box repeats it, with the most accidental variations. Moreover, and perhaps this is the most important feature, one cannot give very much sense to the idea that a bird has chosen *that* sequence of notes from among the alternatives available to him, simply because that sequence appeals to him. For the idea of choice has no application here – we cannot think of the bird as trying out sequences of notes to see which one fits: he just sings, and the notes come. If he repeats what he sings we do not say 'He must have liked the sound of that phrase', and certainly not 'I wonder why he liked the sound of that phrase?': we say, 'That's his song', and nothing more. A man, on the other hand, will prefer one phrase to another: certain things sound right to him, others do not, and it is in virtue of this fact that the concept of understanding comes to be applied to musical enjoyment. It is one, sophisticated, expression of musical understanding that one should compose, and composing is not doing something that birds can do any day at the drop of a hat. A man feels that the development of a certain phrase is right, and this is something that a bird cannot feel. We do not seem to have the circumstances in which it makes sense to say that the bird, in continuing his song, is developing something already given. All that we can say is that he sings this and *then* that. He does not sing that *because* he has sung this (except perhaps in a purely causal sense). In no sense does what he has already sung provide a reason for what he goes on to sing.

Musical understanding involves, then, the sense of rational development. Phrases and notes are felt to connect with each other in various ways. How are we to analyse this phenomenon? The principal point to grasp, I think, is that the capacity to understand music in this sense is an auditory capacity: it is a matter of being able to hear certain things. It is not a matter of being acquainted with a body of principles or rules. Suppose, for example, that I fail to understand twelve-note music: I simply do not understand why any note comes where it does. It is of no help to me to be told that the note must come there, say, because the series has exhausted itself and must start again. If I have a sensitive ear I may realize that Ex. 1 has exhausted all of a twelve-note series except for one note – G sharp. And I may as a result learn to anticipate G sharp at this point. But this does not mean that I *hear* the sequence as incomplete in any way, nor that I am particularly satisfied or impressed when the sequence is completed and the 'melodic line' proceeds as in Ex. 2. Indeed this may sound ridiculous to me. Before I can grasp the sense of the passage I need to master a whole new idiom, and while a theoretical understanding may help me to do this it is neither sufficient in itself nor necessary.

Ex. 1   A. Webern: Variations op. 27

Ex. 2

Many people have learned to appreciate twelve-note music by coming to understand the analogies between the tone-row theory and classical principles of musical structure. The two bodies of rules may then seem to constitute similar attempts to cast the boundaries of an auditory space. Within the limits imposed by the media analogous constraints apply, and analogous felicities may be achieved. But to understand this analogy is still not to hear twelve-note music as it is meant to be heard. Until the rules have been translated into auditory experiences that make sense in themselves they must inevitably seem arbitrary.

It seems, then, that we must treat musical understanding as at least partly an auditory capacity. This capacity can best be studied through a very simple and basic example of it: the understanding of sequence and melody. When I hear a piece of music I hear the notes as grouped together into phrases and themes. For example, I hear the opening bars of *Tristan* as composed of two juxtaposed melodic fragments, as in Ex. 3, and not as the single Brahmsian phrase of Ex. 4, even though this second phrase *can* be heard in the passage. There are, of course, differences of timbre which separate the two fragments of Ex. 3, but it is not this that is the determining factor: one hears the opening bars correctly even

Ex. 3 Wagner: Prelude to *Tristan und Isolde*

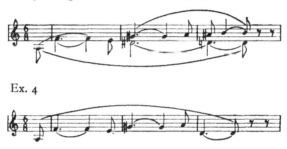

Ex. 4

Ex. 5 Prelude to *Parsifal*

when played on the piano, and besides, there are many examples of melodies that contain different and changing timbres, as in the fragment from *Parsifal* in Ex. 5. Here there is not only a change of timbre from the first phrase (A) to the second (B) (caused by the entry of an oboe); there is also a clear change of tonality from C minor to E minor. And yet one hears the second phrase as a natural continuation of the first.

Associated with musical understanding on this very basic level are such phenomena as hearing a sequence of notes as a melody, or as an accompaniment, hearing a melody in a sequence of chords, hearing one theme as a variation of another, or hearing two simultaneous melodies in a sequence of chords (as one hears the two melodies of Ex. 7 in the chords of Ex. 6), and so on. In common to all these cases is the close relation of 'understanding' to something that we would unreflectingly call an experience. Indeed, if it were not for the connection with the activity of understanding music generally, it would be unnecessarily pedantic

Ex. 6   Mozart, Quartet from *Don Giovanni*

Ex. 7

to speak of understanding a sequence of notes as a melody, rather than of hearing the sequence as a melody. But it must be noted immediately that when we speak of hearing in this context, we mean not hearing but '*hearing as*', and there are grounds for saying that 'hearing as' is not simply an experience, in the way that hearing may be.

'Hearing as' is an interesting concept from our point of view, partly through its close relation to 'seeing as', and partly through the light that it casts on the understanding of art in general. First of all, we find that we cannot analyse 'hearing as' in terms of hearing: the difference between a man who hears a sequence as a melody (or as containing a melody), and the man who simply hears it as a sequence of notes is not a difference in what the two men separately *hear*. They may each hear the same notes, and for the sake of argument we can imagine that they each are able to tell us what these notes are. It may seem at first sight that this is very far-fetched. For how could someone discriminate sounds so completely and yet be unaware of melodies? But, in fact, we need suppose no such general incapacity. We know of many particular cases where even the most sophisticated listener may fail to hear a sequence as a melody while knowing exactly what he hears. In the passage from Brahms in Ex. 8 it is impossible not to be fully aware of the powerful bass line, with its emphatic octaves counteracting the melting treble part. But how many listeners are able to hear the melody of the treble repeated in these muttering octaves? It may require considerable effort to hear these notes as a melody even though, from the very nature of the case, one knows already what the melody is. The difference between hearing this sequence as a melody and hearing it as a jumble of disconnected notes is a difference in the experience, and not in its (material) object. What is this difference? It is not that, in the mind of one man, the notes linger so that he hears them conjointly with the notes that follow.

Ex. 8   Brahms: Variations on a theme by Robert Schumann

To hear the melody in this way would be to hear it as a chord. Nor is the difference one of memory: the two subjects may each remember what has gone before as they hear the new notes played.

But suppose that we attempt to explain the notion of 'hearing as' in terms of the 'seeing as' analysed in Chapter Eight. Immediately a difference becomes apparent. For it is sometimes said that to see a portrait as a man, say, is to see it according to a concept: it is to 'bring a concept to bear' on one's visual experience. But this only begins to seem like an explanation of 'seeing as' because we are able to identify independently what the concept *is* according to which the picture is seen. Our possession of the concept 'man' can then be construed as logically prior to our ability to recognize the man-aspect in a picture. But it is useful to study the case of 'hearing as' partly because it demonstrates the inadequacy of this approach to 'seeing as', and, in doing so, leads us to a further refinement of the theory of aspect perception given in Chapter Eight. The case of hearing notes as a melody is unlike the case of seeing a group of coloured patches as a man, in that we do not have independent access to the concept of a melody. All we know of melodies is derived from our capacity to have *this* kind of experience (if 'experience' is the proper word). Hearing a sequence as a melody is more like seeing a group of lines as a pattern or figure than it is like seeing a pattern of lines as a face. Here the 'organisation' of experience cannot be described in terms of the application of some independently specifiable concept.

Now, someone might still wish to construe the difference we are attempting to define conceptually: in terms of the concept of a melody (or, in the visual case, the concept of a pattern or figure). And the application of these concepts could be supported by the application of various others – such as those of a continuation, a development, an answering phrase, and the rest. It is important to see why this answer is wrong. The idea of concept-application is that of classifying. But suppose our two subjects each classified sequences as melodies or otherwise: must we assume that their classifications will necessarily be different, just because one of them hears the melody and the other does not? In any case, we seem to have inverted the natural order of things: it is as though we were trying to analyse the difference between the blind man and the sighted man purely in terms of certain conceptual capacities. If there are differences in their conceptual capacities (and it is not clear that there need be), then this is because of certain other differences, which are in some sense prior. The case is exactly similar with the musical and the non-musical man.

Despite this lack of analogy with the cases of 'seeing as' previously considered, we find that hearing a melody possesses formal properties of the same order as those of aspect perception generally. Consider the melody in Ex. 9, from Verdi's *Rigoletto*.

Ex. 9   Verdi: 'Caro Nome', from *Rigoletto*

Ex. 9a

In one sense this is no more than a detached sequence of notes, which stand separated from their nearest neighbours by pauses as long as themselves. And yet one hears a process begin in the first note and carry through to the last – moreover, one can divide the process into definite episodes. The second seems to answer the first, and so on.

Now what is it to hear a melody begin? It is here that the analogy with 'seeing as' is most striking. Clearly it is not adequate just to think of a certain sequence as a melody, since I can have this thought before or after hearing, or failing to hear, the beginning of a melody, and it will not in itself affect the question whether or not I really did hear the beginning. Moreover, not only does hearing something as a melody have a precise beginning in time: it also has a precise duration. In other words, it has the sort of relation to the temporal sequence that we normally think of as characteristic of experiences (such as sensory experiences and bodily sensations). Again, the feature of variable intensity can also be attributed to 'hearing as'. My experience of one melody may be more or less vivid than my experience of another, while being at the same time just as total, convincing and complete. In Ex. 9, for example, there are two melodies played simultaneously, separated by the interval of a sixth. But it is undeniable that the experience of one is more intense than the experience of the other: the upper melody stands out, while the lower melody is a mere echo, with no proper life of its own. This is not simply a consequence of the fact that the striking melody is in the upper part: any part can acquire a vivid character, irrespective of what goes on above it or below – if this were not so, counterpoint would be impossible.

But if we do say that 'hearing as' is an experience, then, like 'seeing as', it is an experience of a peculiar kind, as is shown by the fact that we cannot attribute such an experience (as I have already argued) to an animal, however much the animal may literally hear. 'Hearing as' shares with 'seeing as' a formal relation to the concept of (unasserted) thought. For example, it is to some extent within voluntary control. I can sometimes stop myself from hearing a sequence of notes as a melody; or I may voluntarily group notes together in contrasting or conflicting ways. There are two ways of hearing the beautiful passage from the *Diabelli Variations* given in Ex. 10: one may hear the sequence as grouped in the manner of Ex. 10, or else as grouped in the manner of Ex. 11, and depending on how one hears it, the remarkable ending will sound relaxed or tense. Beethoven's symphonies (the Fourth in particular) abound in similar effects, and someone who could not bring his auditory experience under the appropriate kind of voluntary control would be unable to appreciate their characteristic subtlety of construction.

Moreover, I cannot count as hearing a melody in a sequence of notes if I can say nothing at any point about what has gone before (for example, whether the theme was progressing upwards to the note in question or downwards, whether it was fast or slow, and so on). In particular, I must be able to say whether or not other phrases that I am now played correspond to what I previously heard: otherwise there is reason to doubt that I heard the sequence

Ex. 10   Beethoven: *Diabelli Variations*

Ex. 11

as a melody. In other words, I must be attending to what I hear if I am to hear it as a melody: 'hearing as', like amusement, is a mode of attention, and this suggests that it has the same close relation as amusement to the concept of thought. This again is unlike the normal experiences involved in hearing or seeing. It also suggests that one of the principal expressions of 'hearing as' will lie in what is said: in this respect the case is again somewhat similar to 'seeing as'.

This intuitive connection with thought is exemplified in the rationality of musical understanding: my knowledge of a piece of music may influence the way I hear it, by providing reasons (and not just causes) for my hearing it in a certain way. To return again to Ex. 9: this melody creates in me certain harmonic expectations – derived from the parallel sixth – and I hear it according to this harmonic pattern. The leap up of a sixth can, therefore, come to acquire a 'logical' character which in other contexts it would not have, and the decorative flourish of sixths in the final phrase of the melody seems entirely natural. We hear it as natural because of what we have learned to expect. In a similar way, our knowledge of a theme may enable us to hear it in a variation: hearing a variation involves a particular kind of thought process. It is not sufficient – nor is it necessary – to remember the original melody while hearing its variant, nor is it sufficient to think of the variant as similar (since there are many similar melodies that are not related in the manner of theme and variation). In hearing a variation we hear the variation as the original theme: we can recognize the original melody in it. (Compare thinking someone to look like his father, and then suddenly being struck by the similarity, so that one sees the father in his son's features.) This process is rational in the following sense: hearing the new theme as a variation (hearing Ex. 9a as a variation of the third phrase of Ex. 9, for example), is like discovering a relation between the two themes. But the peculiar feature is that this relation is something that we hear: we do not simply 'have it in mind' as we listen – it comes alive in the notes themselves. If this 'transformation' – as it might be called – of thought into experience were not possible, then there could hardly be such a thing as the criticism of abstract music. But the rationality of thought is transmitted to the experiences that depend on it: in reading criticism, for example, I may have my attention drawn to similarities and relationships between themes that – sometimes by an effort of will – I am afterwards able to hear in the themes themselves. As a result of this process my whole appreciation of a piece may be entirely altered. Whether or not I attempt to hear certain relations, or whether they become at all important to me, will depend largely on my sense of their significance. What is most important in music is clearly the way in which an intellectual grasp of structure and meaning can in this way become part of an auditory experience. In Hegel's words: 'what appeals in music is the formal unity which the unity of consciousness transfers to the temporal process, and which is thus re-echoed back to our conscious life.'[3]

Before drawing conclusions about the nature of musical understanding, we should reflect a little on the previous discussion of 'seeing as'. I argued that seeing X as Y is in some way like thinking of X as Y; on the other hand, I attempted to show that, in so far as it might be useful to conceive aspect perception as the sensory 'embodiment' of a thought, we must recognize that the thought itself can never be fully specified independently of the 'perception' in which it is embodied. We can now see that there are cases –

[3] *The Philosophy of Fine Art*, tr. Osmaston, vol. 1, pp. 333–4.

the hearing of melodies, and the seeing of patterns – where the element of thought has been reduced to something entirely formal. There is no way of achieving even a partial description of the *content* of the musical thought: we can only point once more to the experience in which it is 'embodied'. And yet the formal properties of thought remain, removing the experience of music from the realm of merely animal mentality. We have, then, taken the idea of a perceptual thought well beyond the point at which it could even be indicated apart from a perception. And what is interesting is that such thought-impregnated perceptions seem to lie at the heart of our understanding of art. It is because we can see patterns and figures that we can see representation in painting, and it is because we can hear melodies and sequences that we can hear expression in music. In other words, the media of painting and music are of their nature open to just the kind of imaginative interpretation of experience that we have placed at the heart of the aesthetic attitude: the possibility of aesthetic appreciation is intrinsic to the media themselves.

It is worth touching on another problem relating to the general idea of 'seeing as', a problem that I passed over in Chapter Eight, but which can now be tackled more directly. It will be asked, what is the precise difference between the man who hears a melody in a sequence of notes and the man who does not? The intuitive description of 'hearing as' that I have given is partly phenomenological: that is, it relies on metaphors that attempt to convey what the 'experience' is *like* without indicating how such an experience might be *ascribed*. What is the publicly observable basis for attributing experiences of this kind? It is reasonable to suppose that this basis will have some similarity to the circumstances in which we attribute normal perceptions (seeing, hearing, and so on), and also some similarity to the circumstances in which we attribute thoughts. Now the attribution of thoughts requires a certain background of behaviour. I can only attribute mathematical thoughts to someone who is able to display a measure of mathematical competence. In a similar manner there must be a recognized background of 'musical behaviour' before we can meaningfully attribute musical experiences to a man, and this behaviour will be in certain respects like the background behaviour of thought. It will involve preferences, choices, intentional activity, a sense of what is right and wrong. It is arguable that no such background is presupposed in the attribution of sensory experience (even though a background of *some* kind is required). Just as a man cannot understand a joke unless he has a sense of humour, or understand a proof unless he has a mastery of mathematics, so he cannot understand a melody unless he is in some way musical. In other words, in attempting to elucidate the notion of understanding music we are brought back immediately to just the capacities for enjoyment and appreciation that we attempted to describe. The understanding of music involves no process that cannot be assimilated to our account of aesthetic experience. Note that certain important consequences follow from the comparison with 'understanding jokes': for one thing, music is like humour in that there is more than one way of being musical. The background of musical behaviour is culturally determined, and its place in human thought and feeling is given by its place in a culture as a whole. Similarly musical understanding, like a sense of humour, may be educated and developed; it may also be 'morally' refined in certain ways that I shall not attempt to indicate.

Now if we return to the original problem – what is the difference between the man who hears the melody and the man who does not? – then we see that it may be very difficult to describe this difference in terms of what we may observe at the time. For they both hear the notes of the melody and they both may attend to what they hear. If, therefore, we rely only on the normal criteria of auditory experience we may be forced to say that their experiences are identical. The difference may lie only in the background of 'musical behaviour'. To insist that there must be some further difference at the time of hearing is to make a mistake about the nature of thought. The only reason why we can locate 'hearing as' in time with any precision is because it has an element of experience that carries with it the normal properties of exact occurrence and precise duration. But it is not sufficient for the ascription of 'hearing as' that we should locate a mere experience – 'hearing as' shares some of the properties of thought, and thought need not be related to the temporal sequence in the same exact way. The full difference between our two subjects may only come out later in what they say or do. But this cannot imply that the difference between them will not be logically adequate as a basis for describing their 'experience' differently.

I have argued that musical understanding involves certain capacities for experience that are in a sense *sui generis*. The discussion has concentrated on only one of these, but clearly there are many more: for example, the capacity to understand the sense and direction of an interval. Built on these elementary capacities is a whole structure of rational enjoyment, to describe which would be a formidable task. But if someone were to ask what is the value of the 'experiences' I have referred to, then it would be necessary to attempt a description of musical appreciation as a whole. What is important for present purposes is the conclusion that 'understanding' is here in part an experiential concept, and that its analysis does not involve any move away from the description of aesthetic appreciation that has already been given.

What is true of music is true of architecture: the understanding of architectural forms cannot be elucidated in theoretical terms alone. We must experience the balance of masses in St Peter's, just as we must see the rhythm of the columns in S. Spirito.[4] If architecture can have meaning over and above what is implied in these experiences, then this is only because we have first acquired the basic capacities which these experiences entail. The deeper significance of buildings, like that of paintings and symphonies, must be described in other terms: we must refer to the characteristics of representation, expression, imitation, and the rest. It is with these concepts, therefore, that our problems chiefly lie.

At first sight, however, it may seem that the above account of musical understanding can have little to do with the understanding of literature. Here, it might be said, what we call understanding *must* be divorced from the mere 'experience' of its object. It is worth going some way towards meeting this objection, since it serves to show the peculiarity of the relation of literature to sensory experience.

First of all, to understand a poem is not to understand what it literally means: Blake's poem *The Sick Rose* expresses a thought that could be grasped by anyone with a knowledge of the language, whether or not he also understood it as a poem. Although one may not understand a poem – *A Nocturnal upon St. Lucie's Day*,

---

[4] I develop this point at length elsewhere, through analysis of architectural experience and its relation to the experience of music. See 'Architectural Aesthetics', *B. J. A.*, 1973.

for example, or *Une Saison en Enfer* – because one does not understand what the poem says, it is I think, a commonplace of
criticism that there is more to literary understanding than merely
literal comprehension. On the other hand, it is also said that to
understand the *thought* that Blake's poem expresses is to understand more than the literal (that is to say, paraphraseable) meaning.
Poetic thought is more subtle, and has many levels beneath the
literal surface. And yet it might be argued that understanding is
none the less cognitive through being constrained beyond the
merely literal significance of words.

This theory, while persuasive, employs a notion of 'thought'
that obscures the problem with which I am trying to deal. In the
sense in which one may understand the thought of a scientific
or historical treatise the identity of a thought is secured not by the
identity of its expression but by the identity of the conditions for
its truth. That is, identity of what is said is, in the normal case,
independent of the identity of expression. To deny the distinction
between thought and expression in poetry is to deny that interest
in poetry is merely an interest in what is said (in the propositions
or thoughts that are expressed). Thus we find Eliot arguing
that metaphysical poetry expresses not thought but its emotional
equivalent, since emotion, unlike thought, can (logically) be
thought of as constituted by a single expression. But this emphasis
on the 'particularity' of an emotion relies, as I have argued in
Chapter Six, on a mere play of words: it is certainly the emptiest
explanation of why the poet's words cannot be paraphrased without loss of 'meaning'. All that this approach teaches us is that if
to understand a poem is to have knowledge of the thought or
feeling that is expressed by it, then 'thought' and 'feeling' are
being used in such a way that neither can be considered separable
from a given form of words. And this simply brings us back to
the main problem: what is it to understand the particular form of
words that constitutes the poem?

We may note first of all that, just as in the case of music, the
understanding of poetry brings with it a range of preferences:
certain ways of continuing a line will seem more appropriate
than others, even though the 'thought' that is expressed may in
each case be the same. Moreover, these preferences will involve
the *performance* of the poem: ways of reading it. (This point is
not affected by the fact that poetry need not be read aloud.)

Take the following lines from *Absalom and Achitophel*:

> Then, *Israel's* Monarch, after Heavens own heart,
> His vigorous warmth did, variously, impart
> To Wives and Slaves: And, wide as his Command,
> Scatter'd his Maker's Image through the Land.

It will be part of my understanding of this passage that I should wish to read it in a certain way, acknowledging the commas in the second line, pausing on the false rhyme of 'And', emphasizing the first syllable of 'Scatter'd' in such a way that the line seems to rush away after it to the end. My wanting to read the poem in this way is a direct consequence of my knowledge of what it means: I feel that the sound suits the sense. Clearly, then, the experience of hearing the words in a certain way may be a part of understanding. But it would be wrong to think of the understanding of poetry as simply another case of the 'hearing as' typical of musical appreciation. True, there have been attempts to explain the experience of literature in terms of a basic apprehension of structure and pattern, as we might explain the experience of music,[5] but such attempts court absurdity in failing to make clear that we appreciate poetry for what it means, and not, primarily, for its sound. To experience poetry as pure sound is not to understand it. Nor do we understand poetry in thinking of it as a combination of two separable elements – sound and meaning – with independent criteria of success. It is precisely when the two elements become separable in this way that poetry degenerates into bombast, as in certain works of Dylan Thomas.

However, the 'gestalt' experiences proper to music and painting also find their replica in the appreciation of literature, and it is a replica of a particularly interesting kind. For one's ability to hear words in a certain way cannot be described independently of one's grasp of their meaning: the experience of language and the 'experience' of meaning are inseparable. It is nonetheless true that, in hearing or reading words, one 'groups' them together in various ways, and this 'grouping' is part of the experience of hearing or reading in the way that the perception of a melody is part of the experience of hearing its constituent notes. Indeed, the experience of 'grouping' words together is so familiar to us that we borrow

---

[5] An example of this procedure is to be found in D. W. Prall, *Aesthetic Analysis*, ch. IV.

the vocabulary with which we normally refer to it to describe the musical 'gestalt': we say that a phrase is like a sentence, or a question (cf. the 'Muss es sein?' of Beethoven's Quartet in F op. 135); we speak of musical 'punctuation', musical 'phrases'; and so on. And yet our 'grouping' of words is also a part of our conception of their sense: we hear as grouped together those words that seem to make up a meaningful totality. This is so whether or not we also understand the words: we 'phrase' a foreign language in this way, even before we understand it. It is in this respect that poetry differs from the other arts. Our experience of poetry does not arise purely out of what is given to sense, but is consequent on a prior understanding of the medium of poetry as a means of discourse, with a semantic dimension that cannot be thought away. Thus, although the appreciation of poetry is, like the appreciation of all the arts, essentially perceptual, we see that its relation to sense is at once more subtle and more abstract than that of the other arts.

At the heart of our understanding of poetic metre and diction lies, then, a variety of experience not wholly unlike the 'hearing as' that determines musical enjoyment. And indeed we find that, at every point where a poem presents something that needs to be understood, understanding comes to rest in an 'experience', and not in a mere hypothesis or paraphrase. It is not the sense, but the impact of the line 'See, see, where Christ's blood streams in the firmament!' that requires the added syllable. And if there is a sense in which poetry is 'untranslatable' it is because we inevitably hear the words as 'filled with their meaning' when we attend to them aesthetically. A certain word sounds right in a certain place, and in aesthetic appreciation to sound right is to sound irreplaceable. In Mallarmé's beautiful lines

> Que non! par l'immobile et lasse pâmoison
> Suffoquant de chaleurs le matin frais s'il lutte,

we experience a heaviness in the word 'suffoquant' that would vanish if we attempted to put 'étouffant' in its stead. And it is this experience of heaviness that enters our understanding of the poem – our understanding of its mood.

Without this emphasis on the aesthetic experience it is indeed very difficult to account for the nature of criticism. Even the art

historian's scholarly comparisons have as their aim the transformation of experience. Take the following example: faced with
Cranach's *Adam* I may be disposed to treat the figure in the
manner of Renaissance nudes, whose nudity is of their essence,
the sign of a physical and moral confidence. But on reading
Wölfflin's analysis I find myself less prepared to see Cranach's
painting in such a way.[6] I shall now be conscious of its analogy
with Gothic art. The figure will approximate in my thought not
to those of Cranach's Italian contemporaries, but rather to the *S.
Sebastian* of Martin Schongauer, with its delicate form, and its
unified flow of body, tree and fluttering loin-cloth, and thence to
the tradition of Gothic drapery, with its emphasis on line at the
expense of structure. As a result of this comparison I see the
fragility of Cranach's figure more strongly emphasized. Indeed,
it will hardly be possible now to regard Adam as naturally naked:
he will seem like someone unable to brace himself for lack of
clothing. Cranach's Adam possesses a vulnerability of which even
Masaccio's Adam knows nothing. One might say that, as I come
to understand the picture, and the tradition behind it, its aspect
begins to change. Even here, the complex process of comparison
comes to rest in an 'experience'. And, formally at least, this
experience is analogous to the process of understanding music.

This is not to say that there is no more to understanding art
than the ability to 'perceive aright'. There is a sense in which no
one unfamiliar with religious experience can understand the late
quartets of Beethoven, no one ignorant of medieval civilization
can understand the *Divine Comedy*, and no one unversed in Counter-
reformation attitudes can understand the Oratory of Borromini.
But we should be able to prove that even here interpretation leads
to experience, in the sense that, only when knowledge alters the
experience of a work of art does it become part of one's understanding. But this leaves us with a new problem. For the further
levels of significance that affect our understanding of art – the
levels of representation and expression, for example – seem to
demand just the kind of cognitive analysis of aesthetic interest
that I have in this chapter been combatting. We must, therefore,
turn our attention to representation and expression, and attempt
to describe their place in the appreciation of art.

[6] Heinrich Wölfflin, *The Sense of Form in Art*, pp. 21–85.

CHAPTER THIRTEEN
Representation

At first sight it seems natural to account for representation and expression in terms of an entirely cognitive theory of appreciation, and this will be at variance with any view – such as ours – that gives precedence to the aesthetic experience. For representation and expression seem to be semantic properties – ways in which a work of art refers beyond itself to objects and properties with which it is not identical. To see what a work of art represents or expresses might, therefore, be like seeing what a sentence refers to: it might involve learning to understand the work of art as one symbol among many, with a function that is primarily referential. Understanding a work of art will be analogous to understanding a sentence: it will involve a grasp of certain propositions about the objects represented and the states of mind expressed. And it is tempting to say that once this understanding is achieved a large part of the significance of a work of art has been grasped. If, then, so much of the significance of a work of art is to be given purely in terms of semantic properties, how can we argue that understanding and appreciating a work of art is not primarily a cognitive matter – that it is not, for example, like understanding the meaning of a sentence?

This new form of cognitive theory must be distinguished from that which explained aesthetic appreciation as the 'perception' of aesthetic features. The semantic view does not confine appreciation to a knowledge of specific features of its object. What is known, according to the semantic theory, is not a fact about the work of art itself, although appreciation depends on having some knowledge of the work of art. From works of art we learn not about themselves but about the world to which they refer. They are systems of symbols which transmit to us, much as a language transmits to us, an awareness of the world in which we live. The semantic theory can, therefore, offer a more intelligible picture of aesthetic appreciation than the theory of aesthetic perception discussed in Chapter Three.

To treat aesthetic appreciation as a species of cognition is, of course, by no means new. Perhaps the most famous exponent of such a view was Hegel, who conceived art as a mode of human knowledge contrasted with philosophical thought; art seeks to arrive at an order in experience through the achievement of an embodied concept. For Hegel, as for the idealists generally, there can be no sharp distinction between cognitive and non-cognitive mental states. All mental life is a mode of thought, an attempt to impose order on the flux of experience, and knowledge is the successful achievement of an order that would otherwise not exist. Similar views have found expression in works of aesthetics in the analytical tradition: in Susanne Langer's *Feeling and Form*, for example, and, most notably, in Nelson Goodman's *Languages of Art*. It is interesting that Goodman – whose views I shall have cause to refer to several times in this and the following chapter – takes over many of the idealist's premises. In particular, he refuses to acknowledge a clear division between cognitive and non-cognitive states of mind. He attacks the view, which he associates with attempts to describe aesthetic appreciation in terms of 'empathy', that the emotions are essentially *contrasted* with thought. On the contrary, he affirms, emotion is itself a mode of cognition.[1] Thus even if we do find arguments for saying that emotion has a large part to play in aesthetic appreciation this does not show that aesthetic appreciation is not a search for truth. For Goodman, as for the Idealist, the aesthetic and scientific attitudes are contiguous members of a single spectrum; the motive of each is curiosity and the end awareness.

It is of some interest to examine the semantic approach to representation since the semantic theory offers a direct challenge to all that has already been said. If the theory of previous chapters is correct, then it seems that the purpose of representation will be to guide the imagination, so that the thoughts involved in

[1] Op. cit., p. 248.

aesthetic interest will refer to predetermined objects. But to be interested in an object as a representation is not necessarily to be interested in it as a means for presenting these thoughts. On the contrary, the thoughts themselves may be essentially bound up with the perception of an aesthetic object, in the manner of 'seeing as'. To see an object as a representation is to see it under a description, a description which may be part of one's reason for attending to it, and hence part of the basis of aesthetic interest. However, only certain ways of analysing 'representation' will be compatible with this Kantian point of view. In particular we will find that our analysis must restrict the place of 'truth' in aesthetic interest. Moreover, representation may occur in a variety of ways, according to the medium – through the presentation of aspects in painting, for example, or through direct description in works of literature. We must also show that these separate forms (depiction and description) are from the aesthetic point of view analogous.

For the semantic theory there is no difficulty in showing this. The analogy is held to lie in the fact that depiction and description are both symbolic and must be understood semantically. Indeed, it is through the study of representation that a defender of the semantic theory will wish to show how our understanding of pictures resembles our understanding of words. It seems but a small step to go on to describe both representation and expression in terms appropriate to our ordinary understanding of symbols and signs. Even if we must conclude that there is something special in our understanding of art – so that works of art are only 'presentational' symbols, say[2] – it may still be that we have discovered in the theory of symbolism the clue to much if not all of our understanding of the forms of art, as well as to much of the value and significance of art.

The semantic theory starts from the premise that no account of depiction in terms of resemblance, or in terms of similarity of appearance, can possibly account for the relation between a picture and what we might call, for convenience' sake, its 'object'. Our knowledge of what a painting represents depends at least in part on our understanding of certain conventions governing the portrayal of perspective, movement, light and shade. Such con-

[2] Susanne Langer, *Philosophy in a New Key* and *Feeling and Form*.

ventions cannot be explained in terms of a notion of identity of appearance between painting and object. Goodman,[3] following Gombrich,[4] has argued that the whole notion of an identity of appearance shows a misconception of the problem. We can only speak of identity of appearance if the appearances which are to be compared are already, in some sense, brought under a classification. We cannot, for example, compare the appearance of a representation with the way something looks to the 'naked' eye – there is no naked eye. Any specification of the way a thing looks will already involve *descriptions* of it whose claim to denotational accuracy is founded no differently from the claims of a picture.[5] A picture cannot, therefore, be compared for accuracy with an appearance, and spoken of as a representation to the extent that it copies or shares that appearance. The only thing that has the appearance of a picture is another picture, but this is not what the picture represents.

It is tempting, in view of these difficulties, to assimilate the concept of representation to that of reference. Plainly, it is because words refer that novels represent. So why should reference not be the core of representation, even in the visual arts? Such is the view of thinkers like Gombrich and Goodman. Representation, according to Goodman, for example, is simply a species of denotation, and, like denotation it is, in its primary occurrence, fully extensional. Thus a picture of the Duke of Wellington is *ipso facto* a picture of the man who won the Battle of Waterloo. And whatever the difficulties that might stand in the way of explaining *how* denotation or reference arises out of extensionality, it might be argued that these difficulties are no more easy to solve in the case of language than in the case of pictures. Once we grasp how the construction '*a* is a picture of *b*' can be interpreted extensionally, then the analogy between depiction and description becomes very impressive. For a description denotes an object in virtue of its sense – that is, by attributing a character to it. Similarly, we might say, it is the sense of the picture that enables it to denote. It attributes a definite character to its object. Moreover, like a completed sentence, the picture goes on to tell us something

---

[3] *Languages of Art*, ch. 1.
[4] E. H. Gombrich, *Art and Illusion*, pp. 297–8.
[5] Goodman, op. cit., p. 9.

about the object that it denotes, and it is a faithful picture to the extent that what it 'says' is true.

Clearly, then, we should account for the representation of a fictional object as we would account for empty description. The fictional painting has a definite sense, but no reference. Painting an imaginary object is like writing a story. If we speak of adequate, correct, or telling representation in these cases, it can only be because the painting or the story convey information about the *kinds* of things to which their fictional objects belong. It would seem then that realism in literature and realism in painting are related notions.

But it is here, I think, that the analogy with language breaks down. If depiction is like reference, then it is arguable that there must be both an extensional and an intensional construction of the form '*a* is a picture of *b*', according to whether the picture is a portrait or an imaginary scene. Thus we have the construction '*X* is a picture of a unicorn', which conveys no reference to a unicorn. If we are to explain what is important about the extensional interpretation of '*a* is a picture of *b*' (in which this sentence entails $(\exists x)(x = b)$), then we should be prepared to explain the supposed intensional interpretation too. We must establish the connection of *sense* between the two constructions. For if we are to take the analogy between pictures and symbols as seriously as the semantic theory suggests, then we should not allow that whether or not there *is* an object corresponding to what is 'shown' in a picture has any bearing on the nature of the picture as a symbol, or on its place in the scheme of symbols that enables it to denote. It is the property of a picture that is marked out by the intensional use of '*a* is a picture of . . .' that we must analyse if the semantic view of art is to have the cogency and value that it claims for itself. We must show that this property is a property which belongs to a painting as a member of a scheme of symbols, and that it can, *as such*, play the part in aesthetic appreciation that representational properties are generally thought to play. Clearly, aesthetic appreciation of a picture is directed towards its representational properties in this (intensional) sense, and not to the further property, that it may or may not have, of actually denoting, or corresponding to, an item in the world.

The difficulties for the semantic theory can be clearly seen through an examination of Goodman's views. Goodman argues that the proposition 'X is a picture of a unicorn' is, when construed intensionally, not relational. It must be construed as the combined assertion of two propositions 'X is a picture', and 'X is of-a-unicorn', where 'of-a-unicorn' is construed as an unbreakable one-place predicate.[6] But now the question arises 'How do we account for the meaning of this predicate "of-a-unicorn"?' To this question Goodman gives a nominalist answer. We learn, he says, to classify pictures as unicorn-pictures; that is, we learn to apply the predicate 'of-a-unicorn' to them, and that we *do* classify them in this way is a fact as basic and as little in need of explanation, as the fact that we learn to classify objects as 'red' or 'men', 'horses' or 'unicorns'. 'All that directly matters', he says,[7] 'is that pictures are indeed sorted with varying degrees of ease into man-pictures, unicorn-pictures, Pickwick-pictures, winged-horse pictures, etc., just as pieces of furniture are sorted into desks, tables, chairs, etc. And this fact is unaffected by the difficulty, in either case, of framing definitions for the several classes or eliciting a general principle of classification.'

But it can be immediately objected to this that it fails to explain the sense in which our classification of pictures is secondary to our classification of the objects they portray. We would not know what was being said in applying the term 'man-picture' to a picture unless we knew what was said in applying the term 'man' to an item in the world. But Goodman thinks that he has an answer to this:

> We can learn to apply 'corncob pipe' or 'staghorn' without first understanding, or knowing how to apply, 'corn' or 'cob' or 'corncob' or 'pipe' or 'stag' or 'horn' as separate terms. And we can learn, on the basis of samples, to apply 'unicorn-picture' not only without ever having seen any unicorns but without ever having seen or heard the word 'unicorn' before. Indeed, largely by learning what are unicorn-pictures and unicorn-descriptions do we come to understand the word 'unicorn'; and our ability to recognize a staghorn may help us to recognize a stag when we see one.[8]

[6] *Languages of Art*, op. cit., and reply to Wollheim, *J. Phil.*, 1970.
[7] *Languages of Art*, p. 24.
[8] Ibid., pp. 24–5.

It is doubtful, however, that this reply is able to rebut the spirit of the objection. For the objection could equally be phrased the other way round, asking how it is that our knowledge of the application of 'unicorn-picture' could possibly enable us to learn the application of 'unicorn'? The point is that, unless the word 'unicorn' means the same when it stands alone and when it stands in the unbreakable predicate 'of-a-unicorn', we have no explanation of how it is that we can learn the meaning of both locutions together. This is not a small difficulty, for we now see that we lack an explanation of why we react to pictures of unicorns as we do (why they make us think of unicorns), and that we also lack an explanation of how we can extend all our ordinary language for talking of the world to talk of pictures without having to learn the trick afresh for every picture that we come across.[9] *Merely* to assert that the predicate 'of-a-unicorn' is unbreakable does not explain the fact that we use precisely this predicate to locate the picture's place in a scheme of symbols. What is the function of the word 'unicorn' here?

It is important to see that this question is not simply a request for the kind of explanation of the meaning of a term that the nominalist forbids. We need not object to the nominalist presuppositions of Goodman's theory, even though these presuppositions might have encouraged the view that appreciating art is like understanding language. The objection could be phrased without arguing against nominalism. For suppose that it is true that there is no explanation of the fact that we apply the description 'man' to all men, other than the simple fact that this is how we classify. Then, of course, there will be no explanation why we call a man a man, why we use the term 'man' to apply to just this thing. But it does not follow that there will be no explanation of why we include the term 'man' in a complex predicate that denotes pictures of men. Indeed, we saw in Chapter Four that there could be explanations of the meaning of a word in a new application in terms of its previous meaning, and these explanations did not in any way presuppose the falsity of

[9] Compare the difficulty encountered by traditional theories of *oratio obliqua* in explaining how it is that an understanding of ordinary speech can enable one to understand reported speech. See D. Davidson, 'On Saying That', in D. Davidson and J. Hintikka (eds.), *Words and Objections*.

nominalism as a view about the ultimate basis of our classificatory scheme.

That there must be an answer to the question why the term 'man' can occur within the scope of the intensional context '*a* is a picture of . . .' is suggested by considering not the nature of representation but rather the way in which representation is appreciated. If a picture of a man is to be properly appreciated it must at least be possible to see the picture as a man (to see a man in the picture). Now we speak of 'seeing a picture as a man' and clearly we mean to refer to a relation between this process and others that we call 'seeing a man', 'thinking of a man', and so on. It is a peculiarity of the first and third of these locutions that in standard cases one cannot allow quantification into the position occupied by the expression 'a man', whereas one can allow this in the case of the second locution. But of course it would be absurd to conclude that, just because the term 'man' occurs in the first locution as part of what is in this sense an unbreakable two-place predicate ('. . . sees . . . as a man'), the term 'man' has a different sense here from its normal sense. On the contrary, the term must have the same sense in either case, for in order to explain what it is to see something as a man we must take for granted an ability to apply the ordinary concept of a man, and it is in terms of this ordinary concept that our explanation will be couched.

A theory of representation must, therefore, enable us to explain the connection of meaning between 'man' and 'man-picture'. But can the semantic theory really do this? A natural way of attempting the needed explanation would be to invoke the supposed parallel between paintings and verbal symbols. Thus we might say that a painting belongs to a scheme of symbols which are used to denote objects such as men, mountains, rivers and horses. It is by understanding this feature that we learn to classify paintings as pictures of men, and so on. Now it is unobjectionable to suggest that, if this is so, a painting can have a place in the symbol scheme that is proper to being a man-picture without actually *denoting* a man. Its place in the scheme is fixed not by its reference but by its sense. It is, therefore, the conventions of the symbol-scheme (the meaning-rules) that would enable us to understand that a given symbol is of the kind that could denote a man. In other words, we explain the notion of a man-picture or unicorn-picture on the analogy of the place of terms in a language (such as 'man' and 'unicorn') that are used referringly. But we can imagine giving 'sense' to a picture (in the way we give 'sense' to words) in an indefinite number of ways, and the aspect of the picture need play no part in determining this 'sense'. So the relation between representation and visual appreciation will now be entirely arbitrary. Explaining the notion of representation in *this* way has the consequence that representation is of no relevance to aesthetic interest. Moreover, if we explain the notion of a man-picture through the analogy with the place occupied by certain denoting-phrases in a language, then it seems extremely odd that pictures do not have a standard use in communication, as words do. If we speak of words as denoting or referring to individuals this is not merely because singular terms sometimes occur extensionally. Extensionality of occurrence is not sufficient to secure reference. It is necessary also that the sentences in which terms occur extensionally can be *used* to refer to individuals. In other words, the semantic property of reference or denotation arises out of the pragmatic property of a referential use. Now a picture *can* be used on occasion to stand for what it represents, but here its role is determined by quite different considerations from those that are active in aesthetic interest. It is essential to the notion of a denoting phrase in language that it should be possible to use it in assertions, in questions, in conditionals, in commands, and so on: in speech-acts where reference occurs. Now truth and falsity belong primarily to assertions, not to questions and commands. It would, therefore, seem that, if we are to use the analogy with language to show how a picture can be a true or false picture of what it denotes, we must say that pictures can have a standard use in communication, and that in this use they occur in assertoric form. But it is arguable that we can only speak of assertion where there is at least the possibility of other speech-acts, such as questions and commands. We can imagine pictures being used to make assertions, but the circumstances in which we can imagine this are also circumstances in which pictures could be used to ask questions or make commands. In these circumstances – which, of course, will have nothing to do with aesthetic appreciation – pictures would function like semaphor signals. But it is not the context of aesthetic interest that gives this use to pictures. We can indeed learn from a picture how a certain man looked, but there are normally no grounds for supposing that the picture is being used to *assert* that this is how he looked. For this to be possible, we should have to be able to tell when the picture is not asserting, but rather questioning whether this was how he looked, commanding that he should look like this, supposing that this is how he looked, and so on. It is because these notions have no application to the part of pictorial representation which is the object of aesthetic interest that the semantic theory breaks down as an account of appreciation.

It might be argued that when we cannot quantify into a context, then we should first look for an explanation of this fact in terms of a reference to some mental item – intention, experience, belief or desire – whose 'intentional object' causes reference to fail. If '*a* is a picture of *b*' were to mean '*a* is intended to resemble *b*', or '*a* can be seen as *b*', then '*b*' would occur in each case as part of a complex psychological predicate, and serve to identify the so-called 'intentional object' of a mental state. If this were so, then we can explain the failure of reference while conserving the connection of meaning between the extensional and intensional constructions of '*a* is a picture of *b*'. We might compare knowledge with belief: if I know that *p* then what I know is what I believe when I believe that *p*. Suppose that *X* knows that *Fa*. It follows from this that $(\exists x)(Fx)$, although this does not follow from '*X* believes that *Fa*'. Yet '*Fa*' has not changed sense from the first context to the second. The difference between the two contexts can be explained immediately: the first involves at least two separate propositions: '*X* believes that *Fa*' and '*Fa* is true'. The second of these carries the reference to *a* that is lacking in the first. Similarly, someone might plausibly argue that the difference between the extensional and the intensional senses of 'to represent' amounts to no more than the difference between, say, '*a* can be seen as *b* and $(\exists x)(x = b)$', and '*a* can be seen as *b*' (where '*a*' and '*b*' are singular terms). The intensional sense would then be prior, the central component of meaning in either construction. Such a theory would, of course, encounter none of the difficulties that have so far been raised.

However, there are other difficulties that this rather simple aspect theory is unable to overcome, and for the sake of completeness I shall suggest various ways in which the theory might be amended. First, the theory is unable to distinguish between genuine representations and other objects (such as clouds, shadows, etc.) in which aspects can be seen. Secondly, it does not sufficiently restrict the range of objects (in the extensional, or material sense) of a given picture. For example, a portrait executed before the time of Wellington may, nonetheless, have the aspect of Wellington, but it can hardly be a portrait of *Wellington*. Thirdly, the theory gives no account of the place of convention and tradition in our understanding of what a picture represents. Finally, it gives no criterion of realism; unlike the semantic theory, which analyses the notion of realism in terms of the ease with which accurate information is conveyed, the theory gives no grounds for distinguishing between a realistic and an unrealistic representation of a single object.

The aspect theory must allow for the fact that representing is something that human beings do, and an object is a representation only in so far as someone has made it to represent something. Cliffs, clouds and trees, unlike pictures, do not typically represent what we see in them. Moreover, it is not always possible to see pictures as what they represent (e.g. the child's incompetent drawing of his father). It is because of such considerations that the semantic theory has immediate appeal. Denoting, like representing, is something that human beings do; it is not judged in terms of how we see the final product.

Clearly, the aspect theory must be amended to include a reference to the painter's intention: we must say that a painting is a painting of X only if it is *intended* to be seen as X. It would follow from this definition that it is the products of human activity that have representational properties; moreover what they represent is independent of how we can see them. But there will be nothing more to pictorial representation (from the point of view of appreciation) than the presented aspect – the aspect of the painting is the true object of aesthetic interest, and gives the description under which the painting must be seen.

This simple emendation also enables us to overcome the second objection. The artist's intention will serve to restrict the (material) object of a portrait. For a to be a picture of b in the extensional sense it is necessary that *a* should have been produced with the intention that it should be seen as *b*. It is not sufficient that *a* should have the aspect of *b* and that *b* should, as a matter of fact, exist. In this sense depiction differs from photography; for while the material object of a picture is identified through an intention,[10] the material object of a photograph is given by a relation that is purely causal.

The inclusion of a reference to intention further enables us to answer the third objection. In order to know what a painting represents it is necessary to understand the artist's intention, and it is clear that convention and tradition may well have an important part to play in revealing intention. Intention requires a background of pre-established expectations, together with a medium of action in which the intention's fulfilment is possible. The artist will, therefore, lean on those features of tradition and convention that will enable his intention to become clear, for our understanding of his intention will influence how we see his picture. It might be objected that if revealed intention has such an important part to play in our understanding of art, it is surprising that paintings are not accompanied by written instructions which explain how they must be seen. It might seem odd that artists have to rely on such devices as convention and tradition, which are comprehensible at best only to someone with an established habit of looking at pictures. But there are two replies to this objection. First, many paintings do have, in the form of a title, some instructions as to how they should be seen. Secondly, it is necessary to remind ourselves of the complexity of the phenomenon of 'seeing as'. It is intrinsic to the notion of an aspect that it should be indeterminate, and hence ambiguous. Even the most straightforward picture is a picture of an object some of whose properties are not determined by what we see. We assume that the lady whose

[10] Here we should take note of two interesting features of the analysis. First, it requires us to quantify into an opaque context (in order to explain the sense in which a picture can be *of the Duke of Wellington*). Secondly, it commits us to assertions of 'intentional identity', as when I say that *X* is a picture of the object represented in *Y*, without meaning to imply that such an object exists. But these are not objections to our theory. On the contrary, it is a merit in the analysis that it does justice to the obvious logical complexities of the sentence '*X* is a picture of Pickwick', rather than ignoring them through the invention of an unbreakable predicate, as Goodman does.

portrait we are studying has another side, here invisible, just as we assume that a half-size painting of fighting men is not a life-size depiction of embattled dwarfs. These assumptions determine our experience, even though they are themselves undetermined by the picture. Now if tradition and convention play a part in the understanding of a painting it is not because they help us to see it as, say, a seated woman in a garden (although they may help us to do this). The function of the conventions and traditions that a painting invokes may be to draw attention to fine shades of expression and gesture, to relations and contrasts that it would be otherwise difficult to see in the configuration of coloured patches. But these fine shades and relations are seen in the picture, just as the physical outline is seen. We see not only a woman's face, but also a face that has known suffering, a face that someone has admired, and so on. To rely on verbal instructions to convey these fine shades of thought and feeling would be to disrupt the observer's interest, to remove his attention from what is visual precisely where he most needs to look and see. Convention and tradition imbue the painting with a sense of intention; the artist's meaning becomes through their aid a visible reality. The observer is always able to ask 'Why did the artist draw attention to *that*?', a question which, outside any determination of what should and what should not be portrayed in a painting, scarcely makes sense. The least we can say is that, without conventions, there could be no dramatic significance in art.

As an example, we might consider Manet's exploitation of Venetian conventions in his *Olympia*. By keeping to Titian's formula, involving an accompanying figure, and a rich embellishment of drapery, Manet was able to create a visual relation between his model and her Venetian prototypes that reveals – as a predominantly visual impression – much of the woman's character. In Titian the drapery and the accompanying figure are characteristically used to offset the naturalness of the naked body, to bring it into relation with normal worldly commerce. As a result, the sexuality is mellowed, and the dignity of the human figure emphasized. In Manet's picture, on the other hand, the atmosphere has been shattered by one or two small but immensely suggestive touches – the cord around the neck, the vulgar *sabats* on the feet – which restore a kind of sexual unrest on a quite different level.

The picture acquires a sad, urban, desultory sensuality, and because of this we can see the character of the woman in the picture, just as we see her strange surroundings. Manet was able to achieve this quite peculiar value by leaning on a tradition from which he departed with the greatest economy of means, so that our expectations are simultaneously encouraged and betrayed. It is precisely because his intention can only be seized through a visual impression that it plays such an important part in our aesthetic interest.[11]

It should be noted that I have treated convention not as a part of the analysis of depiction but rather as one factor among many that affect our interest in it. Convention functions as a direct and intelligible index of the artist's intention. But this is by no means the only effect of convention in art, and later I shall return to survey some of its wider significances. It is worth remarking, however, that, introduced in this way, through the notion of convention, the emphasis on intention by no means implies the heteronomy of aesthetic judgement.

The final objection is the most interesting of the four. How is it possible to explain the concept of realism in pictorial represent-ation? It is agreed that we will find no criterion for realistic representation in the notion of resemblance, since a picture resembles another picture more closely than it resembles anything else. The most a picture can do, it will be said, is resemble the *look* of its object. But how can we account for this kind of resemblance except by invoking once again the notion of an aspect? Thus Goodman criticizes the resemblance theory of realism on the grounds that in referring to the realism of a depiction we can only mean to be referring to the *ease* with which we recognize it visually as a symbol for its object. There is no independent criterion of what it is for two objects to look alike: certainly there is no criterion to be discovered in the science of geo-metrical optics, on which theories of perspective are usually based.[12]

But this criticism of the resemblance theory is, I think, too hasty. Certainly Goodman's alternative to it will not do; the

[11] A similar and yet more daring exploitation of the same traditional 'repertoire' occurs in Gauguin's masterpiece: 'The Spirit of the Dead Watches'.

[12] *Languages of Art*, pp. 10–19.

child's picture of his father may be more easily recognizable than the realistic portrait in *chiaroscuro*. Moreover it is wrong, as the earlier discussions should have made clear, to analyse the notion of an aspect in terms of an identity of appearance. An *animal* may notice an identity of appearance, but it cannot, logically, perceive an aspect. Of course, some pictures also *look like* what they can be seen as, and the extent to which they do this is a matter of degree. One duck actually looks like another, a decoy duck looks very similar, a naturalistic life-size colour photograph of a duck is also (from certain angles) a plausible likeness, and so on in a descending scale until we reach the ducks that can be discerned in the unjoined dots of a puzzle picture, or in the folds of a painted garment.[13] The most important difference between cases at either end of this spectrum is that, whereas in one case you have to be thinking if you are to see the aspect in the picture, in the other case (the case of same appearance) you do not need to think in order to be struck by the similarity – your natural inclination is to take the object before you *for* a duck, and this does not necessarily involve the perception of an aspect at all.

This immediately gives us a criterion for distinguishing the case where X sees a as b from the case where a looks to X as b looks. In the latter case we may say that a looks to X exactly as b looks (a looks the same as b to X) if, under normal circumstances, and going only on the basis of the way a looks, X would take a to be b (believe a to be b). In other words, identity of appearance involves the permanent possibility of illusion. This is not to say that X will actually be deceived: in many cases he will possess further information – such as that he is looking at a picture – which prevents him from taking a for b. But this is no objection to our account of sameness of appearance. In order to make the definition clear, however, we should have to specify what is meant by the phrase 'going only on the basis of the way a looks'. This would involve reference to such facts as X's eyes being open and directed at a, X being conscious, a causing in X, by the mediation of his eyes, the belief in the existence of something that X would naturally take to be b, and so on. But, however this notion of 'looking' be analysed, the solution to the problem of the identity of appearance remains.

[13] Cf. S. Freud, *Leonardo da Vinci*.

Now the normal case of 'seeing as' does not involve identity of appearance in this sense – if it did, then most painting would be *trompe-l'œil*. 'Seeing as' exhibits no tendency to illusion. We might put this point by saying that while the central expression of a sensory experience is also the expression of a perceptual belief, the central expression of 'seeing as' is the expression of a thought that is 'unasserted'. If we were to look for an analysis of realism in terms of identity of appearance, therefore, not only should we be forced to conclude that the number of realistic paintings is extremely small, but we should also be committed to the naïve, illusionistic, view of aesthetic experience that was rejected in Chapter Nine.

It might be said, none the less, that 'seeing as' involves the perception of a *similarity* of appearance, and that we should define realism in terms of this 'similarity'. But we find that, either this invocation of 'similarity' says nothing at all, or else it renders the recognition of realism quite mysterious. The notion of a 'similarity of appearance' can be construed either intentionally or materially. By the intentional construction I mean the sense in which a similarity of appearance depends on a similarity between the *experience* of seeing an aspect and the *experience* of seeing the object. In Chapter Eight I argued that there is indeed such a similarity, but I also argued that it must be construed as 'irreducible'. It can be explained only as the similarity that exists between the experience of seeing X as Y and the experience of seeing Y. In the present case, therefore, it gives us no independent criterion of realism. By the material construction I mean the sense in which 'similarity of appearance' is explained in terms of a greater or less congruence in visual features between the painting and its object (or between the painting and some object that is identical in appearance with the object of the painting), together with some specification of the 'direction' of congruence. For example, one might test similarity of appearance by scanning the picture and its object from left to right, top to bottom, matching points of colour against each other. (A variety of procedures suggest themselves.) But now we shall be unable to explain why the recognition of realism is immediate, and depends on no piecemeal comparison between the picture and its object.

In fact we can define realism more usefully if we ignore 'appearance' altogether: in this the semantic approach to representation is surely right. But it does not follow that we must also discard the notion of an aspect. A realistic representation *a* of *b*'s face is not one where *a* looks like *b*'s face, but one where *the face I see in a* is like *b*'s face. This explains why the recognition of realism is immediate, for the face I see in the picture, being an 'intentional' object of sight, presents its features to me 'immediately'. Now there is a definite sense in which what is seen in a picture imposes conditions on the appearance of the picture. If *a* is seen as *b* then, if *b* is many-featured, there must be a multiplicity of observable features in *a*. I cannot see a round face in a square outline, nor can I see a face with ears in a smooth circle. Suppose that I see the following figure as a face. Here there are certain questions that do not apply: for example, 'What kind of ears does the face have? What kind of hair? Nose? What colour is it?' and so on. And if I ask what shape is the face that I see then the answer must be 'Square' – a feature that no face can have. The more questions of this sort to which there is either no answer, or else an answer that gives some feature which the represented object lacks, the less realistic the representation.

This account of realism enables us to draw an interesting conclusion. Not every feature of the face that I see in the picture is a feature of its appearance (i.e. a colour or a shape). Hence a realistic depiction of the appearance of a face might in other respects be unrealistic. It makes sense to say that, while Guido Reni's head of Christ is a realistic portrait of the appearance of a suffering face, the Christ of some more primitive master (such as Cimabue) is more realistic as a depiction of the suffering: it *reveals more* of the suffering. Realism is always realism *in a certain respect*. One can also argue that the Florentines were right to hail Masaccio as the discoverer of a more realistic mode of painting. What is realistic is after all not relative to the ease with which information is conveyed.

In other words, the definition of depiction in terms of the presentation of an aspect leads naturally to an intelligible concept of pictorial realism. A painting represents *b* if it is intended to be seen as *b* (where '*b*' stands proxy for a name, a definite description or an indefinite description). The painting is a successful representation to the extent that it can be seen as *b*, and it is realistic to the extent that it is naturally seen as an object that resembles *b*. Such an account should leave us in no doubt as to how the appreciation of representational features in painting can be part of aesthetic interest, as this was described in Chapter Ten.

Note, however, that we must depart from our previous account of the logic of aesthetic description. For in saying that a painting represents *b* I am referring to a genuine property of it: I am saying that it is intended to be seen as *b*. This is a fact about the painting that I can know whether or not I see it as *b*. But this departure should not worry us – indeed, we shall discover the need for a similar departure in analysing the concept of expression. Although the important facts about both representation and expression must be stated in terms of our reactions to works of art, the logic of these two notions is (or, in the case of expression, can be) a logic of description. It is for this reason that they lend themselves so readily to a cognitive theory of aesthetic interest. This departure from the standard logic of aesthetic judgement has no serious consequences for our theory of appreciation.

So far I have said nothing about representation in forms of art other than painting. In what way is pictorial representation like representation in literature? And does it make sense to attribute representational properties to music? The answer to the first of these questions is clear. We speak of representation in literature not only because of the formal similarities with depiction noted by the semantic theory, but also, and primarily, because there is a place for description in the appreciation of literature which is exactly similar to the place of depiction in the appreciation of visual art. We may summarize the similarities as follows: first, in understanding a piece of literature as a representation we may suspend our judgement of its literal truth; we appreciate it not as a means for conveying information, but rather as a vehicle of thought in whatever form. The thought involved in appreciation of literature is, characteristically, 'unasserted', but this does not mean that *truth* is irrelevant to aesthetic interest. On the contrary, without an interest in truth, it would be impossible to be interested in meaning, and hence impossible to be interested in literature at all.[14] Now there is a sense in which one may appreciate a poem,

[14] This point has been well defended by R. K. Elliott, 'Poetry and Truth', *Analysis*, 1967.

say, for the truth of what it says, as one appreciates Blake's lines:

> Love seeketh only self to please,
> To bind another to its delight,
> Joys in another's loss of ease,
> And builds a Hell in Heaven's despite.

Similarly one may admire a play or a novel for the truthfulness of its vision, where truthfulness means truthful depiction. Here the 'unasserted' thoughts involved in understanding the work may depend for their existence on the recognition of certain complex truths conveyed by the novel or the play. It is part of the 'impurity' of the novel that, more than other literary forms, it hovers in this way between assertive and unassertive discourse. But in none of these cases is truth the *object* of appreciation: if it were such then the content of the work could be phrased in any abstract way, and one's interest would not outlive the perception of its truth. An interest in truth alone must treat all works of literature as documentaries, in the manner of 'socialist realism'.

Secondly, representation in literature is like representation in painting in that it is partly dependent on the author's intentions. Since the intentions are realized, if at all, in language, and since the language of literature is, in general, the language of the readers of literature, it might seem that there should be little discrepancy between the intention and the final result. But once again, we must remember that what is represented in literature is not only the gross outlines of human life, but also the fine details – shades of behaviour, and complexities of motive. Awareness of an author's intention can be an important guide in our thought of these elusive things. A sense of intention may thus infect our whole way of reading literature, and without an understanding of the conventions through which intention is focused, it is often impossible to acquire any sense of literary tone. Thus, an awareness of intention determines our appreciation of such devices as irony, which in turn determines our awareness of what is being described. When, in Joyce's *Ulysses*, the two heroes, Bloom and Stephen, are finally brought together, the imaginary narrator of 'Ithaca' contrives, in a series of devastating questions and answers, to destroy the sense that anything has passed between them. In this device we recognize an intention to neutralize dramatic possibilities. (For no

relationship could be formed in this meeting that is not sentimental or banal.) We come to understand that, while Stephen's
presence elicits from Bloom a sense of paternal responsibility,
so that for the first time he fully conceives himself as an individual
standing against the current of mere animal existence, inheriting
consciousness and passing it on, Stephen cannot be the object of
this feeling. On the contrary we recognize it as the natural fulfilment of Bloom's experience, tying up the ragged ends of his day's
adventure, and bestowing on him the nimbus of moral authority
that he has struggled all day to deserve. In this way our understanding of the character of Bloom is determined by a sense of
the author's ironic intention, an intention that is nowhere stated,
but which reveals itself in the structure and language of the work.
It is through such discrete revelations of intention that literary
styles develop, and it is through the development of style that
literature becomes capable of representing at a stroke what the
common reader would take a lifetime to observe.

Finally, there is room for a notion of realism in literature:
realism is the description of particular things as things in general
are. 'Realism' has also come to name, not a particular mode of
representation, but a particular choice of subject-matter: the
objects that a 'realistic' writer describes are chosen because they
exemplify a norm. But this sense of 'realism' is, from the logical
point of view, a curiosity.

Roughly speaking, then, 'representation' has a place in literature
comparable to its place in painting, even though it arises in a
different way; what representation *gives* to the spectator of art is in
each case the same. In each case representation is a property,
rooted in intention, and realized in forms that have a degree of
inter-subjective regularity – a recognizable visual aspect, and the
agreed structures of English syntax. In both cases the central core
of representation is 'intensional', divorced from reference. This
is a natural consequence of the fact that our interest in art is not
an interest in literal truth. This 'intensionality' of representation
can be observed most clearly in the theatre. What goes on when I
see a play is very like what goes on when I see certain things
happening in life. Thus I can point to an actor on the stage and
say 'There is King Lear'. The stage is like an illusion and my
appreciation of what takes place on it, like my appreciation of the

visual arts, is half mingled with belief. But it is interesting to note
that when I point and say 'There is King Lear' my pointing gives
no denotational significance to my words. For what I point to
(speaking 'materially') is determinate in all its properties – it is a
man of middle age who lives in Grantchester and who sells an-
tiques on the market. But this description, although it fits what I
point to, does not fit King Lear. There are questions that can be
meaningfully asked of what I point to that cannot be meaningfully
asked of Lear. To some questions about King Lear there is,
logically, no answer. For King Lear, like all fictions, is inde-
terminately characterized. Asking what he ate for breakfast is like
asking what Piero's St Catharine looks like from the other side.

We have seen that what makes representation possible in both
painting and literature is the existence of a medium in which an
artist can effectively direct our thoughts to pre-established objects.
There is no room for doubt that a painting has the aspect of a
man, or that a sentence describes a certain state of affairs, and it
is these facts that make possible the intention to convey the
thought of determinate objects. Can we say that the medium of
music bears a similar relation to the things that it might be held
to represent? We certainly speak of music as though it had
representational powers: indeed, the whole theory of the *leitmotif*
is based on this supposition. And in explaining musical representation we can once again point to the experience of 'hearing as'.
But a problem immediately arises. Just as a painting is seen as
something visible, so, it might be argued, must a phrase, chord or
symphonic poem be heard as something audible. Now the only
audible feature of an object is its sound, and this property can
scarcely match the complexity of what can be seen in a picture or
described in a narrative. The wood-bird's music in *Siegfried* can
certainly be heard as the song of a bird, just as passages in *La Mer*
can be heard as the sound of waves or the call of seagulls. But if
this were all musical representation amounted to then it would
be of little interest.

In fact, we also speak of music as representing things other
than sounds: Love's redemption, the World's End, the fragility of
Melisande – these are all correlated with recognizable *leitmotifs*.
Nor is 'representation' in this sense the exclusive property of
romantic symbolism: if it were so then perhaps we should treat it

as a curiosity. In the tradition of French keyboard music, for example, a subject has often been regarded as essential. Witness, for example, 'Les Petites Crémières de Bagnolet' from Couperin's *Dix-Septième Ordre*, or 'Les Pas dans la Neige' from Debussy's first book of preludes. We see that what passes for representation in music is by no means the prerogative of opera, nor does it result always from a 'code' of auditory symbols of the kind used to such astonishing effect by Wagner.

There seems at first to be no *a priori* reason why music should not represent in the manner of painting – through the intentional presentation of an aspect. For when we learn of a piece of music that it has a representational status then its aspect may change for

Ex. 1   Debussy: *La Mer*, III, 'Dialogue du vent et de la mer'

us, even when what it 'represents' is not a sound. But consider the bars from *La Mer* in Ex. 1. We may take the music here as representing the slow silent swell of the sea. When we do so we find that the aspect of the music changes for us: we begin to hear an enormous power and tension in the musical line, comparable to the invisible straining of a quiet sea. But what is represented is something inaudible. Can we say, then, that we *hear* the music *as* the slow swell of the sea?

Here we come across what is perhaps the most powerful objection to the view that representation has a place in music comparable to its place in the other arts: one can understand a 'representational' piece of music without treating it as a representation, indeed, without being aware that it has this status. On the other hand, the very suggestion that one could understand Rembrandt's *Nightwatch*, for example, while being indifferent to, or ignorant of, its representational status is absurd. The suggestion has, of course, been made, since every conceivable absurdity has at one time or another been entertained in the theory of art, but it is plainly of little interest. If we imagine a painting that can be understood independently of its representational status, then we imagine an abstract painting. And while abstract paintings sometimes have titles their representational status is as much in doubt as the status of music.

To return, then, to our example. In being reminded of the sea one is being led to grasp an aspect of the music, but it seems that this aspect is independent of the representation. There is no absurdity in supposing that I could hear the tension in the musical line while being unaware that it represents the sea. Representation does not determine our understanding of music in the way that it determines our understanding of painting or prose.

Another peculiarity of music is here worth mentioning. When music attempts direct representation, it has a tendency to become 'transparent', as it were, to its object. Representation gives way to reproduction, and the musical medium drops out of consideration altogether as superfluous. Thus the tinkling tea-spoons in Strauss's *Domestic Symphony*, and the striking of anvils in *Rheingold*, are not so much sounds represented as sounds reproduced, which in consequence detach themselves from the musical structure and stand out on their own. Rarely does one have an example of music that can be heard as some sound while not reproducing it. The Wood-bird's song already mentioned is one such example, but perhaps a more interesting case is that of the dance music from Act II scene 4 of *Wozzeck*. In *Don Giovanni* Mozart placed a light orchestra on the stage, but this orchestra did not 'imitate' the sounds of popular music; it recreated them. Representation was achieved purely through the non-musical convention that what is on the stage is part of the action. In *Wozzeck*, on the other hand, we find the stunning effect of an imitation of Viennese dance music written in the prevailing a-tonal idiom of the work (see Ex. 2). The music has a part to play in the total representation,

Ex. 2   Berg: *Wozzeck*, Act II, Scene 4

over and above the fact that it is performed on the stage. For the music must be *heard as* the robust tonalities of Johann Strauss, and yet at the same time can be *understood* only in a-tonal terms.

It needed Berg's extraordinary genius to achieve this effect, and I think that we should regard genuine representation in music as a rare and peripheral phenomenon. Of course, it has been a commonplace since Aristotle that music can 'imitate' such things as the movement of the waves, the flight of a bird, the pulse of anxiety and the nobility of a gesture. But 'imitation' is here being used to refer to a feature of art that we have not yet analysed. For musical imitation is evocative rather than exact; it conveys the idea of the thing rather than the thing itself. Hence, when we speak of music as representing the movement of the sea, or the inexorability of fate, and when we speak of music not as representing but as expressing these things, then we are speaking of one and the same phenomenon. And this transition from representation to expression is by no means a peculiarity of music. Picasso's *Guernica*, for example, which represents the bombardment of a provincial town, also represents the horrors of bombardment; and here representation and expression coincide. It is to the question what it means to describe works of art in this way that we now must turn.

CHAPTER FOURTEEN

Expression

There have been many attempts to analyse the aesthetic concept of expression, which has always proved recalcitrant. The difficulty arises, I think, from a conflict between two important features of the concept. On the one hand, expression in art must be related to the common activities of expression – to the public display of thought and feeling. On the other hand, aesthetic expression is always a value: a work that has expression cannot be a total failure. These two features seem to constrain the analysis of the concept in two separate directions, and in this chapter I shall attempt to show how they might be reconciled.

The second feature – the connection with value – leads in the direction of an 'affective' theory of expression. If to 'recognize' expression is already to respond in some way to an object, then it becomes impossible to regard expression with indifference. This was the principal argument for Santayana's famous theory of expression in terms of 'fused' associations:

> If expression were constituted by the external relation of object with object everything would be expressive equally, indeterminately: expression depends upon the union of two terms, one of which must be furnished by the imagination: I could regard expression with indifference, it will not be a beauty until I suffuse the symbols themselves with the emotions they arouse and find joy and sweetness in the very words I hear.[1]

Santayana's theory – while it rests on an unexplained idea of

[1] *The Sense of Beauty*, p. 197.

'fusion' – gives an account of emotion terms not unlike the one I have been defending. But can it really cover the more complex cases of expression, cases where the judgement that an object expresses sadness cannot be replaced without loss of meaning by the judgement that it is sad? In fact Santayana's theory is unable to explain why we use the word 'express' to convey the relation, judged to be so important, between a work of art and a state of mind.

In defence of the affective theory it might be objected that we are not *constrained* to use the word 'express' in this way. The term 'expression' does not impose itself in the description of art. If this is so then clearly a mistake is made by those theories that regard expression as the principal value of art, while insisting nonetheless that expression is here the ordinary phenomenon that we meet with every day. Indeed, it is often the case that instead of saying that a song expresses melancholy we might have said that it captures, is redolent of, possesses or even evokes melancholy. What we wish to say about a song in calling it an expression of melancholy can often be said just as well in some other way, by using terms that in other contexts do not have the same meaning as the terms that they here replace. It may be, then, that the idiom of 'expression' is, properly speaking, a rather precarious one.

An interesting feature of the aesthetic use of the term 'express', in this respect, is that it is generally replaceable by the term 'expressive'. In art there is no expression without expressiveness; a work of art is an expression of grief only if it is expressive of grief. This implies that the aesthetic concept of expression cannot be identified with the non-aesthetic concept of natural expression (or evincing). A gesture is a natural expression of some feeling if it is a symptom of that feeling, and a symptom need not be expressive. 'Expressiveness' has to do with impact: an expressive gesture is a revealing or eloquent gesture. Expression becomes expressiveness only when it is in some sense successful, and the concept of success has no clear application to the notion of a symptom. On the other hand, it does have ready application to language, where a man can be more or less successful in conveying what he means. To the extent that his choice of words is successful it is apt to be called expressive of its subject – cf. 'He spoke very expressively of the King's predicament'. This might suggest that it is to language that we should turn for a full analysis of the concept of expression in art.

Unfortunately, as I shall argue in more detail later, the analogy with language remains no more than an analogy. Language is expressive through the conventions that give it reference: it is expressive because it expresses thoughts. But a work of art is not expressive in this way. For one thing it is often very difficult to identify *what* is expressed in a work of art. Indeed, it may be unimportant to know what is expressed, even though it is always important to grasp the expressiveness of a work of art. This has led to the view that expression in art is essentially intransitive; 'expression' means 'expressiveness', and an expressive work of art no more needs to express something definite than a passage marked *espressivo* in an instrumental score.[2] On the other hand, the whole purpose of linguistic expression is thwarted if the hearer is unable to discover what is being expressed. (Which is not to say that language cannot also be expressive in the manner of a work of art – indeed it can, since poetry is possible.)

But while natural and linguistic expression provide inadequate models for artistic expression, there are other activities that are more closely related. It has been argued that 'evincing' and 'expressing' are quite different things, and that if we sometimes use the same word to cover both activities this should not blind us to the fact that there are crucial differences between them. For expression is primarily *intentional*. When one expresses one's feeling one does not only do something *because* of the feeling, one also puts the feeling *into* what one does.[3] As a result, there is a definite intention that lies behind expressive activity.

Now this might lead us to suppose that expression in art is after all explicable in terms of some non-aesthetic paradigm. For expression, like representation, is an aesthetic feature that belongs only to works of art; hence it is not unnatural to regard it as defined, like representation, in terms of an intention. Our interest in expressive works of art is continuous with our interest in certain things that people do under the stress of emotion.

[2] This view has been well defended in Eduard Hanslick, *On the Beautiful in Music*, and E. Gurney, *The Power of Sound*, pp. 313 ff.
[3] On this point, see Richard Wollheim, 'Expression', in *The Human Agent*.

To understand expression in art we must first understand the intention that underlies expression in life. But if we approach the concept of expression in this way then we find that we are offered no real alternative to the 'affective' theory. For we are led back once again to the concept of expressiveness: a concept which may be analysed without absurdity in a way that the affective theory demands. Normally, if I do something to express my feeling then my intention is to produce something expressive of my feeling: this is so, whether or not I also express my emotion *to* someone. I might express my grief by building a monument or writing an elegy, and the monument or elegy arises out of my intention to produce something expressive of my emotion. Similarly, I may express my love to X by doing something expressive of my love, in order that X may come to see what I feel. I will do something expressive because this will be the best way of conveying to X the strength and seriousness of my feelings.

In other words, we are led back once again to the possibly affective notion of 'expressiveness'. If this is so, then we are able to heal the apparent fracture between the two features of artistic expression mentioned earlier. For when I say that a funerary monument expresses grief I may mean one of two things: (a) it was intended to be expressive of a man's grief, (b) it succeeds in being expressive of grief. The first of these is descriptive, while the second is (perhaps) affective: and yet the connection of sense between them is entirely straightforward. Moreover, feature (b) is clearly a mark of success, and has more than an analogy with expression in art. It is also a feature that is at least partly independent of intention, and can, therefore, be attributed to the monument, whether or not the monument was ever intended to be expressive, and whether or not the grief it purports to express was real. The passer-by can notice the expressiveness, even though he may have no reason to take the monument as a real expression of grief. The same is true of works of art.

But how are we to analyse the idea of expressiveness? Being expressive is related to being evocative – I cannot find an object expressive unless it 'reminds' me of something. But the precise character of this reminiscence is difficult to determine. Expressiveness may be loosely defined as the power to remind us, call up for us, evoke, or 'symbolize' (in a loose sense that must not be confounded with any semantic idea) objects, such as emotions and states of mind. It lies, therefore, at the intersection of a complex network of feelings and thoughts, and it will be impossible to describe the recognition of expression in any simple or unitary way. In the next chapter I shall show in more detail how expression might be analysed. For the present, the best indication of what it is to recognize expression is through examples: we can point to what a man says, thinks and does when something – a poem, say – strikes him as expressive. There is no need to suppose that, when this happens, he should also know what the poem expresses: he may be overwhelmed by a sense of the expressiveness of the poem, even when he cannot put its feeling into words. For example, the lines:

> O body swayed to music, O brightening glance,
> How can we know the dancer from the dance?

suggest a powerful and extremely precise emotion, but it is quite beyond my powers to put it into other words. Indeed, I have no desire to do so. The knowledge of a description of the feeling is no part of the enjoyment of these lines – unlike the 'knowledge by acquaintance' of the feeling itself. Thus we arrive swiftly at the expressionist's conclusion. There may be no place in the 'recognition' of expression in art for the knowledge that some particular feeling is expressed. But this conclusion is divested of its usual air of paradox. It follows immediately from the fact that our interest in expressiveness and our interest in the description of what is expressed are two different things. The recognition of expressiveness belongs in parts to 'knowledge by acquaintance', and cannot, therefore, be fully replaced by description.

This does not imply that expressiveness is always the same phenomenon, or that it exists in detachment from the expression of particular states of mind. Rodin's hands, Brancusi's birds, and Bernini's fountains are all expressive, but in very different ways. On the other hand, the sense of their affinity with certain states of mind may be so strong that no other way of referring to these states will seem equally effective. Someone with sufficient culture and experience will grasp from these works something that he may be unable to put into words. Their value resides partly in the fact that one can learn from them what an experience or state of mind is like, even when no words can convey this knowledge in their stead.

It is often true, nonetheless, that I can analyse the effect of a work of art, and thus diagnose the origin of its expressive nature. And I can do this even when I am unable to say precisely what the work expresses. Take the following lines:

> And sometimes like a gleaner thou dost keep
> Steady thy laden head across a brook:

I do not know exactly what these lines express, but I can none the less give a partial description of their effect. For example, the break that comes before the word 'steady', imposed by the metre, vividly brings to mind the precarious movement that is being described. The lines are partly expressive of this precarious movement. On the other hand, the very suggestion that we could say what is expressed by the lines:

> Dans l'interminable
> Ennui de la plaine,
> La neige incertaine
> Luit comme du sable . . .

is absurd: in understanding such a poem we come to see that its atmosphere is indescribable.

Here we might raise an interesting question about the identity of expression. Normally, there is no problem as to when two gestures express the same thing. My gesture and yours both express anger: in this sense they have identity of expression. Expression is constituted by the relation to a state of mind, and two gestures coincide in expression to the extent that the states of mind to which they are related are identical. But when our interest is transferred from the state of mind expressed to the expressive quality of the gesture itself, we discover a problem. For how are we to decide when two gestures have the same expressive quality? We might wish to say on occasion that two poems express the same thing, or that the accompaniment of a song expresses the same thing as the words, and in such cases we mean to invoke a notion of the identity of expressive quality. But clearly we must resist the temptation to say that what happens in the case of a successful setting is that the poem expresses a certain feeling, and the music expresses a certain feeling, and that the feeling is in each case the same. For what is our criterion of identity? If there is a criterion it is one that makes sense only in the context of attributing 'expressiveness' to a work of art, and not one that bears a resemblance to our normal criteria for the identity of feelings. And properly speaking, since expressiveness is an affective notion, the 'identity' of expressiveness is not determined by the application of an external standard. The identity is the identity of an experience – the experience of 'recognizing expression' – and for this no criterion (in our own case) is required.[4]

This problem about the identity of expressiveness can be taken as further confirmation of the affective theory of expression. For it explains more convincingly than the expressionist's argument from the 'particularity' of feelings why there should be a 'heresy of paraphrase'.[5] If paraphrase is a search for identity of expressiveness, then paraphrase cannot be determined by any external rules – such as rules of meaning. For what is sought is an identity of experience, and this cannot be secured in any such simple way.

This is only the preparation for a theory, some of the details of which will be explored in the following chapter. It is unlikely, moreover, that it could be extended without considerable modification to cover all the uses of the term 'expression' in aesthetics. But it suffices, I think, to show that the concept of expression need present no special difficulty to our theory of aesthetic experience. An object is expressive if it 'corresponds to', or 'symbolizes' a state of mind, where correspondence is a matter of evocation, not of reference. How this 'correspondence' arises in any given case is not properly a philosophical, but rather a critical question, to be answered by individual analysis. But such a theory will fail if it can be shown that there is some independent property of the work of art that determines our description of it as an expression. It is precisely this that the semantic theory tries to show. The semantic theory attempts to 'objectify' the symbolic quality of the work of art, by showing that it arises as all symbol-

[4] On this point, see the example of the mimic, discussed by Wittgenstein, *Lectures and Conversations* etc., p. 32, and by Sartre, *L'imaginaire*, pp. 55–63.
[5] Cleanth Brooks, *The Well Wrought Urn*, ch. 11.

ism arises, through a cognitive relation between the work of art and a state of mind.

There is one way of formulating the semantic theory that rapidly becomes empty, in just the way that expressionism is empty. For example, we might argue with Mrs Langer[6] that works of art stand in a symbolic relation to the feelings that they express, but that this relation is not to be explained in terms of any rule of reference. Works of art are 'presentational' symbols, whose relation to their objects is purely morphological. The symbol and its object are related through possessing the same 'logical form'. It follows that what the symbol expresses cannot be re-stated in words; words do not present the 'logical form' of individuals; they only summarize the properties and relations that individuals possess. But explained in this way, the relation between a work of art and a feeling cannot be described as a semantic relation. Our ordinary understanding of the relations between words and things cannot be extended to the understanding of artistic expression. For one thing we are no longer able to explain why we say that a work of art expresses a feeling, and not that the feeling expresses a work of art: for the relation of 'expression', explained in Mrs Langer's way, is clearly symmetrical. In this it is, of course, wholly different from any normal semantic relation.

We might suspect that Mrs Langer's theory becomes trivial through its over-simple solution to what must be the most powerful objection to any semantic theory of expression: what is a work of art supposed to *say* about the state of mind that it expresses, and how is the state of mind identified? We find that Mrs Langer's theory rules these questions illegitimate. The kind of symbolism peculiar to art is not to be explained on the model of 'reference and predication'. Artistic symbolism is *sui generis*, involving not statement or comparison but rather 'presentation', the revelation of an individual thing.

Like expressionism, this theory is a direct descendant of the Kantian view that aesthetic experience is free from concepts. In aesthetic experience objects are neither compared nor described but rather 'given' in their entirety. Croce likewise argued in defence of his cognitive theory of aesthetic appreciation that art and the appreciation of art are forms of non-conceptual know-

[6] *Philosophy in a New Key, passim.*

ledge. Reduced to its barest terms the distinction between art and science lies in the fact that the first involves *intuition*, or the knowledge of particulars, while the second involves *conception*, or the knowledge of universals. Croce argued that the work of art as a whole presents an intuition, even when it contains parts – as in a novel – which taken alone would have purely conceptual import.[7] In effect Croce tried to unite in a single formula two separate aspects of the Hegelian view of art: the view that art and the appreciation of art are forms of knowledge, and the view that art is a sensuous and not an intellectual medium. Croce connects these views in such a way as to derive the important consequences that what art says, and what it gives knowledge of, cannot be said or known in another way, since this would contradict the assumption that the object of art is not a conception but an intuition.

It is a small step from this kind of expressionism to Mrs Langer's version of the semantic theory: the conclusions are the same, and the reasons for them equally difficult to interpret. In fact, even with semantic theories that are both more subtle and more genuinely explanatory than Mrs Langer's, the same conclusions are yielded, and the same inadequacies of explanation arise. This should lead us to suspect that, however refined the semantic theory might become, it is ultimately as empty a theory of aesthetic appreciation as the doctrine of 'presentational symbols'. I shall attempt to illustrate this conjecture through a brief consideration of Goodman's views.[8]

Goodman analyses the relation between a work of art and what it expresses in terms of the common notion of reference, thus avoiding many of the difficulties that stem from Mrs Langer's recourse to 'presentation'. He argues that expression is a species of exemplification, and that an object exemplifies a property if it both possesses the property and refers to it, in the way a tailor's sample exemplifies the pattern of a particular cloth. Expression is distinguished from other kinds of exemplification by the fact that in expression the property exemplified is possessed metaphorically

---

[7] See, for example. *Breviario di Estetica*, pp. 26–31. The argument is also implicit in Hegel. See *Introduction to the Philosophy of Fine Art*, tr. Bosanquet, p. 133.

[8] *Languages of Art*, ch. 2.

and not literally. In other words, expression consists in the reference to an attribute that is 'metaphorically possessed'. Goodman feels at liberty to use the terms 'attribute' and 'predicate' interchangeably, on nominalist grounds. Equally true to the premise of nominalism is his refusal to give an explanation (other than genetic) of how a predicate is metaphorically applied. There is no room for the suggestion that understanding a metaphor might involve very different capacities from those involved in understanding a literal truth: the question has already been partly begged against a non-cognitive analysis of aesthetic appreciation. But it is not necessary to argue this point again. Nor need we argue against Goodman's view by pointing out that not every quality that a work of art is said to express is also attributed to it metaphorically ('grief' is but one example). The fault might lie, after all, in our ordinary sparingness with metaphor. It is true that Goodman's analysis needs to be amended slightly if it is not to be open to certain counter-examples. Clearly it is not sufficient for expression that a poem should be both sad and refer to sadness, since the reference could arise in an irrelevant way. (Sadness might simply be mentioned in one of the lines.) Goodman's discussion includes several suggestions as to how this kind of difficulty might be overcome. All we need say, I think, is that the poem must refer to sadness in virtue of being (metaphorically) sad.

Now Goodman denies that his theory enables us to tell what any given work expresses: no philosophical analysis framed in nominalist terms could give us this power. It follows that we cannot compare Goodman's theory with our prior intuitions about expression and see it vindicated. Besides, it seems that these intuitions are extremely vague. Every judgement that has been made about expression has also been hotly contested, and set beside this instability in critical language most philosophical theories of expression have a detached and paradoxical air. We do not know how to apply them to works of art; nor do we know what follows if they are true. This very lack of an established body of intuitions renders Goodman's analysis, in terms of necessary conditions, rather curious. The theory presents an '*analysans*' without identifying its '*analysandum*'. If the arguments given earlier about the recognition of expression are correct, then it is difficult to assess what is shown by the fact (if it is a fact) that some works of art possess the property of referring to an attribute that they also metaphorically possess.

The burden of Goodman's analysis must lie in the condition of reference: it is this feature that ultimately explains the symbolic relation between a work of art and whatever is expressed by it. It is in terms of reference that the relation of 'correspondence' is analysed. What does this feature amount to?

For Goodman, the various forms of art are, like natural languages, symbol schemes. They symbolize objects and properties, the one by representation or description, the other by expression or exemplification. Representation involves denotation, which is both less immediate and more literal than exemplification, but the core of both expression and representation is the property of reference, which can exist in these and many other forms. Reference recurs in other symbol schemes, and could be understood from the study of any of these. Symbol schemes are differentiated partly in terms of certain formal properties, some semantic (derived from what Goodman calls the 'field of reference' of the scheme), others syntactic (belonging to the structure of the scheme itself). If certain of these properties are present and others absent, then it is possible to develop a notation for the scheme; otherwise not. Not all these formal properties need be shared by any two schemes of symbols. (Thus natural languages, unlike pictures, are syntactically differentiated, or articulate, and unlike musical scores are semantically undifferentiated, or dense.)

Now suppose we were to ask, what is the content of saying that the separate art-forms constitute symbol schemes? What do they symbolize, and what kinds of thing do they enable us to say about what they symbolize? A first reaction to these questions might be to construe them as unproblematic or else once again to rule them illegitimate, as Mrs Langer does. The art-forms are symbol schemes in that they share certain roughly formal properties with other symbol schemes, and in that they have a 'field of reference' with which they can be correlated. There is no content to the notion of a symbol scheme that can be given independently of these features. If it is asked *what* is symbolized by works of art then the answer is objects and properties (or, in nominalist language, individuals and predicates): these exhaust the field of reference of art as of most schemes of symbols. If it is now asked what works of art *say* about these objects, then it will be replied that an answer is neither necessary nor possible. To understand an utterance in the 'language' of music is simply to understand the references that are made by the individual utterance, in accordance with the conventions and practices of music. There is no need to refer to what the music *says* in order to explain how we understand it. In any case, the music says nothing that could be put into words: there is no reason why the translatability that characterizes natural languages should show itself in other symbol schemes. We cannot speak of a musical utterance as 'equivalent' to a piece of English; the notion of equivalence is itself tied to linguistic utterances, and marks a relation between sentences alone. To suppose that a musical utterance could be understood by being translated into a verbal utterance is to suppose that the former belongs to a symbol scheme to which it does not, in fact, belong. To understand a musical utterance is not to know of some utterance in another symbol scheme which somehow says the same thing; there is no reason for saying that such another utterance could be found. In any case, suppose one does find this further utterance: how does one understand *it*? Not, surely, by knowing yet another utterance in the same – or another – symbol scheme: to insist that understanding must always proceed in this way is to generate an infinite regress. Understanding a musical utterance must be considered as a purely *musical* ability, much as understanding a sentence is purely linguistic.

I give this argument since it seems to do some justice to the extreme radicalism of Goodman's approach and to his determined rejection of all 'ultimate explanations'. But this radicalism also has its drawbacks, and while on one level it seems to render the analysis impregnable, on another level it opens it to serious criticism. It is not an irrelevant fact that natural languages can be translated. It is of their essence. For translation is a possibility as soon as there is an interpretation, and all natural languages are inherently interpreted. In other words 'reference' in a natural language seems immediately to open the possibility of translation. For reference to particulars cannot occur in a scheme of symbols that does not admit the possibility of predication, and hence the possibility of assigning truth-values. (I rely on the usual Fregean arguments for a connection between reference and truth.) Truth introduces the idea of equivalence, and hence of translatability. Now we are supposed to assume that this translatability is not a feature of the symbol scheme of music even though reference occurs in that scheme. It immediately becomes doubtful that we can explain what is meant by 'reference' in terms of a *linguistic* practice. But, if this is so, the term 'reference' as employed by Goodman becomes as obscure and unhelpful as Mrs Langer's 'presentation'. As in the theory of representation, Goodman rests his analysis on a supposedly semantic property which must nonetheless be divorced from almost all the normal activities in which reference occurs: assertion, denial, questioning and command. The work of art picks out an object (in this case a feeling), but predicates nothing of it. The work of art has no truth-value; to say, therefore, that understanding the work of art is cognitive is to say very little. It is to say only that it involves attention to an object, and hence more than the simple stimulation of feeling or sense. If we can speak of the work as having a relation of reference to that which it expresses it is not so much like the reference that occurs in 'This is green', but more like that which occurs in 'Look at this!' To obey such an order, and to understand the reference it contains, does not involve any determinate judgement about the object that is referred to.

This seems to suggest that a semantic theory of art does not really say anything about appreciation that could not be said in less misleading terms. It does not have the implication that understanding art is cognitive in the way that understanding a language is cognitive, nor does it have the implication that the work of art is a symbol in the way that words are symbols. Artistic symbolism is entirely *sui generis*: it does not express knowledge of universals; instead, it conveys a sense of individual existence. It is for this reason that works of art cannot be translated. Art is not conceptual, but rather 'immediate' or 'intuitive'. The apparatus of the semantic theories does no more than preserve in more daunting form the central tenets of Crocean expressionism. But it is impossible to explain the terms of the semantic theory in a way that will cast any light on the Crocean doctrine. On the contrary, the doctrine remains as obscure as ever, despite the superficial persuasiveness of the terms in which it is now expressed. To say that a work of art 'presents' or 'refers to' a certain feeling, where 'reference' is detached from truth, and where no rules of reference can be given, is to say no more than that the work in some way (but in no particular way) calls some feeling to mind. And this we need not deny. To go on to argue that appreciation is cognitive is at best misleading, and to call a work of art a symbol is to use the word 'symbol' in an attenuated sense. Being a symbol no longer implies being used to symbolize. If the red shirt is a symbol of communism and the black shirt a symbol of fascism this is because people have used the colours of their shirts to declare their political allegiances. To wear a red shirt, in the right circumstances, and to say 'I am a communist' are equivalent acts, even though one may be appropriate and effective where the other is not. The fascist who attends a communist demonstration in a red shirt is guilty of dissimulation: he is telling a lie in his mode of dress. Anyone who thought that a work of art symbolized feeling in a similar way would find the activities of aesthetic judgement and appreciation impossible to explain. As we shall see, symbolism in art is a matter of suggestion rather than reference.

In arguing that appreciation is not primarily cognitive I have intended to maintain that the aesthetic attitude is not one of discovery, and its end-point not the knowledge of facts, whether about the work of art or about the world to which it 'refers'. No cognitive theory of aesthetic experience can explain why one should desire to listen to a symphony again, any more than one should wish to re-read a scientific treatise, or repeat a successful experiment.[9] Although judgement is a necessary pre-condition of aesthetic experience – as the reading of any novel will make clear – it is not the experience itself. An attitude of discovery, while it is essential to, is not sufficient for aesthetic appreciation, and the effects of art cannot be summed up in terms of propositions that we learn or come to believe through studying it. The cognitive aspect of appreciation can only be described in terms of certain experiences, of which the 'understanding' analysed in Chapter Twelve gives the general form. It is in this way that we must now attempt to describe the 'recognition of expression'.

[9] I owe this point to Mr R. K. Elliott.

CHAPTER FIFTEEN

Symbolism

So far our conclusions have been negative. Expression in art has both an intentional and an affective side, and we have found reason to consider the second of these as primary. But what is this affective side? What is the experience of 'recognizing expression' and how does it arise?

We must emphasize at this juncture the distinction between nature and art. Imagine a cliff face somewhere, in which the action of wind and water has engraved a figure closely resembling the Olympian Hermes. It is impossible to approach such a figure with the attitudes, assumptions and expectations that we reserve for works of art. We regard the cliff face 'sculpture' as an accident, and however much we may study it for its beauty it will be impossible to appreciate it as we appreciate the Greek original. Let it resemble the Hermes as closely as you will, it will never be possible to observe in the cliff face the niceties of representation and of expression which affect us so deeply in art. If I am interested in the expression on Hermes' face, then I am interested in the expression that Praxiteles (supposing it were he) gave to that face, and if it has value for me it is partly because I recognize in this expression a particular intention of the artist.

The recognition of intention cannot, then, be discounted as irrelevant to our interest in art. Nor is there a clear contrast, after all, between an 'affective' and an 'intentional' approach to the concept of expression, for the very reason that a sense of intention will determine our experience of art. The work of art is 'transparent' to intention, so that at any level intention may operate through the medium of art, refining and transforming its effect on us.

This is true not only of expression but also, as we have seen, of representation. Indeed, it is often difficult to distinguish the two phenomena, as is clearly shown by the example of mimicry. In both cases the fundamental experience may involve the recognition of an aspect, rather than the judgement of a similarity. And in both cases the 'stability' of this aspect depends on a sense of intention. At first I 'recognize' Mr Heath in the mimic's gestures, just as I might 'recognize' Mr Wilson or the Queen. But when I see that it is Mr Heath who is *intended* through the gesture, then my experience changes; the aspect becomes more stable, and more immediate. Now I allow my experience to pursue a familiar course; I give myself up to the impression, and situate my perception of the performance in the framework of thoughts and attitudes relating to Mr Heath. If the mimic is accurate, and his intention clear, then I am amused by this performance.

This example, used by both Wittgenstein and Sartre,[1] serves to show, I think, that the very same capacities may be involved both in the understanding of expression and in the understanding of representation. Mimicry lies on the boundary between the two phenomena, and our experience of mimicry is related both to our understanding of representation in the theatre and to our appreciation of expression in ballet and music. Representation and expression are alike forms of 'imitation', and our experience of each of them derives from imagination, not belief.

But this is not all that needs to be said in connection with the concept of expression. As it stands the notion of an aspect fails to elucidate all the phenomena that we might bring under this concept in discussing art. In particular, it seems not to cover the phenomenon of atmosphere, in which a large part of the 'expressiveness' of works of art consists. Certain works seem to be 'suffused with' emotion – such as Watteau's *Embarcation à Cythère*, or Tennyson's *Ulysses* – and this is a phenomenon that calls out for analysis. These are prime examples of artistic 'symbolism'; such works of art are treated as perfect expressions of a state of mind and in this task of symbolism we can think of no prosaic statement that could stand in their place. How do we describe the 'recognition of expression' in cases like these?

Artistic symbols, it is often said, are distinguished from lin-

[1] *Lectures and Conversations* etc., p. 32, and *L'imaginaire*, pp. 55–63.

guistic utterances in being iconic. The term is Peirce's[2] and it is used to suggest that the relation between the artistic symbol and what it stands for is somehow 'direct' in a way that linguistic symbolism is not. Part of what is meant by this is that artistic symbolism is not mediated in the manner of linguistic symbolism by rules of reference, but proceeds directly, through the intrinsic ability of the symbol to call some object to mind.

This invocation of a respectable distinction is harmless enough, so long as we do not think that anything is explained by it. To say that artistic symbolism is iconic is to give an indication of what it is not. But this does not tell us what it is, nor how it arises, nor when it is successful. Peirce's own explanation of iconicity – in terms of similarity – is scarcely likely to account for the way in which *L'Invitation au Voyage* is related to emotional surrender, or the way in which Schumann's *Kinderszene* is related to the experience of a child.

Now it is not only works of art that stand in affective relationship to objects and states of mind. Thus, a landscape may convey the joys of childhood to someone who had once been happy there. Indeed, in Baudelaire's famous sonnet the whole of nature is involved in the *Correspondances* that we experience in waking life, and Freud's discovery of a dream symbolism takes as its starting point a notion that is closely related to the idea of symbolism that infects contemporary aesthetics. This Freudian conception has its analogues in anthropology and comparative religion, and, in fact, we discover in every branch of human experience forms of 'symbolism' which are not semantic in the narrow sense of verbal utterance, but affective in the manner of works of art.

It might be objected that the continuity between artistic and non-artistic symbolism cannot be assumed simply because we sometimes use the same rather vague vocabulary in describing both. But let us take an example. Suppose I am sitting by an estuary in hazy sunlight watching the boats and listening to the murmur of their sails. I find the scene evocative, and by this I mean that it calls certain emotions to mind. These emotions I 'entertain' in imagination, but if asked for a description of their nature I find myself at a loss for words. Suppose, however, that I am able to describe them as a mixture of peace and longing. Now

[2] *Collected Papers*, Vol. V, sections 213 ff.

we cannot say that the estuary is the 'object' of this feeling in any straightforward sense: I do not imagine a feeling of peace and longing that is *directed towards* the estuary, as my present interest is directed towards it. Nor is the estuary merely the occasion of this feeling. The experience is not caused by the sight of the estuary in the way that it is caused by the wine that I have just been drinking. For the feeling that I imagine is intimately related to what I see, in the sense that what I see is integral to a full description of the feeling. If I were to attempt to produce a description that was not vague and general in the manner of the one just mentioned, I should find myself constrained at some point to refer to the estuary and not just to the feeling that the estuary arouses. Without pursuing the matter further we might say that I am here treating the estuary as a 'symbol' of a state of mind.

Suppose now that in reflecting on this state of mind I discover a work of art that perfectly expresses it. On hearing the lines:

> Vois sur ces canaux
> Dormir ces vaisseaux
> Dont l'humeur est vagabonde;

I exclaim 'That's exactly what I felt!' If I am speaking sincerely, then here my word is law.[3] Would it not be odd to say that the poem, which expresses to me precisely the same feeling as the feeling that was conveyed by the estuary, nonetheless, stands in a quite different relation to the feeling? After all, the poem is expressive partly in virtue of what it describes, and what it describes is what I see when I look at the estuary. In other words, while the poem expresses the feeling more completely, it stands in a relation to the feeling that is essentially similar to the relation that exists between the feeling and the estuary. It follows that, although the recognition of intention must modify and deepen our experience of symbolism, the experience itself belongs to a kind that can be described without reference to the intentions characteristic of art.

Let us follow our usual practice and confine our attention to the third-person case. What must be true of a man if he is to be said to regard a work of art as the symbol of a certain state of

[3] Cf. The problem discussed in the last chapter of the identity of expressive quality.

mind? It seems to me that, once we transfer our attention from the aesthetic object to the subjective experience, the enterprise of listing necessary conditions can be carried through. The first three conditions are suggested immediately by our theory of imagination:

A. It is necessary that the subject should be able to call the feeling in question to mind, and thus 'imagine what it is like'. The knowledge that is gained from the recognition of expression is, in this as in every case, a form of knowledge by acquaintance. The subject is made familiar with something which he may not be able to describe in words.

This leads at once to a second condition:

B. The feeling should be called to mind by the work of art. That is, the thought or perception of the work should cause the subject to think of, or entertain, the feeling. We cannot say, in the abstract, which features of an object might give it this evocative power, and this accords well with the intuition that what makes a work of art expressive of some emotion cannot be laid down in advance of the particular case.

Finally, we must make clear that the recognition of expression forms part of our experience of art:

C. It is necessary to perceive or have perceived the work of art if one is to take it as an expression. That is, the experience of symbolism cannot be obtained at second hand. This condition needs, I think, no further comment.

It is in attempting to advance beyond these minimal conditions that philosophers have wished to invoke such vague notions as the 'fusion' of which Santayana speaks. The poem comes to have a symbolic value when the idea (or perception) of the poem becomes fused with the idea of the feeling. This reminds one of the attempt to explain aspect perception by saying that here experience has become informed by a concept. It seems to suggest that our experience consists of *two* elements, united in a certain specifiable relation.

But if we try to give a non-metaphorical explanation of this 'fusion' we run into difficulties: either we invent some new metaphor, or else we turn back in a circle, and explain 'fusion' in terms of symbolism, insisting the while that here symbolism is *sui generis* and not to be explained in terms of some linguistic or semantic paradigm. Of course, one can give a *critical* account of the process of fusion. By this I mean that one can name those features of a poem in virtue of which it comes to be expressive of a certain state of mind. But the critical survey of thought, diction and connotation can be seen as providing us with the genesis of symbolism, not with its analysis. It is because the poem awakens all these thoughts, and draws them together in a particular form of words, that it acquires a symbolic value. But this does not tell us what it means to say that the poem symbolizes a certain stare of mind. In another context it might be necessary to give an entirely different explanation, even when the state of mind in question is as similar as can be. (In this respect we might well compare Watteau's *Embarcation* with Herrick's *Corinna*.)

We must, then, attempt to put something in place of the empiricist's 'fusion'. And it might seem that we already have an alternative in our theory of imagination. When we translate the metaphor of 'fusion' into philosophically acceptable language, does it not lead us once more to the idea of an aspect?

Unfortunately, the matter is not so simple. Of course, we can regard the recognition of sadness in music as a case of aspect perception. But this does not bear on our present difficulty. For we need some term with which to denote the more subtle relations between music and emotion, relations of 'suffusion', or symbolism in the affective sense. The experience of symbolism cannot be described simply as the direct and unmediated perception of a relationship, in the manner of 'seeing' or 'hearing as'. When I recognize that the *Embarcation à Cythère* expresses an attitude towards the transience of happiness then, while my experience is in certain important ways analogous to the perception of an aspect, I have referred to no 'aspect' in this description of the painting. We cannot say that seeing the painting is like seeing an expression (in some more literal sense) of this attitude. For this does not give a description of anything that could be seen. To invoke the notion of an aspect in order to explain the recognition of expression in a case like this is, therefore, at this stage quite unhelpful. It is not yet clear what it means to say that a picture can be seen as something that is in itself invisible. (In this sense, the case is exactly parallel to that of *La Mer* discussed in Chapter Thirteen.)

More needs to be said, then, about the precise relation between thought and experience in cases of this kind. Suppose a man sees Watteau's painting as an expression of some attitude towards the transience of happiness. It is not sufficient to say, as we have so far said, that he is simply led by the painting to think of this attitude. There are many irrelevant ways in which this thought could arise out of the perception of the picture, and it is for this reason above all that we must reject the doctrine of the 'association of ideas'. A first step in overcoming the difficulty might include some reference to emotion. Thus we might consider adding the following condition:[4]

> D. To see *a* as a symbol of *b* is to react in some way towards *b*, as a result of perceiving *a*. It is possible that this reaction should exist in imagination only – 'entertained' rather than adopted; and if *b* is itself an emotion, then the reaction will have a 'sympathetic' character, as when one responds to the grief in the music of a requiem.

Such a condition might well seem natural, since it goes some way towards explaining the importance and value of expressiveness. But there is a problem that we have already mentioned: the problem of 'double intentionality'. In discussing the example of the estuary it became clear that the estuary could be considered neither as the object of my imagined feeling (in any normal sense), nor merely as its occasion. And yet the feeling seemed to be dependent on the estuary not merely for its existence, but also for its proper description. The feeling could not be fully described without at some point referring to the estuary.[5] The expression

---

[4] This condition, and the next, are to some extent suggested by Bishop Alison, (*Essays on the Nature and Principles of Taste*, Vol. I, ch. 2), who saw that mere association of ideas is not sufficient for aesthetic judgement.

[5] On this point, and related problems in the analysis of expression, see John Casey, *The Language of Criticism*, chs. IV and V.

of such an imagined feeling in words and behaviour must be quite distinct from the expression of a reminiscence (which may take the form 'It makes me think of . . .' rather than 'It expresses . . .'). Part of the expression of this state of mind will reside in the desire to go on observing a particular object, and this is why we might wish to say that interest in 'symbolism' is always aesthetic: for it always involves attention to a particular sight or sound.

This phenomenon of 'double intentionality' is, of course, precisely what we observe in the case of aspect perception (although here it is a question of the intentionality of a perception rather than the intentionality of a feeling). When I see *a* as *b*, or see *b* in *a*, then my perception has two immediate objects: *a* (which is also the material object of perception), and *b*, the aspect, these two objects being fused in the sense that *what I see* must be described in terms of both of them. I think we must recognize that 'double intentionality' is here entirely primitive. If this is so, then the similar 'double intentionality' observed in the recognition of symbolism – as indeed in every exercise of imagination, and hence in aesthetic experience of whatever kind – will be sufficiently clear once its relation to aspect perception is explained. And in fact this suggestion proves to be fruitful.

Let us return to the case of the painting or poem that expresses an attitude towards the transience of happiness. Here the emotion that is felt or imagined cannot have as its object only the state of mind expressed in the work of art: it must also be directed in some way towards the work of art. The following analysis of the phenomenon seems natural:

> E. Although the subject's feeling is expressed towards what is symbolized (the attitude, in this case), it is directed also towards the work of art itself in the sense that the subject is disposed to describe, and perhaps to justify, his emotion in terms of features of the work. (He describes the lassitudinous postures of the people in Watteau's painting; he refers to the sombre final lines of Herrick's *Corinna*, and so on.)

In this way it might be held that the work of art provides the elaboration of the subject's feeling. For to give a complete account of the thought on which his feeling is founded, the subject must refer to the work of art that is before him. This is so despite the fact that the object of his feeling – which is defined by this thought – is not the work of art itself, but rather something beyond the work which it 'symbolizes'.

This suggestion is promising, but as yet incomplete. Let us return, then, to the remarks on intentionality in Chapter Six. I argued there that intentionality can be explained, for the most part, in terms of the notion of thought, where 'thought' covers belief, judgement, and the unasserted states of mind, some of which have been discussed under the heading of Imagination. Suppose one were to ask: what makes my fear of X fear of X? The answer can be stated quite simply: my fear depends for its existence on a thought about X (the thought that X has some frightening feature). But it is not just any thought about X that will serve in this way to direct my fear. I must think that X is a proper object of fear. In a similar way, if, on looking at the Watteau, I come to feel regret at the passing of happiness, then there must be some thought about the passing of happiness on which this emotion is founded. And this thought must be such as to render the passing of happiness regrettable in my eyes. And it is here that the painting may play its role in the elaboration of my feeling. For the features of the passing of happiness that give rise to my emotion might be features which the picture itself brings home to me. (It is the critic, not the philosopher, whose task it is to name these features.)

But there are two related difficulties for this approach, which must be overcome. First, it seems to make the recognition of expression once more a merely cognitive activity: I learn from the work of art certain facts, say, about the human condition, as a result of which I come to sympathize with a certain attitude towards the passing of happiness. There is no sense in which the recognition of expression involves the *appreciation* of the particular work of art, and indeed, in so far as I recognize anything at all it is something that could be brought to my notice in an indefinite number of other ways. Secondly, there is the familiar problem caused by emotional ambiguity. To return to 'seeing as'. I could see the ambiguous figure as a duck and yet at the same time be able to justify to another quite cogently the perception of the figure as a rabbit. I need only point to the figure's rabbit-like features. But to engage in this process of justification is not also to see the figure as a rabbit. Analogously, I might experience a work of art as a symbol of regret, while producing reasons for treating it as a symbol of the frivolity of courtly existence (assuming that the Watteau, or some similar painting, will bear both interpretations). In other words, the idea of justification does not in itself suffice to explain how my feeling is 'directed' at the picture.

In fact, we may overcome both of these difficulties through one and the same strategy:

> F. What the subject learns from the painting – what the painting 'brings home to him' – is something that he learns in the *experience* of the painting, and only in that experience.

This suggestion corresponds to the Hegelian (and to some extent Kantian) theory that a work of art has expression through being the 'sensuous embodiment' of an idea. Such a theory can be freed from the obscurity of its idealist prototype in the following way. In describing the intentionality of my feeling in terms of the painting, I refer to the way the painting *looks*, and it is in such a way that my thought is dependent on experience. It is the look of the picture that provides the elaboration of my thought. For example, it is the observable postures of the figures in Watteau's painting, and the particular light that suffuses them, that give so vivid a sense of regret at the transience of happiness. I describe what moves me in this transience partly in terms of these features of the painting, but they are exclusively visual features. Only someone who has seen the painting, and seen a particular aspect of the painting, will fully understand to what I am referring.

In other words, to agree to my description of what is expressed in the painting is to come to see certain features of the painting in a certain light. And it is possible that we can return at this point to the doctrine of 'seeing as'. For if my thoughts depend so closely on the appearance of the picture, then it is possible that I should see them embodied in that appearance. The thoughts may transform the 'look', so that I shall wish to describe it differently. The experience of a 'look' so transformed by thought will be formally analogous to the experience of seeing an aspect. But it will also resemble the 'understanding' that was described in

Chapter Twelve, in that it will be impossible to say in other words how the details of the painting must be *seen*. All we can say in the abstract is that they are seen in such a way that the interpretation of the painting as a symbol becomes immediate.

This experience of recognizing symbolism is, like all the phenomena that share the formal properties of imagination, within rational control. There is such a thing as defending an interpretation as appropriate to a given work of art, and in doing so one may persuade another, by means of reasons, to experience the work in a certain way. These reasons may once again point to analogies – as when I describe the rhythm or melodic line of a piece of music in terms of the 'dynamic' properties of an emotion.[6] But the judgement of 'appropriateness' is, once again, *sui generis*, and by no means limited to analogies. Take the final lines of Herrick's *Corinna*:

> Then, while time serves, and we are but decaying,
> Come, my Corinna, come, let's go a-Maying.

Here we are forced suddenly to recognize that what is expressed is not merely argumentative, in the manner of *To His Coy Mistress*, but also infected with sorrow. But, of course, there is no *analogy* with sorrow here. The effect depends on what is said, and on the peculiar halting rhythm of the verse.

The 'recognition' of symbolism in art is by no means a detached or curious phenomenon. Indeed, it has much in common with certain other forms of 'recognition' that infect our awareness of the world. Now, in the normal way, 'recognition' denotes a cognitive process of which even animals are capable: a dog may recognize its master, just as I recognize a man whom I pass in the street. Here recognition is a matter of *knowing whom the man is*. It is as though I say to myself: 'Here is Mr Smith'. But there is another sense, in which 'recognition' has a dimension of 'fullness', and in this sense, recognition cannot be explained simply as a case of realizing that a certain proposition is true. While I may know (realize) that this is indeed Mr Smith, I may nevertheless not 'recognize' him, in that I may not see in him the physical and moral nature I know to be his. Moreover, I may as a result be

---

[6] Cf. The 'smiling through tears' of Beethoven's B-flat quartet, Op. 128.

unable to attach to my perception of Mr Smith the attitudes and feelings that I normally reserve for him. I may not find my expectations reflected in the face I see. In this way, indeed, the expression on another's face may become strange to me, simply because my own attitude to the other has altered. In *War and Peace* Tolstoy describes Rostov's perception of the Princess Mary in the following terms:

> Nicholas immediately recognized Princess Mary not so much by the profile he saw under her bonnet as by the feeling of solicitude, timidity, and pity, that immediately overcame him.

While there is perhaps something exaggerated in this, we also recognize, I think, a grain of truth. Our emotions are often inseparably bound up in this way with our perceptions, so that the character of each is transformed. This is, I think, nothing but a further instance of the 'double intentionality' characteristic of many of our reactions to art.

I have taken examples from the representational arts alone. But there is no reason why conditions A–F might not be satisfied by our experience of music or architecture. But while the account may be generalized in such a way, we must recognize that there will always be uses of the term 'express' that it cannot cover. The uses of this term in describing art are extremely varied, and if I have chosen only one of these it is because it seems to me the most important and, at the same time, the most difficult to understand. I have been concerned to analyse a phenomenon rather than a word, and if I choose to appropriate the terms 'expressiveness' and 'symbolism' in describing this phenomenon this is not because I find myself compelled to use these terms in such a way. A poem like Bishop King's *Exequy* expresses grief in the direct way that words and gestures express grief. If it is also 'expressive' in my sense, this is a separate feature the significance of which goes beyond the import of 'expression', whether natural, conventional or acquired. In general, we find that a work of art, like any other human activity, can be taken as the expression of every state of mind that went into its making. But this feature is of course independent of expressiveness. The same applies to many other kinds of 'expression' in art – for example, the artistic representation of expressive behaviour. Thus we say that Beatrice's much ridiculed speech from *The Cenci*:

> . . . O
> My God! Can it be possible . . .

expresses horror. But it is expressive of nothing.

Although we have seen how the recognition of expression might after all be a proper part of aesthetic experience, we have also seen that certain of the idealist's doctrines must now be accepted. In particular, it is no longer possible to argue that art is not in some sense a form of knowledge. In recognizing expression I am brought to an awareness of what is expressed. But what I learn can itself be described only in terms of an experience of 'seeing', 'hearing', or 'grasping the meaning of' a work of art. If I also gain knowledge of what is represented or expressed then this knowledge belongs to 'knowledge by acquaintance' and can be conveyed in no other way. It is the experience of the work itself that summarizes what I know. Recognizing expression has, in fact, precisely the experiential dimension that was discovered in 'understanding' art, and in this chapter I have done no more than to extend the analysis of 'understanding' until it covers the dimensions of reference that until now have seemed inexplicable. But we have yet to give an indication of the value of aesthetic experience as I have described it. This is one among a group of questions that I wish finally to consider.

CHAPTER SIXTEEN
Objectivity and Value

I have discussed the basis of aesthetics in the philosophy of mind, and it will perhaps be wondered how the argument bears on the practice of criticism. In particular, I have offered no solution to the critic's most vexing problems: the problem of objectivity and the problem of value. Any detailed treatment of such issues would require arguments at least as complicated as those I have already given, but I shall conclude with a few suggestions.

First, then, the question of objectivity. Even if we leave evaluation aside, we find that our account of aesthetic description presents an awkward problem. For the meaning of many aesthetic descriptions has been explained without reference to their justification: nothing has been said that will provide rules for the application of 'aesthetic' terms. It must not be assumed, however, that the use of aesthetic descriptions is entirely arbitrary, or 'subjective', any more than the description of an aspect is arbitrary or subjective. A figure with several aspects may be seen in several incompatible ways; but aspect descriptions are not for that reason subjective. It cannot be held, therefore, that the possibility of rival interpretations of a work of art demonstrates the subjectivity of criticism. It is perhaps possible to see Othello as either noble or self-indulgent, and these rival interpretations give rise to quite different experiences of the play. But neither interpretation is for that reason subjective.

It might be thought that, in arguing that aesthetic descriptions need have no truth conditions, I have in effect made it impossible to describe them as 'objective'. But this is not so. Objectivity and

Truth belong to separate categories. Take the parallel case of moral judgement. Suppose it is true that moral judgements express attitudes and not beliefs: the condition for their acceptance involves a decision or a desire. It follows that there is a sense in which moral judgements do not have truth conditions – their truth does not consist in their 'correspondence' with a state of affairs. But it by no means follows that moral judgements are not objective. It may still be possible to support them with reasons 'valid for all men', reasons which one must accept on pain of being irrational. It may be true that, in the absence of truth conditions, there can be no such thing as a conclusive reason that is not itself 'evaluative' (since 'conclusiveness' derives from deducibility, which is a relation subordinate to truth-value). But practical reasons might nevertheless be objective, in the sense of being rationally acceptable to all men whatever, irrespective of their personal desires.[1]

But how do we secure the objectivity of critical judgement? To what may we appeal? The theory of aesthetic perception argues that the objectivity of an aesthetic judgement is founded no differently from the objectivity of judgements ascribing secondary qualities – in the 'agreement in judgements' of mature observers.[2] But such an approach is at best indecisive. For although it is clearly true that most judgements about *aspects* are in this way objective – in that it is a necessary truth that a man with normal sensory capacities and normal abilities as a language user will agree with others about a wide range of aspect-judgements – it is by no means certain that this appeal to agreement can support the objectivity of all aesthetic argument. Certainly, at least some aesthetic features are, like aspects, dependent for their recognition on a visual or auditory experience, but in aesthetic judgement we no longer find the same kind of spontaneous agreement. The particular experience of seeing an aspect is pre-determined by the first-order features of its object in a way that aesthetic experience is not. We can, therefore, no longer make a direct appeal to agree-

---

[1] Thus Kant believed that moral judgements are *imperatives* (and, therefore, without truth conditions), and that they are founded on reasons valid for all men: practical, not theoretical reasons.
[2] Such a view is defended by Sibley in 'Objectivity and Aesthetics', *A.S.S.V.*, 1968.

ment in order to establish the objectivity of aesthetic description. The recognition of an aesthetic feature, unlike the recognition of an aspect, is not the prerogative of the 'standard observer'. Even if there were *de facto* agreement in aesthetic judgement, this would still not establish objectivity. For a man can be reasoned out of a critical interpretation in a way that he cannot as a rule be reasoned out of the perception of an aspect, and in a way that he can never be reasoned out of the perception of a secondary quality. We say that one must 'see for oneself' in aesthetic judgement, but it must be remembered that this process of quasi-perception is founded on a complex 'understanding', without which it can hardly be said to exist. A man does not 'see' that a work of art is sincere, sad or sentimental if he does not understand it. It does not need understanding to see that a picture is red, or even to see that it has the aspect of a horse. It is because this understanding can take many forms, and can be altered and educated by reasoning, that we cannot use 'agreement in judgements' as a criterion of objectivity. It is significant in this respect that, while we can give rules for the construction of aspects, we cannot give rules for the production of aesthetic features.

If there is objectivity in aesthetic description, then, it must be discovered at a deeper level than that of *de facto* agreement. We must investigate the roots of reasoning in aesthetics – in particular, we must attempt to discover whether anything like objectivity can be attributed to the reasons offered in favour of an experience or response. Those philosophers who think of practical reasons as all relative to desires will, of course, reject the objectivity of aesthetics. But such a view of practical reason is grotesquely narrow: there is, after all, such a thing as the justification of a desire itself, and hence of an emotion, and hence of a response, and hence of an aesthetic judgement. The question is, whether objectivity can be obtained here, where it is both clearly believed in, and in some sense required. We can rest content with the knowledge that this is not a question for aesthetics alone, nor is it a question for which only the empiricist lacks an answer.

Although it is difficult to prove the objectivity of critical reasoning, it is certain that we demand objectivity, or at least that we demand the kind of rational agreement in attitude that may here have to stand in its place. Whether or not this demand can be met, its presence is felt in all our reactions to art, and it is for this reason that we cannot treat aesthetic judgement as the subjective expression of a personal taste. The 'normative' character of aesthetic interest demands that subjectivity be suspended in aesthetic judgement, and that it be replaced by a search for rational agreement, and hence by a search for standards. But now, it may be wondered, why do we make this demand for agreement when we do not even know that it can be met?

This question, which Kant clearly considered to be the most serious in aesthetics, was laid aside in Chapter Ten; we must now attempt to answer it. We find that it is precisely here that we need to call on a theory of art. For it is in the experience and judgement of art that the demand for agreement is most apparent, and it is in attempting to explain this demand that we might again wish to resort to a cognitive theory of aesthetic interest. It is art that gives to aesthetic appreciation the importance in our lives signalled in the 'universality' of aesthetic judgement. But if art is not a form of knowledge, then we seem to have nothing left with which to explain its value, other than a set of autonomous and incommunicable experiences. Traditionally, empiricists attempted to account for appreciation in terms of pleasure: to say that art is a source of pleasure at least offers some slight excuse for it. But this jejune theory offers no explanation of the 'universality' of aesthetic judgement. An answer to our problem will be satisfactory, therefore, only if it assigns a proper significance to art.

We can see at once that there need never be a shortage of reasons for a critical judgement, and this ready availability of reasons might at least excuse, even if it does not justify, the demand for rational agreement. For a critical judgement, of whatever kind, must be founded in a perception of its object, and we have seen that any change in this perception – such as attention to some hitherto unnoticed feature – may undermine the appropriateness both of the judgement and of the experience that is expressed by it. Given the complexity of works of art there will always be scope for a critical explanation or analysis that draws attention to features previously unperceived, and hence which gives reasons for a change of judgement. It might be thought that such an analysis can hardly provide 'reasons', for its endpoint is not an action, nor even an attitude, but rather an experience, which the critical judgement is used to express. But it must be remembered that aesthetic experiences are of a peculiar kind. Even in their purest 'perceptual' form they are closely analogous to processes of thought that are subject to rational control. It is true that the influence of reason is less immediate and less predictable than in thought and imagery, but this does not alter the fact that, in any proper division of the contents of the human mind into 'active' and 'passive', it is certain that aesthetic appreciation should be situated on the 'active' side. There is such a thing as accepting a reason for an aesthetic experience; an aesthetic experience can feature as the conclusion of a practical syllogism.

However, this ready availability of critical reasons cannot *justify* our demand for agreement, since it does not explain why we should be interested in making such a demand. Why, then, do we regard agreement in aesthetic matters as important? It is here, I think, that we might appeal to the connections between art and morality, and between moral and aesthetic experience. For the 'universality' of moral judgement needs no explanation: the purpose of morality requires us to take an interest in the moral views of others. We should justify the demand for 'universality' in aesthetics, therefore, if we could show that a sufficient relation exists between aesthetic and moral preferences.

There are two ways of conceiving this relation, corresponding to two rather different attitudes to art. I shall refer to them as the 'external' approach and the 'internal' approach, since they differ in that while the first regards the appreciation of art as related only externally to considerations of morality, the second regards the appreciation of art as internally related to the moral point of view.

It is characteristic of the external approach to locate the value of art in its effects on the man who appreciates it. Art is held to be a form of education, specifically, an education of the emotions. It would seem to follow that the two questions 'How are works of art evaluated?' and 'What is the value of art?' must be treated independently. For it would be natural to argue that works of art are to be evaluated purely autonomously, by reference to standards of success that are internal to the realm of aesthetic interest. Beauty and moral depravity can, therefore, coexist. The defender of the external approach would then argue that art is in some general way beneficial. As such one might wonder how far art is replaceable by a more effective discipline. For example, Johnson praised Petrarch, saying that he 'refined the manners of the lettered world',[3] and it might seem that such a beneficial effect of Petrarch's poetry could have been as well secured by some other schooling. The true value of art lies in a moral end to which art is only one among several instruments.

There is a flaw in this approach. For suppose someone were to deny that art has beneficial effects, as Plato did. Must he, therefore, abandon the 'universality' of aesthetic judgement, show no further interest in agreement, and replace all criticism with expressions of subjective taste? I think not. It seems that we aim at agreement in aesthetic judgement whatever our opinion about the effects of art. The internal approach will, therefore, provide a more plausible explanation of 'universality', provided it can be shown that aesthetic preference is in some sense continuous with the moral point of view.

Now there certainly seems to be an internal relation between aesthetic and moral judgement. In moral judgement it is usual to praise a man for certain qualities, and these qualities may be such that the question 'Why is that a reason for admiring him?' normally requires no answer. Similarly, the analogous question asked of the aesthetic features of a work of art may also require no answer. And it is interesting to discover that the features of men and the features of works of art which are in this sense intrinsically admirable tend to coincide.[4] We admire works of art, as we admire men, for their intelligence, wisdom, sincerity, depth of feeling, compassion and realism. It would be odd to acknowledge this, and yet to deny that there is a relation between moral and aesthetic judgement.

But we need to say more than this. For even this internal approach is compatible with the fact that art is of merely instrumental value, and hence with the fact that a better substitute for art may one day be discovered. For aesthetic interest might involve no way of appreciating these moral qualities that is not available to the philistine. It may be unnecessary to look to art in

---

[3] *Lives of the English Poets*, Vol. I, p. 4.
[4] On this point see John Casey, *The Language of Criticism*, chs. VIII and IX.

order to admire the values that are conveyed by art. Perhaps, we should end our discussion on this note of scepticism. For it is not obvious that art can lay claim to any more autonomy than we have already assigned to it. On the other hand, it also seems that works of art bring to what they represent a value that can be appreciated only by someone who has aesthetic judgement. What is so important, after all, about the sincerity of a symphony, when the sincerity of a laundry bill arouses no admiration or respect? Surely, then, aesthetic interest must bestow some additional value on the moral qualities of its object? I shall attempt to explain how this is possible.

The example of amusement is helpful once more. In one sense it is absurd to ask of something said to be amusing: 'And what is good about *that*?' (although there may be other reasons for disapproving of it). This is not because amusement is a valuable reaction that needs to be cultivated: the value of an amusing *object* does not derive from the value of *amusement*. (Similarly, we might urge in favour of the internal approach that the value of the aesthetic object does not derive from the value of aesthetic experience, any more than the value of another's courage derived from the value of our own approval.) In liking something for its amusing quality one is liking it for an intelligible reason – and the same goes for intelligence, profundity, sincerity and the other 'virtues' that may be attributed to works of art. Amusement, like aesthetic experience, is a mode of attention to its object, and its appropriateness is measured in terms of its object alone. Similarly, our experience of a work of art can be made inappropriate only by its object, and not by its effects. Thus amusement can be shown to be inappropriate only if its object is shown not to be amusing, that is, only when its object is inappropriate. If I am amused it is for a reason, and this reason lies in the object of my amusement. Amusement involves a particular pattern of thought about its object, and if this pattern of thought is shown to be wrongheaded, childish or corrupt it will no longer be possible to be amused.

This judgement of 'appropriateness' that we discover in amusement is similarly involved in all appreciation of art, and is the inevitable outcome of aesthetic interest. When I react to a work of art I also think of it as an appropriate object of my reaction. Hence we say that aesthetic experience involves not only pleasure but also the exercise of taste – taste in the sense of reasoned discrimination, and not in the sense of savouring impressions. And taste brings certain normative attitudes in its train. A partial explanation of these attitudes will be achieved, then, if we can give some indication of the place occupied by taste in our experience as a whole.

The first thing to notice is that the exercise of taste is by no means confined to the experience of art. We exercise taste when we judge what is appropriate in manners and behaviour, and it is precisely here in regulating our sense not of what is right and wrong, but of what is decent – that taste shows its continuity with moral sentiment. Moral attitudes do not and cannot exist in isolation. On the contrary, they form part of a continuum of normative opinions which mutually sustain one another – as manners and morals sustain one another. Clearly, then, the exercise of taste cannot be described if we confine ourselves to the study of art alone: only in the context of an entire culture can the importance of taste be fully demonstrated.

The second thing to notice is that we speak of what is appropriate only where there exists some established practice – of etiquette or art – with its body of generalities and rules. The notion of the appropriate only makes proper sense against this background of agreed practice. Without this background it would be pointless to distinguish the exercise of taste from the display of arbitrary preferences (tastes, in the more common meaning of the term). This is not to say that what makes a taste other than arbitrary is its conformity to rule, but rather that once an established practice exists then the concepts of the normal and of the appropriate can gain a foothold. (Looked at from the point of view of the third person, there is nothing surprising in this.) Once this foothold has been gained then it seems quite legitimate to turn the judgement of taste on the very conventions that first gave rise to it, criticizing them as shallow, say, or inappropriate.

Rules, conventions and artistic forms have an immense importance in art, and this importance cannot be accounted for in any simple way. Nonetheless, we seem to have discovered one reason for their importance. In daily life our sense of what is appropriate must be held in abeyance, and only in the enjoyment of art is it allowed total freedom. In art everything that occurs is deliberate and reasoned; art presents us with a world entirely circumscribed by human intention. Every work of art is created in a medium, under the guidance of pre-established rules which may be broken but never ignored, for they embody the tradition of thought without which no work of art would be meaningful. Each word or gesture on the stage strikes us as in place or out of place, and no feature of the work of art can escape making some contribution to the effect. In the absence of rules and traditions our sense of what is appropriate could hardly be aroused, and appreciation of art would remain inchoate and primitive. But our sense of the appropriate, once aroused, entirely penetrates our response to art, dominating not only our awareness of form, diction, structure and harmony, but also our interest in action, character and feeling. It is inevitable, therefore, that we should make the connection between artistic and moral experience.

Even in the realm of abstract art, there is no way in which moral and aesthetic judgement can be neatly separated. If music were as abstract and unfathomable as is sometimes thought, then it would be impossible for there to be irony in music, or the deliberate exploitation of character. If we were unable to recognize bad taste in music, then we should not be amused by its dramatic exploitation in the operettas of Kurt Weill, nor moved by its poignant setting in the symphonies of Mahler. In the opening bars of *The Seven Deadly Sins*, for example, Weill deliberately exploits the language of the American musical, and the dramatic irony is missed if we do not intuitively contrast the sweet and endearing sentiments of the text with the gross self-indulgence of the music. Our appreciation of the music is entirely determined by our reaction to the vulgarity of its message.

In our search for an explanation of the 'universality' of aesthetic judgement we have been led to suggest connections between moral and aesthetic experience that are of the first importance for criticism. It would seem to follow that if there are to be standards of critical judgement, then they cannot be divorced from standards of practical reasoning generally. The relation between moral and aesthetic judgement suggests that standards for the validity of the one will provide standards for the validity of the other. To show what is bad in a sentimental work of art must involve showing what is bad in sentimentality. To be certain in matters of taste is, therefore, to be certain in matters of morality: ethics and aesthetics are one.

Bibliography

This is a list of works referred to in the text. I use the following abbreviations:

P.A.S.	*Proceedings of the Aristotelian Society*
A.S.S.V.	*Aristotelian Society, Supplementary Volume*
Phil.	*Philosophy*
Phil. Rev.	*Philosophical Review*
Phil. Q.	*Philosophical Quarterly*
Phil. and Phen. Res.	*Philosophy and Phenomenological Research*
B.J.A.	*British Journal of Aesthetics*
J. Phil.	*Journal of Philosophy*

J. Addison, 'The Pleasures of the Imagination', in *The Spectator*, 1712.

A. Alison, *Essays on the Nature and Principles of Taste*, Edinburgh, 1790.

G. E. M. Anscombe, 'On Brute Facts', *Analysis*, 1958.

G. E. M. Anscombe, 'The Intentionality of Sensation: A Grammatical Feature', in R. J. Butler (ed.), *Analytical Philosophy, Second Series*, Oxford, 1965.

St Thomas Aquinas, *Summa Theologiae*.

Aristotle, *De Anima*.

Aristotle, *Politics*.

D. M. Armstrong, *Perception and the Physical World*, London, 1961.

B. Aune, *Knowledge, Mind and Nature*, New York, 1967.

J. L. Austin, 'The Meaning of a Word', in *Philosophical Papers*, 2nd ed., ed. J. O. Urmson and G. J. Warnock, Oxford, 1970.

Charles Baudelaire, 'Obituary Notice of Eugène Delacroix', reprinted in *L'Art Romantique*, ed. J. Crépet, Paris, 1925.

E. Bedford, 'Seeing Paintings', *A.S.S.V.*, 1966.

Clive Bell, *Art*, London, 1913.

B. Bosanquet, 'On the Nature of Aesthetic Emotion', in *Science and Philosophy*, London, 1927.

Cleanth Brooks, *The Well Wrought Urn*, London, 1949.

Edmund Burke, *A Philosophical Enquiry into the Origin of our Ideas of Sublime and the Beautiful*, London, 1757.

John Casey, *The Language of Criticism*, London, 1966.

Stanley Cavell, 'Aesthetic Problems in Modern Philosophy', in Max Black (ed.), *Philosophy in America*, London, 1965.

R. Chisholm, *Perceiving, a Philosophical Study*, Ithaca, N.Y., 1957.

S. T. Coleridge, *Biographia Literaria*, ed. J. Shawcross, Oxford, 1907.

R. G. Collingwood, *The Principles of Art*, Oxford, 1938.

Peter Collins, *Changing Ideals in Modern Architecture*, London, 1965.

B. Croce, *Estetica*, come Scienza dell'Espressione e Linguistica Generale, 7th ed., Bari, 1941, tr. *Aesthetic*, Ainslee, 2nd ed., London, 1923.

B. Croce, *Breviario di Estetica*, Bari, 1913, tr. *Breviary of Aesthetic*, Ainslee, Houston, Texas, 1915.

D. Davidson, 'On Saying That', in D. Davidson and J. Hintikka (eds.), *Words and Objections*, Dordrecht, 1969.

D. Davidson, 'Truth and Meaning', *Synthese*, 1967.

John Dewey, *Art as Experience*, New York, 1934.

Mikel Dufrenne, *La Phénoménologie de l'expérience Esthétique*, Paris, 1953.

Roy Edgley, *Reason in Theory and Practice*, London, 1969.

R. K. Elliott, 'Poetry and Truth', *Analysis*, 1967.

B. N. Fleming, 'Recognising and Seeing As', *Phil. Rev.*, 1957.

Phillipa Foot, 'Morality and Art', *Proceedings of the British Academy*, 1970.

G. Frege, *The Philosophical Writings of Gottlob Frege*, ed. P. T. Geach and M. Black, Oxford, 1952.

S. Freud, *Leonardo da Vinci*, a psychosexual study, tr. A. A. Brill, London, 1948.

P. T. Geach, 'Good and Evil', *Analysis*, 1956.

P. T. Geach, *Mental Acts*, London, 1957.

P. T. Geach, 'Assertion', *Phil. Rev.*, 1965.

E. H. Gombrich, *Art and Illusion*, London, 1960.

N. Goodman, *Languages of Art*, London, 1969.

N. Goodman, 'Reply to Wollheim on Languages of Art, *J. Phil.*, 1970.

H. P. Grice, 'Meaning', *Phil. Rev.*, 1957.

H. P. Grice, 'Utterer's Meaning, Sentence-meaning and Word-meaning', *Foundations of Language*, 1968.

E. Gurney, *The Power of Sound*, London, 1880.

Stuart Hampshire, 'Logic and Appreciation', *World Review*, 1953, reprinted in W. Elton (ed.), *Aesthetics and Language*, Oxford, 1954.

Eduard Hanslick, *On the Beautiful in Music*, tr. G. Cohen, New York, 1957.

R. M. Hare, *The Language of Morals*, Oxford, 1952.

G. W. F. Hegel, *Introduction to the Philosophy of Fine Art*, tr. B. Bosanquet, London, 1886.

G. W. F. Hegel, *The Philosophy of Fine Art*, tr. F. P. B. Osmaston, London, 1920.

David Hume, *A Treatise of Human Nature*, ed. L. A. Selby-Bigge, Oxford, 1888.

David Hume, 'Of the Standard of Taste', in *Essays, Moral, Political and Literary*, London, 1741.

Frances Hutcheson, *An Inquiry into the Original of our Ideas of Beauty and Virtue*, London, 1725.

E. Husserl, *Ideas*, English Edition, London, 1931.

Roman Ingarden, 'Aesthetic Experiences and Aesthetic Object', *Phil. and Phen. Res.*, 1961.

Roman Ingarden, *Das Literarische Kunstwerk*, 2nd ed., Tübingen, 1960.

Hidé Ishiguro, 'Imagination', in B. Williams and A. Montefiore (eds.), *British Analytical Philosophy*, London, 1966.

Hidé Ishiguro, 'Imagination', *A.S.S.V.*, 1967.

Samuel Johnson, *Lives of the English Poets*, Everyman Edition, London, 1925.

Immanuel Kant, *Critique of Judgement*, tr. J. C. Meredith, Oxford, 1928.

A. Kenny, *Action, Emotion and Will*, London, 1963.

Susanne Langer, *Philosophy in a New Key*, Cambridge, Mass., 1942.

Susanne Langer, *Feeling and Form*, New York, 1953.

John Locke, *Essay Concerning Human Understanding*, London, 1690.

Ruby Meager, 'Aesthetic Concepts', *B.J.A.*, 1970.

Ruby Meager, 'The Uniqueness of the Work of Art', in C. Barrett (ed.), *Collected Papers on Aesthetics*, Oxford, 1965.

G. E. Moore, *Principia Ethica*, Cambridge, 1903.

Toyoichiro Nogami, *Japanese Noh Plays*, Tokyo, 1954.

C. S. Peirce, *Collected Papers*, Vol. V, ed. C. Hartshorne and P. Weiss, Cambridge, Mass., 1934.

D. W. Prall, *Aesthetic Analysis*, New York, 1936.

H. H. Price, *Belief*, London, 1969.

W. V. Quine, *From a Logical Point of View*, Cambridge, Mass., 1953.

W. V. Quine, *Word and Object*, Cambridge, Mass., 1960.

I. A. Richards, *Practical Criticism*, London, 1929.

Bertrand Russell, 'Knowledge by Acquaintance', in *Mysticism and Logic*, London, 1917.

G. Ryle, *The Concept of Mind*, London, 1949.

G. Santayana, *The Sense of Beauty*, New York, 1896.

J.-P. Sartre, *L'Imagination*, Paris, 1936.

J.-P. Sartre, *L'Imaginaire*, Paris, 1940, tr. *The Psychology of the Imagination*, New York, 1948.

F. C. S. Schiller, *Letters on Aesthetic Education*, Wilkinson and Willoughby (eds.), London, 1967.

Arthur Schopenhauer, *The World as Will and Representation*, tr. E. F. J. Payne, two vols., Colorado, 1958.

Roger Scruton, 'Architectural Aesthetics', *B.J.A.*, 1973.

J. R. Searle, *Speech Acts*, Cambridge, 1969.

F. N. Sibley, 'Aesthetic Concepts', *Phil. Rev.*, 1959.

F. N. Sibley, 'Aesthetic and Non-aesthetic', *Phil. Rev.*, 1965.

F. N. Sibley and M. K. Tanner, 'Objectivity and Aesthetics', *A.S.S.V.*, 1968.

T. L. S. Sprigge, 'The Definition of a Moral Judgement', *Phil.*, 1964.

P. F. Strawson, 'Imagination and Perception', in L. Foster and J. W. Swanson (eds.), *Experience and Theory*, Massachusetts, 1970.

P. F. Strawson, 'Aesthetic Appraisal and Works of Art', *The Oxford Review*, 1966.

A. Tarski, 'The Concept of Truth in Formalised Languages', in *Logic, Semantics*, Metamathematics, Oxford, 1956.

J. O. Urmson, 'What Makes a Situation Aesthetic?', *A.S.S.V.*, 1957.

David Wiggins, 'On sentence-sense, word-sense, and difference of word-sense', in D. Steinberg and L. Jakobovitz (eds.), *Semantics, an Interdisciplinary Reader*, Cambridge, 1971.

B. A. O. Williams, 'Pleasure and Belief', *A.S.S.V.*, 1959.

L. Wittgenstein, *Zettel*, ed. G. E. M. Anscombe and G. H. Von Wright, tr. G. E. M. Anscombe, Oxford, 1967.

L. Wittgenstein, *The Blue and Brown Books*, Oxford, 1958.

L. Wittgenstein, *Philosophical Investigations*, tr. G. E. M. Anscombe, Oxford, 1953.

L. Wittgenstein, *Lectures and Conversations on Aesthetics, Psychology, and Religious Belief*, ed. C. Barrett, Oxford, 1966.

Heinrich Wölfflin, *The Sense of Form in Art*, New York, 1958.

Richard Wollheim, *Art and its Objects*, New York, 1968.

Richard Wollheim, 'Expression' in *The Human Agent*, Lectures to the Royal Institute of Philosophy, Vol. 1, 1966–7, London, 1967.

Index

Page references have been included which denote pages where an author is not named explicitly but where one of his works is discussed or mentioned.